INSIGHT GUIDES

Tenerife
Western Canary Islands
La Gomera
La Palma
El Hierro

Edited by Andrew Eames
Editorial Director: Brian Bell

APA PUBLICATIONS

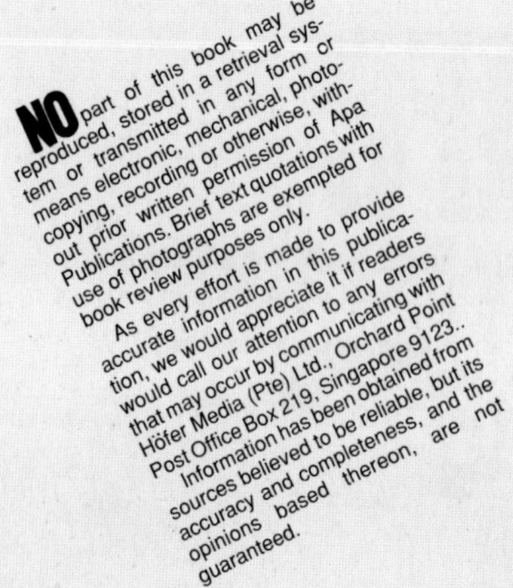

TENERIFE AND THE WESTERN CANARY ISLANDS

First Edition (2nd Reprint)

Printed in Singapore by Höfer Press Pte. Ltd

ABOUT THIS BOOK

The Canary Islands, stepping stones between the continents, have been legendary until very recently; until the 15th century their very existence was more a matter of speculation than of fact. A legacy like that is not quickly overcome. Despite carbon dating and all the modern history techniques, very little is still known about the history and society of the islands before the arrival of the conquering Spanish.

Good literature about the Canaries is similarly thin on the ground—a situation that has been remedied in these pages. Putting the Canaries on Insight Guides' map of the world was the task of project editor **Andrew Eames**, no stranger to Apa's philosophy, having edited *Cityguide: London* and *Insight Guide: The Balearics*. Eames is a freelance writer and editor now living in London. He is the author of *Crossing the Shadow Line*, his travel autobiography, as well as a novel and a cartoon book. In recent years he has worked for the London *Times* and as a freelance magazine consultant.

Resident Writers

The task of finding resident experts on the islands, capable of writing with sufficient authority on a wide range of subjects, was not an easy one to manage from London. Eames enlisted the support of **Austin Baillon**, long-term British resident in Tenerife, and **Mike Eddy**, a British archaeologist living and working on Gran Canaria.

Baillon (chapters on early tourism, news topics and the water problem) lives with his wife Julia in the former customs house in Puerto de la Cruz. Baillon was born on Tenerife, where his father had come to develop the flourishing banana business. Baillon's own career focused on oil exploration, particularly in South America. Now retired to Tenerife, he writes copiously about local history both in English and Spanish, and for many years presented an excellent audio-visual to visitors to the island. He has been awarded the Gold Medal for services to tourism by the Puerto de la Cruz tourist board.

Mike Eddy, with a wealth of information at his fingertips in the Museo Canario in Las Palmas, and with several years of research on the islands behind him, writes in this book about early Guanche existence and traditional customs. His wife, **Moira**, a geologist and teacher, writes about the archipelago's volcanic past.

Carolyn Mowlem, editor of the magazine *Tenerife Property Scene*, first arrived on the island in 1974. A former copywriter, she now writes both commercial and cultural articles, and in these pages she completed chapters on expatriates and fiestas. Mowlem says the islands have become far more sophisticated in recent years; there was a time when she would ask visiting friends and relations to fill their suitcases with goodies from home. Nowadays the islands cater for everyone.

Christopher Goulding (Travel Tips section and Going to Africa chapter) also came to Tenerife in 1974, as the deputy headmaster in the British school. A fluent Spanish and French speaker, and a contributor to local publications, Goulding was flattered recently to be described as *medio Canario*, or half Canarian.

Also resident on the islands are **Sarah Simon** (chapter on the Verdino) and **Chris Taylor** (Nightlife and additional Travel Tips).

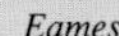

Eames

Baillon

Fernandez- Armesto

The history chapters of this book were the province of **Felipe Fernandez-Armesto**, a fellow of St Antony's College, Oxford. His books include *Before Columbus*, *The Spanish Armada*, and *The Canary Islands after the Conquest*. He is now at work on a major history of Spain for Oxford University Press. Canarian history has been among his most persistent interests for nearly 20 years, and he has been elected to the Instituto de Estudios Canarios, a rare honour. "I detest travel," he writes. "The only journeys I like are made in the imagination, and my favourite means of transport are an armchair and a book."

Visiting Experts

Until recently **Dr Paul Murdin** spent months at a stretch in a lonely spot on one of the most remote of the islands. Dr Murdin, who writes in these pages about La Palma, that very same remote island, is an astronomer with the Royal Greenwich Observatory and the author of several authoritative titles in his field. Dr Murdin played a key role in establishing the observatory on La Palma.

Neil Dunkin, who writes about the northern half of Tenerife, admits to having been a "rabid Hispanophile" since his days as a student of Spanish language and literature at London University. Now a journalist in London working for the *Daily Mirror*, the high spots of his year are holidays on Tenerife, the island which he says comes with a cast-iron guarantee of pure, unadulterated bliss.

Nigel Tisdall, who writes about the southern part of Tenerife and the island of Hierro, comes from the right stock for the job: his parents have also written about the islands and own an apartment in south of Tenerife. Over the years Tisdall has witnessed the rapid development of the islands, observing the advent of tourism with a mixture of fear and fascination; he says he has an "unsentimental admiration" for the traditional values of Canarian life, perhaps most clearly revealed in his writing which focuses on the island of Hierro.

The photography in these pages draws on the work of **Joerg Reuther** and **Thomas Kanzler**, two Munich-based German photographers, and on **Tulio Gatti**, an Italian who has been living on Gran Canaria for longer than he cares to remember.

This book could not have been completed without the assistance of the Canarian tourist authorities, particularly **Señor Jose Torrellas**, and of **Monarch Airlines**.

Supervising the book's progress from conception into print was Apa's London-based editorial director **Brian Bell**. Vital cogs in the production machine were typists **Janet Langley** and **Valerie Holder**, proofreader and indexer **Rosemary Jackson Hunter** and computer tamers **Audrey Simon** and **Karen Goh**.

Tisdall

Dunkin

Mowlem

Goulding

CONTENTS

ABOUT TENERIFE AND THE WESTERN CANARIES

PLACES

FEATURES

MAPS

TRAVEL TIPS

BEHIND THE BROCHURES

The Canary islanders believe they have always existed at the whim of mainland Europe, forced to accept scraps like a dog waiting by a table. It is not just the islands' long history of exploitation that supports that belief; on television, for example, while mainland Spain is watching advertising, Canarios are faced with blank screens. Advertisers on the mainland do not think it worthwhile targetting the Canaries.

Columbus used to call at these islands on his voyages of discovery; more recently early steamers called in to refuel, and latterly airlines did the same. But modern shipping barely stops at all and modern aircraft have increased their range, transforming the Canaries from a bridge across the Atlantic to an island cul-de-sac, with all manner of people and customs accumulating on the shores.

Europe has long treated the islands as a seed bed for various experimental industries; sugar, wine, tomatoes, cochineal, and bananas have all at one time or another completely dominated island trade. During their time these industries have made fortunes for their architects, but they have left little or nothing behind them for the islanders after each crash. Hundreds of thousands of Canarios have emigrated to Central or South America, where life is at least a little more predictable, if not actually easier.

The latest in the series of monocultures is tourism. In the early part of the century ladies and gentlemen of gentility sought out Tenerife for a health cure in the winter, and the elegant guide-books recommended "a discriminatory use of laxatives" to relieve the colic brought on by garlic and olive oil used in the cooking.

Today seven million visitors travel to the Canaries every year, bringing new prosperity; on Tenerife, turnover from tourism amounts to £80,000 per metre of beach. And yet a questionnaire circulated among the sun-flattened tourists on Playa de las Américas, for example, would be poorly answered: does anyone know that Admiral Nelson lost his arm trying to grab a Spanish bullion ship in Tenerife? That the ancient, tertiary-era forests on the lesser-known islands are so damp that the trees are draped in a cloak of moss from top to toe? That Franco started the Spanish Civil War from here? How many are aware of the existence of the islands of Gomera, Hierro and La Palma? Few, if any.

The short tradition of guidebooks to the islands has done little to reveal anything of the extensive corpus of learning that exists about the Canaries. This book does more than its predecessors; it takes the islands seriously, and in so doing lifts the lid off what is effectively a mini-continent, revealing the tapestry of life behind the brochures.

Preceding pages: black sand beach at Las Gaviotas; high-jinks in the wind at Médano; botanical gardens on Tenerife; the banana industry survives still. Left, past and pastimes meet on the shore.

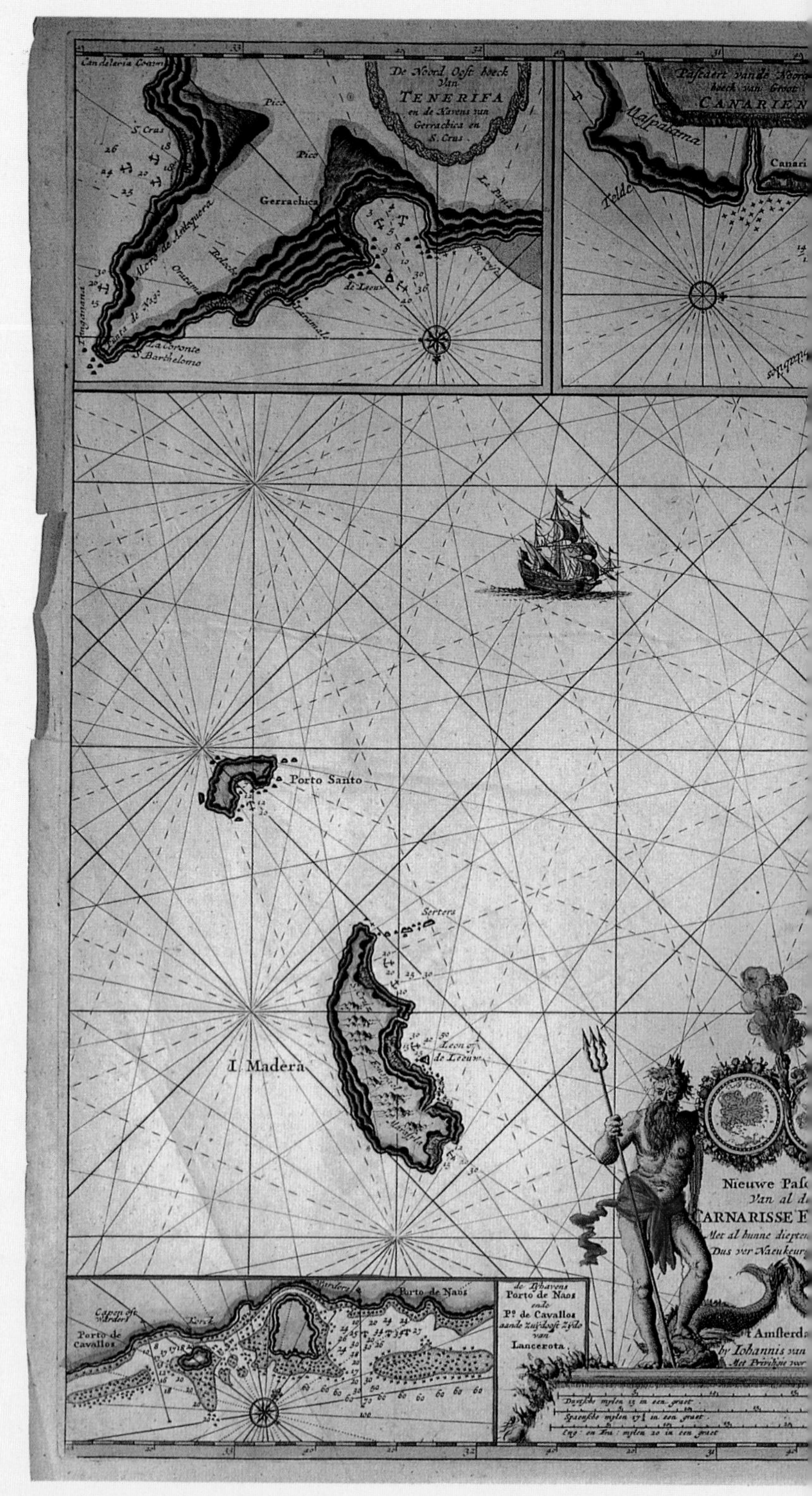
De Noord Oost hoeck van TENERIFA en de Havens van Gerrachica en S. Crus
Gerrachica
Porto Santo
I. Madera
Nieuwe Pas
CARNARISSE E
Porto de Naos
Porto de Cavallos
de Ysthavens Porto de Naos ende Pº de Cavallos aande Zuydoost Zyde van Lancerota.

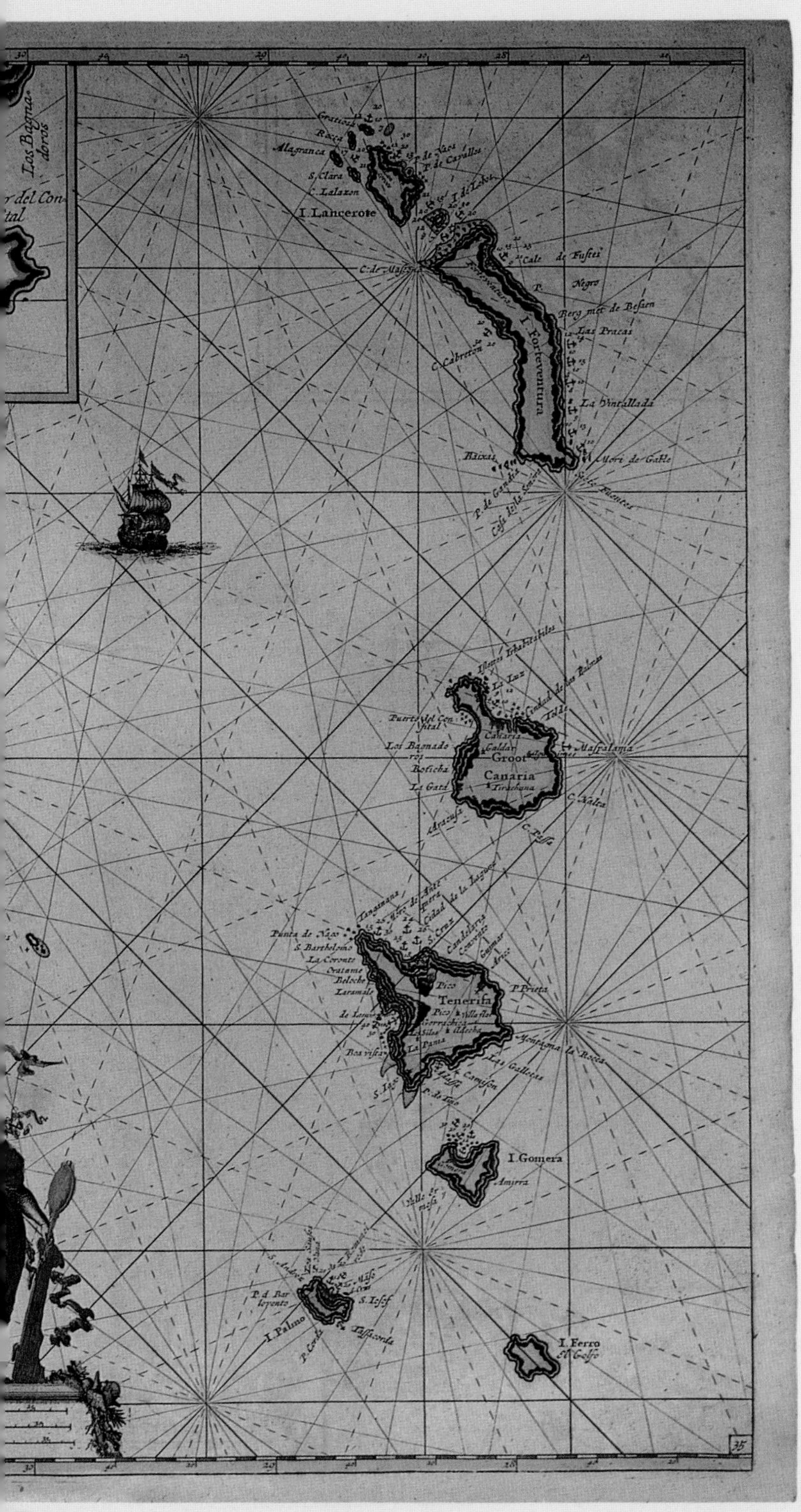

I. Lancerote
I. Forteventura
Groot
Canaria
Tenerifa
I. Gomera
I. Palmo
I. Ferro

THE GUANCHES IN PREHISTORY

Leonardo Torriani, the Italian engineer who chronicled the European colonisation of the Canaries, describes the conquest of the island of Hierro: "The Christians began to disembark, and they were received with great rejoicing and happiness. They seem'd to all the natives to be Gods and not mortal men like themselves; and with this illusion the heathens nearest to the shore began to board the lighters, as they wished to get out to the ships; and so many came on board that the ships were fully loaded. They were all taken to Lanzarote and afterwards they were dispatched from there to be sold in divers places."

Torriani, writing *circa* 1590, goes on to recount how the Europeans came back the following year in order to play the same trick on the naive islanders. Unfortunately on that occasion one of the shore party made too clear his intention to take one of the young women with him and her father struck him with his staff, drawing blood. Realising that gods shouldn't bleed, the girl's father rallied the islanders to prevent yet more Bimbaches (as the islanders called themselves) from being taken into slavery.

Whether Torriani got the story right is a moot point, but he certainly exposes one of the main interests of the European adventurers who visited the islands in the Middle Ages—slavery.

Human trade: Like all slave-raiders the medieval Europeans were mainly concerned with the natives' sales potential and what might be called product availability. "The country (the island of La Palma) is strong and well populated because it has not been so heavily raided as the other islands. They are people of comely proportions and live on naught but meat..."

Likewise on Tenerife, relates one trader, "there live many people, who are the most daring of all the other peoples that inhabit the islands, and they have never been attacked nor led into captivity like those of the other islands". Gomera, too, was first recorded as well-populated by powerful tribesmen, protected from raiders by "the marvellously great and deep ravines" of the island.

But Hierro, the smallest and the most westerly island, had suffered the effects of slave raids even before the con-trick that Torriani exposed. "It was once populated by many people, but several times they were made prisoners and led into captivity in foreign countries and today few people remain... The inhabitants are people of comely proportions, both the men and the women." So hurry now while stocks last.

Preceding pages: an early navigational map. Left, Guanche figures in Santa Cruz. Right, slavers made off with many of the islanders.

The sales pitch of slavers, however, is not the only source of information about the original islanders. The first European conquistador—the Frenchman, Jean de Béthencourt—brought with him two priests (who wrote the descriptions quoted above) to save the souls of the heathen islanders and to protect his own. Like other evangelising priests they took a dim view of Canarian paganism and baptised in the wake of military conquest.

Whilst de Béthencourt raided and conquered throughout the islands, the two priests, de Bontier and Le Verrier, left thumb-nail sketches of each island and their inhabitants among the accounts of deeds performed by their master. De Béthencourt's main territorial conquests were the eastern islands of Lanzarote and Fuerteventura, but he did also sieze Hierro and perhaps gained some control over Gomera.

First impressions: The two priests describe Hierro as, "full of great forests of pines and of laurels that produce berries so plump and so long that it is a marvel to behold… the waters are pure and there is a great quantity of beasts, to wit pigs, goats and sheep and there are lizards as big as cats, but they do no harm… And in the highest part of the countrie there are trees that always distill a fine, clear water which is collected in several pits near the trees…" These are the first accounts of the giant lizards of Hierro and of the famous laurel-tree, Garoë, which was finally blown down in a gale at the beginning of the 17th century.

The early colonial administration, too, recorded aspects of native life. Land grants on Tenerife refer to "land which had belonged to the King of Güimar", or to "land on the Teno road… which the Guanches used to sow". Even court cases, brought in defence of islanders' rights, have something to say about the pre-Hispanic life-style of the native islanders—the first case of its type concerned La Palma and was brought to court before the 15th century was out.

Then there are the accounts by travellers in the islands after the final conquest.

The first Englishman to write about the Canaries, Thomas Nichols in the 16th century, described Tenerife's native society succinctly: "In this island, before the conquest, dwelt seaven kinges, who with all their people dwelt in caves and were cloathed in goat skinnes, as the Canaria people were, and with such like order of dyet as they had… These people were called Guanches by naturell name. They spake another language cleane contrarie to the Canarians and so consequently everie iland spake a severall language."

Nichols' account touches on one of the basic problems for archaeologists and prehistorians writing about the native islanders—what should they be called? Each island had a different name and the people of each also had their own tribal names.

The easiest solution is to misuse the word Guanche, which actually only applied to Tenerife's original inhabitants, and apply it to all the pre-conquest island societies in general. Nevertheless each island had its own pecularities within the overall "Guanche culture".

Origins of the species: The origins of this culture are still unclear, but it was certainly related to the Berber peoples of North Africa. Many modern placenames in the Canaries are also found in Morocco—the island of Gomera and the Moroccan village of Ghomara are obviously similar. Tenerife, too, is echoed in modern Berber placenames—the placename element "Ten-" or "Tin-" is common in nearby North Africa.

Nichols' brief portrait of the Guanches of Tenerife was essentially accurate. The native islanders did live in caves: natural ones adapted for human habitation by levelling the floor with earth and stones and by building front walls of stone and timber. But unlike on Gran Canaria, where there are whole villages of man-made caves, only one purpose-built cave has been found in the province of Tenerife—Cueva de los Reyes, in Güimar.

It it curious that this one cave should be *de los Reyes* (of the Kings). On Gran Canaria man-made, painted caves are traditionally thought to be the homes of the pre-Hispanic kings, but in fact they are more likely to be *harimaguadas*—a sort of convent where young women were schooled in wifely and religious duties.

Left, the mythical Garoë tree, in full flow. Above, Anglo-French expedition to Morocco (from Froissart's Chronicle).

Gran Canaria's painted caves—and painting was almost exclusively a female activity—are rare (only half a dozen are known), and they fall into two types, either large artificial caves with geometric painted friezes, or small natural rock shelters with painted human figures or wavy lines. The Güimar cave probably, therefore, was not a "Cave of Kings"—though in the Guanche culture the female line was as important, if not more so, than the male—but rather a convent.

Several European chronicles mention the key role played by women in pottery-making, basketry, religion, and collecting and storing the harvest. On Gran Canaria geometric art decorates all these activities, but on Tenerife and the western islands there is no such clear link.

Pots, crops and gods: On Tenerife some of the finest pottery vessels are bag-shaped pots with tubular spouts which can be compared with the highly decorated spouted pitchers of Gran Canaria or the slab-mouthed *tofios* of Fuerteventura. The Gran Canarian and Fuerteventuran pots played an important part in religious ceremonies during which women poured libations of milk to the Guanche sky-god, Alcoran.

The spouted pots of Tenerife may well have had the same sacred purpose, though the god worshipped was known as Acguayaxerax.

On La Palma bowls decorated with patterns of incised lines were probably used for libations to Abora. Too little is known of the archaeology of Hierro and Gomera to suggest what form the libation vessels took there, though Gomeran pottery seems very similar to that on Tenerife. Gomerans worshipped a sky-god called Orahan. On Hierro there were two deities—one male, Eroaranzan, who dealt with menfolk and masculine affairs and the other, Moneiba, a goddess who concerned herself exclusively with women and female activities.

On Tenerife men did the ploughing but

women were responsible for tending the crops and for harvesting and storing them. Unlike on Gran Canaria where grain was stored in specially sealed and marked rock-cut pits, the women of Tenerife kept their food stocks in pots inside certain caves. These grain-storage caves were known as *auchones* and were quite different from habitation caves.

The Guanches on all the islands lived in caves, though on Gran Canaria they built villages of substantial houses, too. On Tenerife and the other western islands early stone buildings do exist, but these are little more than huts, often built against rock.

Houses on Hierro may have been grander structures. One European description reads: "Their dwelling was builded thus. First they maketh a circuit of dry stone walling, large and round, in which they leave but a sole entrance by which it is served; and then within this circle were placed beams against the wall, so that the beams remained clear of the earth, like a lean-to, and covered with ferns and branches; and within this circuit lived twenty or more adults with their offspring." Despite this account, no houses of this type have been found on the island.

Where the nobles lived on the western islands is not known; there are no recorded "palace" sites as there are on Gran Canaria and Lanzarote. However we do know something of the political make-up of the islands at the time of their conquest.

Chiefdoms: Hierro, like Lanzarote in the east, had just one "king" or chieftain. Gomera was divided into four tribal areas, though the "royal" families all claimed descent from a single king, Amalahuige. The four Gomeran tribes formed two apparently exclusive zones—an alliance of the Orone and the Agana tribes lived in the west and in the east the Hipalan and the Mulagana tribes were linked in some way. This division was exploited to advantage by the Spanish conquistador, Fernán Peraza, who eventually succeeded in taking the island.

The nine chiefs or *menceyes* of Tenerife also claimed descent from a single king, Betznuriia, and they shared the broad, alpine plains of the Cañadas de Teide as common grazing land. The names of the *menceyatos* or chiefdoms survive as modern place-names, either for regions or modern-day settlements: Anaga, Tegueste, Tacaronte, Taoro, Icod, Daute, Adeje, Abona, and Güimar.

Twelve pre-conquest divisions are known on La Palma, though one of these areas—Acero—is the Caldera of Taburiente and may have simply been an area of common grazing. Another political unit was Tamanca, on the west coast, but the "king" of Tamanca was known as the "king of the three lordships". Was Tamanca divided into three or did it control the adjacent bands of Tihuya and Ahenguarame? There is no clear evidence for either theory.

Among the Guanches of Tenerife the office of *mencey* was hereditary, though the title had to be confirmed by the *tagoror* or council of elders. But the title did not pass directly from father to son, but to the brothers of the former *mencey*. Only when the last brother had passed away did the title finally go to the eldest son of the original *mencey*. As a gruesome part of the investiture ceremony each new chief had to kiss the bones of the first *mencey* of that lineage.

The *tagoror* was not just a political body; it was also a place—a large, flat, circular space with rough-hewn, stone seats, the highest of which was for the *mencey* himself. Each tribe had its own *tagoror*, where justice was dispensed, war plans made and land allotted. Sites of these meeting places exist throughout the islands—a fine, though much altered, example survives at El Julán, on Hierro, but like every prehistoric site in the western Canaries it is closed to the interested public and open to vandalism.

However El Julán is perhaps the most remarkable site in the western Canaries. Its rock-carvings have been known since early last century. Some fine examples of Guanche writing have been found here. The letters, pecked out laboriously in the rock, are in a pre-Roman Berber script but remain undeciphered. Elsewhere in the western islands rock-carvings are mainly simple geometric patterns incorporating spirals, crosses, groups of circles and intersecting lines, though a few human and animal shapes have been recorded on Hierro and La Palma. So far very few rock-carvings have been found on Tenerife and Gomera.

Way of life: According to Nichols the Guanches of Tenerife, like the Gran Canarians, lived on "gelt dogs, goates and goates milke; their bread was made of barlie meale and goats milke, called *gofio*, which they use at his daie" (and modern Canary Islanders still do!). *Gofio* is a finely ground, toasted flour, then made from barley but now of maize or wheat.

Other crops were available, including local fruits and berries, roots and perhaps figs. Goats were the main food animals, though the Guanches also kept pigs and sheep. Fish bones have been found in excavations on La Palma and Tenerife but no deep-sea species have been recorded.

Left, the Caldera de Taburiente, a Guanche grazing ground. Right, a stone mill for *gofio*.

Hunting, like fishing, was a high-status activity. On Tenerife wild cat was hunted along with wild pig and birds like the Barbary partridge and quail.

The peasantry, on the other hand, relied a lot on shell-fish, and shell-middens are known throughout the Canaries. However the only shell-middens to have been excavated (on Gomera) have produced 17th-century dates—well after the conquest.

The land was held in common and apparently shared out by the tribal leaders every year. On all the islands the peasantry had to pay a sort of tax or tithe of their produce to the headman. On Hierro, "They gave to the king each year certain beasts in recognition

of their vassalage, each one giving as he was able and no-one being obliged to give a fixed amount."

The Guanches had no knowledge of metal-working, and there are no ore deposits on the islands. Stone and bone were used instead. From bone they made needles, awls, punches and fish-hooks. Out of basalt they fashioned heavy knives, picks and chopping tools. Finer cutting tools were made from tiny pieces of obsidian, a black volcanic "glass", found in the Cañadas of Tenerife and on La Palma. Porous lava was shaped into circular mill-stones and into mortars for grinding grain.

Containers were made from wood, leather, basketry and pottery. In Canary Island cave sites such materials are finely preserved in the dry, stable atmosphere. Small leather and basketry draw-string pouches are relatively common finds.

The Guanches' main weapons were wooden spears and staves—the spears were not tipped with stone points but hardened with fire. This was, as the Spanish discovered to their cost, just as effective as a stone-tipped weapon. The islanders used sharp throwing-stones to great effect.

Prehistoric tools and other objects used by the Guanches can be seen at the Museo Arqueológico in Santa Cruz, Tenerife, and plans are being drawn up for a Visitor Centre at the Teide *parador*.

Burial rites: The Guanche way of death was remarkably complex, for they mummified their dead—not as well as the ancient Egyptians but quite adequately. The body was first washed in the sea by a caste of specialist undertakers/butchers, who lived a life apart from the rest of society (death and blood were *tabu* for the Guanche nobility).

The body was then dried in the sun once the internal organs had been removed. Finally it was wrapped in leather or basketry shrouds for burial.

These mummies were then placed in caves on wooden litters or platforms of stones, or even stood upright by themselves against the cave walls. Thomas Nichols visited some of these caves on Tenerife: "I have seen caves of 300 of these corps together; the flesh beeing dryed up, the bodye remained as light as parchment."

Many of the burial caves were probably family tombs—the earliest burials were shoved to the back to make room for new arrivals on their way to the other world.

But where did the Guanches come from, and when did they reach the Canary Islands?

The few fragments of the Guanche languages that can be reconstructed from place-names and a handful of recorded phrases show that they were Berber speakers from North Africa. The occasional letters carved on rocks and cave walls throughout the islands are related to scripts used by the ancient Berbers and by the modern Tuaregs. The archaeological remains and what we know of their social customs find many parallels in North Africa. With these links the "where" is relatively easy to establish; the "when' is more difficult.

Much has been made of the racial types that made up the Guanche populations before the conquest—the Cro-Magnon and the Mediterranean—and several waves of invaders have been suggested on this basis. However, since the introduction of scientific dating techniques—especially radio-carbon dating—such racial distinctions have been shown to be totally irrelevant.

All the radio-carbon dates so far point to the first or second century B.C. as the most likely time for the Guanches to have moved across into the islands. There are a couple of earlier dates, around 500 B.C., but these are not directly related to human activity—just a few fragments of charcoal and lizard bones, both of which occur quite naturally on these volcanic islands. Even by the earliest dates the Cro-Magnon and Mediterranean populations around the Mediterranean Sea had been long mixed into early Berber tribes.

Unless further archaeological finds are made and the early writings deciphered, much of the islands' early history will remain the subject of supposition and guesswork from the few materials available.

Left, a Guanche mummy. Right, Los Letreros, Guanche writings on Hierro, as yet undeciphered.

THE STRUGGLES OF CONQUEST

Even in antiquity the western Canaries were more favoured than the neighbouring islands to the east. Pliny's names for these "Fortunate Islands" include Pluvialia and Nivaria—isles of rain and snow respectively, easily recognisable as the modern La Palma or Gomera, which still enjoy relatively high rainfall, and Tenerife, dominated by the snow-capped peak of Mount Teide.

The names betray the islands' secret: in an archipelago where rainfall is precious and permanent waterways virtually unknown, sources of irrigation were vital in pre-industrial times. The legend of the "holy tree" of Hierro, which produced copious dewfalls as if by a miracle, makes the same point: the islanders were delighted by the water available to them.

There are sketchy descriptions of what may be the western Canaries in two 14th-century navigators' tales, but the best evidence about their early exploration is cartographical. Ancient knowledge of them had been almost forgotten by the time Atlantic navigation resumed in the very late 13th or early 14th centuries and it was not until the drawing of the Pizigani portolan chart in 1367 that Tenerife, Gomera and Hierro seem to have been depicted on a map.

In 1375 the so-called Catalan Atlas was made, probably by the Aragonese royal cartographer Cresques Abraham, it is one of the most famous and beautiful maps of the middle ages, as rich and intricate as the spilled contents of a jewel casket. Here only La Palma is omitted, and Tenerife is unmistakably displayed with the gleaming, towering peak of Mount Teide conspicuously sketched.

The *Libro del conoscimiento*, compiled from the legends of maps at about the same time, lists 11 islands of the Canaries and includes the name "Tenerife"—rendered as "tenerifiz"—for the first time. At the same time the roughly contemporary work of the Mallorcan mapmaker Guillem Soler improves on the Catalan Atlas and excels some later maps in placing the archipelago in its true position relative to the African coast.

The depiction of the Canaries was virtually complete: Hierro has been thought to have been omitted but is in fact clearly visible in a version of the Soler map surviving in Florence. By the time of the work of Pasqualini and Viladestes early in the new century, Hierro was reduced to its proper size, though its shape remained odd. The era of exploration was accomplished.

Coveted as the western islands were by the European navigators who began frequenting the Canaries in the 14th century, they were not easy to conquer. Only the smallest, poorest and least populated of them, Hierro, fell to the conqueror of the eastern islands, Jean de Béthencourt, between 1402 and 1405. He settled the island with 120 colonists from his native Normandy; though Castilian settlers joined in subsequent years, existence was precarious, the livings poor, the history of the colony virtually undocumented and its survival surprising.

The conquering Spaniards put the islands on the map. Right, Jean de Béthencourt.

Gomera, La Palma and Tenerife, by contrast, were all populous islands, whose natives saw off de Béthencourt's attacks. In the 70 years that followed the end of his efforts, the next largest island, Gomera, was the only one to fall to Christian invaders.

The Las Casas-Peraza family of Seville, who had a long history of slaving in the Canaries and had been among de Béthencourt's backers, disputed the right of conquest of the western islands with numerous contenders: Béthencourt's heirs, fellow-Sevillian merchant-aristocrats and the Portuguese prince, Henry the Navigator; it was not until the late 1440s that the head of the house, Fernán Peraza, felt secure enough in the possession of the islands of Lanzarote, Fuerteventura and Hierro to give undivided attention to the extension of the conquest. His campaigns were remembered by witnesses at a judicial enquiry some 30 years later and are celebrated in popular verses, still sung in the islands to this day. His attacks on Gomera and La Palma were said to have cost him 10,000 ducats and the life of his son, Guillén, who died on La Palma:

Weep, ladies, weep, if God give you grace,
For Guillén Peraza, who left in that place
The Flower, now withered, that blossomed in his face...
Guillén Peraza, Guillén Peraza,
Where is your shield and where is your lance?
All is undone by fatal Mischance.

The language of the traditional verses is richly chivalric: the invocation of ladies, the allusion to God, the images of shield and lance, the brooding presence of Mischance or Ill-fortune—*la malandanza*—combine to make La Palma seem an island of romance. In reality, the wars of the Peraza family were squalid affairs, waged against neolithic savages who were scarcely fit opponents.

Fear and persecution: In Gomera, the Perazas' methods of exploitation stand equally outside chivalry and outside the normal pattern of the history of the development of Atlantic colonisation. For on Gomera the native population was relatively numerous, and remained so until the 1480s. The traditional economy, yielding cheeses and hides, was not at first disturbed. The Perazas shut themselves up in their crude and comfortless keep of stone—which stands to this day, just outside the island's capital of San Sebastian—and sustained with their "vassals" a relationship of mutual fear.

Gomera's very singularity was its undoing. The Genoese merchants who financed the conquest of Gran Canaria in the early 1480s were unwilling to tolerate indefinitely the abandonment of fertile and potentially exploitable lands nearby to native herders and gatherers.

The recurring tension between the Peraza and their reluctant "vassals" the islanders made the *status quo* untenable, anyway, and gave the Castilian monarchs a pretext for intervention. The natives rebelled in 1478, taking the opportunity of war between Castile and Portugal to "procure favours" from the enemy (the Portuguese), as was alleged by the Peraza and believed by the authorities in Castile. A further rebellion in 1484 can be inferred from the monarchs' warning that

they should obey their lords and pay their tribute. By 1448, they were again in revolt.

In 1488 and 1489, royal forces from Gran Canaria made two brutal incursions, between which the young Hernán Peraza, who ruled the island as a resident lord on his family's behalf, was put to death by native insurgents. In revenge, the rebels were executed or enslaved in droves, with dubious legality, as "rebels against their natural lords", and the island was permanently garrisoned from Gran Canaria.

The treatment of the natives touched tender consciences in Castile; the monarchs established an inquiry by a committee of jurists and theologists into the proprieties of the case; the release of the enslaved Gomerans (largely on the mainland) was recommended and many of them eventually returned to the archipelago to help colonise other conquests. Their native land, however, was now ripe for transformation by European settlers. In the next decade, it became another among many colonial sugar-islands.

A harder task: The conquests of Tenerife and La Palma, meanwhile, were proving elusive. The Peraza family made incursions in the 1460s and 1470s. The tomb of the effective head of the clan, Diego de Herrera, bore an epitaph claiming that he had received the submission of all nine native chieftains of Tenerife. The material results of these efforts, however, were minimal. By the time the conquest of Gran Canaria was finished, and that of Gomera perfected, the crown had no resources left with which to further matters in the remaining islands, against their notoriously indomitable defenders.

The conquests of La Palma and Tenerife, therefore, were left to private sources of money and means of recruiting. Instead of wages, the conquistadores were promised plots of conquered land. Instead of the yield from the sale of papal indulgences or the direct use of the crown's share of booty to meet the costs of the war, booty yet uncollected was pledged as rewards to conquerors who could raise up-front finance elsewhere.

Peraza's tower in San Sebastian, a "comfortless keep of stone." Above, Alonso Fernández de Lugo raises his cross on Gran Canaria.

The conquests of La Palma and Tenerife were thus financed by *ad hoc* companies, in which financiers and conquistadores agreed to share the proceeds. The organiser of the consortia and captain of the hosts was Alonso Fernández de Lugo, a ruthless and ambitious paladin who had held a subordinate command in the conquest of Gran Canaria. Most of his partners were Genoese merchants of Seville who were looking for an investment in sugar-lands.

In neither conquest was success effected by prowess—despite the chivalric postures struck by the Spaniards in the sources—but in the one case by stratagem and in the other by luck. Alonso de Lugo's invasion of La Palma in 1492 was preceded by the missionary activities of a remarkable woman: the native neophyte or new convert, Francisca de Gazmira.

That an episcopal licence should have been conferred on this lay, native, female missionary suggests extraordinary charismatic powers which she seems to have used to good effect among her people. It was perhaps thanks to this preparation that de Lugo encountered little opposition and some help when he landed on the western seaboard. Reinforced by Christian tribes of the west, he marched round the island in a clockwise direction, defeating piecemeal tribes who made no effort to unite in resistance.

The interior was the scene of a fiercer defence, for there volcanic activity and erosion had combined to create a vast natural fortress, La Caldera, which was occupied by a single tribe under a leader whom tradition calls Tanausú. If our sole but tardy source can be believed, Tanausú might have resisted indefinitely had de Lugo not tricked him into attending a sham parley, at which he was overcome and his followers were all captured or killed.

Here, for once, the historical tradition seems to depart from purely heroic and therefore biased version of events. The surviving history text revealing the treachery dates from the 1590s, when such bold revisionists as the Dominican writer, Fray

Alonso de Espinosa, were challenging the received image of the conquest of the Canaries, praising the natural virtues of the natives and defending their rights. Denunciations of conquistador perfidy were in fashion. No doubt the version we have is as warped as the early chronicles, which reflect perceptions of conquest saturated in chivalric imagery. But cruelty and ruthless daring are thoroughly characteristic of everything that is known about Alonso de Lugo.

Partly, perhaps, because of his early reputation for rapacity, de Lugo's operations thereafter were bedevilled by shortage of finance and legal entanglements with his backers. He narrowly averted disaster in both the campaigns to which the conquest of Tenerife committed him. From the first, which occupied the summer of 1494, he barely escaped with his life after being lured into a trap at Acentejo near the mouth of the Orotava valley. The enduring place-name, La Matanza, recalls the massacre of his men. He was probably making for Taoro—the richest of nine territorial chieftaincies into which the island seems to have been divided.

Tenerife falls: De Lugo returned with larger forces, probably late in 1495, disabused of his first facile expectation that the conquest would take 10 months. Now, however, it was the turn of the Chief of Taoro to succumb to overconfidence. That overwhelming native prince had driven four tribes into alliance with de Lugo; the remainder formed a hostile confederacy, which attacked de Lugo's camp near La Laguna in flat terrain suited to the Spaniards' cavalry. The environs gave the islanders little protection from crossbow fire. Today the battle-site is covered by an appropriate memorial: an elegant residential quarter of leafy villas.

Even after the inevitable Spanish victory, de Lugo remained in winter quarters. When he gingerly sallied forth, early in 1496, he found the natives depleted and debilitated by an unidentified epidemic—the first of a series of mysterious diseases, presumably brought by the Europeans, which caused a demographic disaster comparable, on Tenerife's smaller scale, to those which later devastated the New World. De Lugo resumed his march on Taoro. This time, when he reached Acentejo, he was ready. He avenged the former disaster in a definitive victory. The last chief of Taoro sent his despair the way of his hopes and committed ritual suicide, just as some of the defenders of Gran Canaria had done more than a decade before.

Above, the Virgin of Candelaria, once the object of pagan worship.

Surprisingly, no chronicler mentioned this event, but the spot where the Chief ended his life became a celebrated landmark and is referred to in many early land-grants to colonists. After this ritual ending the tribes who remained in arms quickly made their submissions and by June 1496 Alonso de Lugo was able to parade their leaders before his monarchs, under the eyes of the Venetian ambassador, at Almazán.

The fate of the captive natives was the subject of a furious debate. Clerical advocates—especially Franciscans—saw them as the epitype of all that was best in "natural" man: rude but educable, artless but susceptible to the friars' own arts, fully members of a human community.

There was a schism, however, between the friars' perceptions and those of the conquistadores and potential lay colonists. The former exercised influence disproportionate to their numbers, but the latter held sway in colonial society. Of the experts who remained in armchairs back home, humanists were closest, in their image of the primitive, to the missionaries, sharing an appreciative view and emphasising the natural virtue of the natives; jurists, concerned to justify the conquest, provided raw material for conquistadores by scrutinising native society in the light of Christian ideas of "natural law".

Most laymen, however, rejected the images of the natives conjured up by learned tradition. Their expectations were dominated by stereotypes of the sub-human creatures that occupied the nether links of the chain of being. For the German physician, Hieronymus Münzer, who saw some Guanches in 1497, they were "beasts in human form"; Beatriz de Bobadilla denied that the Gomerans could be Christians on the grounds that "they go about naked".

Fate of the natives: Early colonial society was thus an inauspicious milieu for the native. Survivors after the conquest were few, to be numbered in hundreds rather than thousands, even in Tenerife, where they were most numerous. And those whom the slavers and conquerors spared, the newly introduced sicknesses depleted.

Spaniards of the period were more sensitive to differences of class than race and some members of the native aristocracy found ready acceptance and cultural assimilation. Don Fernando Guanarteme, for instance, a Hispanophile Chief of Gran Canaria who was employed in the conquest of Tenerife, was able to marry his daughters to Spanish *hidalgos*; the sons of the Chiefs of Tenerife, though excluded from the most valuable portions of land, were treated as notables by society and accorded the dignifying title of "Don".

But at a lower social level, natives who survived did so mainly as domestic slaves or rebels in the hills, or in such solitary occupations as herdsmen and gatherers, or in enclaves apart from colonial society, like that granted on Tenerife to members of Don Fernando Guanarteme's tribe for survival in an alien island.

Towards the end of the 16th century, when the islanders were threatened with extinction, antiquarian amateurs compiled ethnographic information about them, perhaps in imitation of the great compilations (which were coming to be known in Europe) written by missionaries in the New World. The Dominican Espinosa emerged as the great defender of the Guanches in a work on the Virgin-patroness of the islands.

The image of the Virgin of Candelaria, according to tradition, had appeared miraculously on Tenerife before the conquest and was revered by the natives even before they understood its significance. This seemed to be evidence of the natural piety of the pre-conquest natives.

This story also provided a splendid moral example with which to castigate the imperfections of the Spaniards' own lives: stolen by a would-be conquistador, the Virgin reputedly turned her face to the wall and would not face her ravisher until she was restored to her own shrine, among her pagan followers.

Writing in the 1590s, Espinosa was still spellbound by the traditional debate on natural law. "They did not live altogether outside law," he claimed, "for in some things their actions were according to reason." In other literature spawned by reports or memories of the natives, their image became altogether popular genre of the time: pastoral literature peopled by noble savages. In a play of Lope de Vega, and the poems of Cairrasco and Viana, they led, not real lives, but a bucolic idyll, in idealised simplicity, enlivened by coy love affairs, rhetorically elaborated. "Natural man" had yielded to another, even less apposite literary stereotype.

THE AGE OF SUGAR AND WINE

"Sugar farming", wrote the natural historian, Gonzalo Fernández de Oviedo in the 1530s, "is one of the most profitable businesses there can be in any province or kingdom the world over." He had the enormous success of the sugar trade of Tenerife, Gomera and La Palma in mind.

In the first half of the 16th century the sugar-wealth of the islands became proverbial. It was cited by Bacon as the model of "a wonderful overgrowth in riches". It was copied in the Antilles and Brazil and, ironically, eventually ruined by the cheaper, bigger outputs of the same transatlantic colonies it influenced.

Except in La Palma, the Canary sugar trade collapsed almost as suddenly as it had arisen. But, for its brief day, it was the making and the moulding of the islands' economies and societies alike.

The origins of sugar cultivation were owed entirely to the private initiative of Alonso Fernández de Lugo, who had seen how readily canes sprouted in the soil of Gran Canaria in the 1480s. He introduced the crop to Tenerife and La Palma as soon as he completed the conquests of those islands. He later introduced it to Gomera, too, when the island became his by marriage.

On Tenerife he built two refineries at El Realejos, a third at Daute and a fourth at Icod. On La Palma he built another at Río de los Sauces, which he later mortgaged to an English sugar-merchant, Thomas Mailliard, and to the Genoese financier, Francesco Spinola. It was on land opposite this that the Welzer family and company opened the first of their many ventures in the Spanish monarchy, when they erected a sugar mill in 1513. The water to drive it was shared between de Lugo and the Welzers.

Generally, de Lugo was indefatigable in promotion of the crop, making the land-grants in his gift conditional, in many cases, on the grantees' promise to plant canes or erect a mill, wherever the grant was substantial or well-watered. In 1502 he tried to exclude rival activities from the area of Taoro, in Tenerife, which he designated for sugar production exclusively.

Left, harvesting the local grape. From having once been a major industry, today's Canary wine is rarely exported.

By dint of de Lugo's land-grants, the Orotava Valley and the coast adjoining it, north-west Tenerife (Icod, Daute, Garachico) and Güimar in the east were effectively turned to the predominant cultivation and milling of sugar for export.

Sugar kings: The industry was capital-intensive. Neither the planting of canes nor the building of mills came cheaply. When a refinery was built, huge expenditure was needed to stoke the fires of the "purging rooms" and to pay the specialised and heavy labour the work demanded. Mill owners charged up to 50 percent of revenue from produce brought to them for processing by small cultivators.

Thus the islands acquired, in the first generation of settlement, a capitalist élite, who owned the bulk of irrigable land and controlled the output of the sugar industry through ownership of refineries. Many of them—and almost all of the really rich and successful—were foreigners.

The Genoese Matteo Vigna, for instance, had been an indispensable source of finance for the conquest, "and without me," he could declare, "the island would not be so well peopled as it is". Tomaso Giustiniani, his fellow-countryman, had interests in sugar, dye-stuffs and fish: an indication of his status is that in 1506 the visiting Inquisitors chose to lodge in his house in La Laguna.

Cristofforo Daponte had traded in dyes before the completion of the conquest and was a big sugar-baron from 1497. He went on to marry a niece of Alonso Fernández de Lugo and lived in old age to cheat the Inquisition of his soul: summoned to an interrogation, he was "unable to cross over, owing to great age and many infirmities".

All these, and others like them, served for long spells on the island council of Tenerife, exploiting their economic preponderance for political advantage. Their presence was resented, but their hold unshakeable. Accused by Castilian colonists of favouring foreigners, de Lugo admitted the charge, but appealed to necessity. The islands needed the Portuguese for their hard work, he said, and they needed the Italians for their money.

The presence of Portuguese workers in large numbers made the sugar industry viable, for they were employed to harvest the canes on a share-cropping basis. Thus the Canaries were spared the need to import black slaves on a large scale; the "plantation economies" created by the monocultures of the New World never afflicted the islands.

There were, however, plenty of other sources of social tension. To disputes between Castilian-born colonists and "foreigners" was added hatred between the owners of water-sources and landholders desperate for irrigation for their canes.

The islands seem to have been better watered in the 16th century than they are today. A writer of the 1590s referred to "a large number" of springs, streams and waterfalls in northern Tenerife; but the deforestation that produced the pitch and stoked the sugar-mills in turn diminished the rainfall of the western islands, so that today a stream that does not run dry in summer is a rare find, despite the large numbers of valleys.

Water problems: But surface water was never abundant and exploitation brought problems of its own. In some cases, where the right to use local water was in private hands, it divided the colonists like the distributaries of a stream, while in others, where its use was communal, it brought them together in tense but narrow co-operation. Irrigation communities became a widespread and effective form of social organisation, so that the water that sculpted the soil was institutionally creative, too.

By the mid-16th century, with fortunate consequences for the islands' future, a balance in the distribution of use-rights in water had been achieved. Small men were protected by stable communities of *adulados* or sharers-by-turns. These were equipped with institutions or arbitration or jurisdiction sufficient to resolve day-to-day problems without recourse to the wasteful judicial structure of the realm and without the loss of local capital in expensive appeals to the courts of the Spanish peninsula.

At the same time the monarchs and their representatives firmly resisted any attempts to distribute water more equably or to wrest waters from the control of large-scale cultivators and millers. The murder of one of the most notorious water-monopolists in 1513, for instance, achieved nothing, for his heirs enjoyed redoubled protection from the monarchs and governors. This was just as well. The era of colonisation was a critical one for the economy of the Canary Islands: a radical experiment in a rather unpromising place. Success depended on investment by the few whom the authorities favoured for their wealth and enterprise.

This early colonial society was paradoxically lawless and litigious. The evidence which survives in abundance, especially for Tenerife, in part confirms conventional presuppositions about the nature of "frontier societies". There were evidently plenty of

criminals and fugitives among the colonists of the Canaries, who stood as individuals outside the usual social configurations or groups, and whose links were with others of their kind. Though bigamy—not surprisingly, perhaps, in the case of remote islands—seems to be the most widespread crime of these fugitives, there were numerous instances of violent malefactors and embezzlers settling on the islands, a tradition which has not altogether disappeared even in the modern era.

Vendettas originating among the families of Seville were continued in the Canaries. Prosecution of crime and exaction of justice were exceptionally difficult because of the long distances which separate the archipelago from mainland Spain, and punishment could be delayed or evaded by appeals to the Iberian peninsula.

Locally strong individuals, like de Lugo, could hire and protect thugs for their own purposes and disregard the law themselves. De Lugo, for instance, used his authority to declare that debts to himself and his wife should be discharged before all other outstanding debts on the island.

Matteo Vigna, to whom some 100 debtors owed a total of 450,000 *maravedis* complained to the monarchs and asked them to appoint "a good man from whom he might obtain his just due, for on the said island of Tenerife he could never obtain justice". Even with the foundation of a permanent Royal Tribunal in Gran Canaria in 1526, the western Canaries never acquired adequate and inexpensive judicial institutions for the relief of tension between neighbours.

When Alonso Fernández de Lugo died in 1525, he left rough-hewn his own vision of the islands. The visitor today to the capital he founded at La Laguna can trace the grid-plan of the streets laid out in the Renaissance manner, but he will notice that the elegant square which de Lugo conceived as the heart of the city is still perched precariously on its edge. At de Lugo's death, one side of this square—where the market now stands—was still planted with vines, and it has never really succeeded in becoming the city's heart. This lack of symbiosis is symbolic of the continuous gap between the ceremonious pretensions of colonial government and the rough-and-ready reality of the emulous and often violent settler society.

The lure of the New World was bringing new immigration virtually to an end; an era of demographic stagnancy was beginning. Yet enduring features of the western Canaries—particularly of the three big islands of Tenerife, La Palma and Gomera—were already taking shape.

Left, collecting orchilla for dyeing was an early industry. Above, early representation of La Laguna, with its original lake.

Culture exchange: The primitive culture of the pre-conquest islanders had been overwhelmed by the civilisation of the invaders and replaced by a new society. Ultimately, the ancient Canarios were neither exterminated nor "acculturated" but simply assimilated. Caspar Frutuoso's description of La Palma at the end of the 16th century is an eloquent testimony: the three main elements of the population of that island—Castilian, Portuguese and indigenous—were more or less equally mixed, according to his impression, and interbred already to a great extent; those who conserved their ethnic identity coexisted as equals, by his report, and were indistinguishable in faith and habit.

On Tenerife, evidence of islanders' wills show the settlers to have acquired a creole enthusiasm for the native cult of the Virgin of Candelaria. As in the New World, the "Black Legend" in the Canaries is neither wholly true nor wholly false. The natives—numbered only six hundred in all on Tenerife, where they were most numerous according to an estimate of the island council—who survived in the recesses of the islands until the late 17th century (later "sightings" all seem fancifully inspired). Hints of the sufferings to which these survivors were exposed have come down to us in the pages of their champion Alonso de Espinosa, who found the Guanches of the 1590s sullen, intimidated and uncommunicative towards their new masters.

A generation earlier, Benzoni had encountered only one old native in La Palma, "all whose delight was in getting intoxicated". The syndrome of alcoholism and fear is familiar enough among conquered primitives suffering from "cultural shock". The colonial transformation was at least as thorough as anywhere in the Hispanic world.

Present-day islanders conserve traces of the pre-conquest past in a few area of folklore, diet, dance and the rhythm of popular rhymes. They find myths of Guanche survival comforting. But all save a tiny minority regard themselves as Spaniards. When they recall the conquest, they do not think of it as an alien triumph, like contemporary Mexicans or Peruvians, but, like Costaricans or North Americans of "Anglo-Saxon" descent, they identify with the conquerors.

From sugar to wine: The sugar-based prosperity of the 16th century did not last. The development of sugar plantations in the Antilles and Brazil created a cheap and abundant source of supply which could undercut Canarian production. Nevertheless, the growth of trade with the New World also opened up the possibility of new economic strategies for the Canaries, which the western islands, and Tenerife in particular, were able to exploit successfully.

The sugar market had been confined to the Old World, and to northern outlets in particular, such as England, Flanders and Germany; strong southern wine became the sought-after product to replace sugar, and it was also much in demand in the growing American colonies. The Malvasia grape, in particular, which had originated in the Aegean islands, and had been carried by

Genoese planters in Sicily, and thence to Madeira and the Canaries, proved highly adaptable, especially in Tenerife.

Malvasia was already established in the eastern Canaries by the late 15th century. It yielded specialist, luxury wines, which were uniquely suited to long-distance trade, because, sweet and liquorous, they travelled well, commanded higher prices than drier, thinner local wines and appealed particularly to northern tastes. Malmsey and Madeira are among its modern progeny. By the time Falstaff and Sir Toby Belch were draining "cups of Canary", wine was taking over as the islands' major export. To Bostonians of the late 17th century, the archipelago was known as "the Isles of Wine".

The virtues which made Canary wine so sought-after were admirably summarised by Charles II's historiographer-royal, James Howell: the wines which the islands produced, he wrote, "are accounted the richest, the most firm, the best-bodied and lastingest wine, and the most desecated from all earthly grossness of any other whatsoever: it hath little or no sulphur at all in it, and leaves less dregs behind, though one drink it to excess. Of this wine, if of any other, may be verified that merry induction that good wine makes good blood, good blood causeth good humours, good humours cause good thoughts, good thoughts bring forth good works, good works carry a man to heaven; ergo, good wine carrieth a man to heaven.

"If this be true, surely more English go to heaven this way than any other; for I think there is more Canary brought into England than to all the world besides. I think also there is a hundred times more drunk under the name of Canary wine than there is brought in; for Sherries and Malagas well might pass for Canaries in most taverns, more often than Canary itself. When Sacks and Canaries were first brought in among us, they were used to be drunk in aqua-vitae measures; and it was held fit only for those to drink of them who were used to carry their legs in their hands, their eyes upon their noses, and an almanack in their bones; but now they go down everyone's throat, both young and old, like milk."

Left, today's vineyards on Lanzarote. Right, local wine made the islands happy and prosperous.

The fortunes of Canarian viticulture depended on access to trade. The Italian engineer Leonardo Torriani, who visited the Canaries to inspect the fortifications in the 1590s, realised the islanders' commercial vocation or destiny. "Men's lives in these islands," he wrote, "devoted to manufacture and to trading, are regulated by what is called "effective" philosophy, which is influenced by the mutable sign of Cancer and the variable nature of the moon."

The most important trade routes were those to and from the New World, not only because of American markets for Canary wine but also because the New World trade needed Atlantic staging-posts which would

attract shipping from all over Europe.

In one respect, the Canaries were ideally placed—especially Tenerife, which had a range of fine oceanic harbours, and Gomera, which possessed the most westerly port on the route to the West Indies: the Atlantic wind-system made them ideal ports of call for shipping bound for the New World. It was, however, the policy of the Spanish crown, for almost the first three centuries of transatlantic navigation, to restrict the benefits of the New World trade to Castilian subjects only, and the most effective way of excluding interlopers was to confine all traffic to one or two peninsular ports.

Thus the Canaries became the focal point for every kind of attempt to break into Spain's New World monopoly—smuggling, fraud, piracy were all most easily practised in the islands. In the 1560s, the Spanish monarchy moved to staunch the lesion in Spain's Atlantic artery by introducing strict regulation and vigilance of the archipelago's trade with America. Native traders suffered along with the foreigners.

Short-lived prosperity: No island benefited more than Tenerife from the relaxation of this system from 1610. One of her major ports, Santa Cruz, had been enlarged in 1604. Her wine production considerably exceeded that of other islands, and she had foreign connexions and expatriate residents of long standing.

The consequent prosperity was reflected in rising fortunes that created an aristocracy of *bourgeois gentilhommes* in the island: the Marquesses of Celada were instituted in 1614; of Acialcázar, Adeje, la Breña and Villanueva de Prado in 1666, the last-named builders of La Laguna's finest surviving palace, the Casa Nava Grimón; the Marquesses of la Fuente de Las Palmas in 1679; of Villafuerte in 1680; of La Florida in 1685. The Marquessate of Quintroja and four countships were founded between then and the end of the century.

Foreign capitalists converged on Tenerife to export the wine and cash in on the accessibility of New World routes. In the mid-century there were 1,500 English and Dutch residents in a total population of well under 50,000. In March, 1665, the Canary Island Company was formed in London, with exclusive rights to trade in Canary Island wines in England, and with the aim of cornering the market, but a merchant of Tenerife, Francisco Tomás Alfaro, led the way in defying the monopoly.

The monopoly dispute came at a time of doubling of prices in London but hopes of unparalleled prosperity were short-lived. Tenerife's wines became easy to under-cut, while over-production and poor quality anyway threatened their domination of the market. In July 1675 the island council banned the planting of new vines. In 1685-7, famine and a plague of locusts wrecked production; but there was no market, in any case, with the English imposing a ban on Canary wines in retaliation for the rejection of the Canary Company.

For the present, however, the trade proved resilient enough. 10,000 pipes of Canary a year were still reaching London in the last years of the century—roughly 20 percent

Above, a *lagar*, or wine press.

more than 100 years previously.

The ruin of the English market seems to have been caused not by the aftermath of the Canary Company affair, but by a combination of structural problems and long-term trends. The price of Malvasia made it vulnerable to competition. In 1670, for instance, at £36 for a pipe in London, it was £4 more than Málaga wine, which was similar in character, and twice the price of claret.

Meanwhile, the slow but irresistible rise of Madeira in English esteem was working its effect. The newcomer broke into the English market on a large scale in the 1680s, achieving a mean annual rate of importation of nearly 7,000 pipes. Aided by the Methuen treaty of 1703, which granted favourable terms of trade to Britain's Portuguese allies, Madeira gradually came to displace Malvasia in English taste.

Eventually the War of the Spanish Succession (1701-14) thoroughly wrecked the trade in Canary. Down to less than 2,500 pipes a year by the end of the war, import levels in England never recovered.

Foreign dynasties: The fortunes of the tinerfeño economy revived, and were sustained at a respectable level, in the 18th century, thanks in large measure to the entrepreneurship of a number of merchant-dynasties in Tenerife, many of whom were foreign.

The Irish had peculiar advantages in this era. As Catholic Anglophobes they were welcome in island society. As members of family networks that stretched across the northern Atlantic, often with representatives in England's North American colonies, they were able to exploit the structures of family businesses. And they had the inestimable benefit of dual nationality, as subjects both of the English and Spanish crowns, which enabled them to compete on equal terms both in the Canarian market and in their English and North American outlets.

Representative figures of this profitable and ambivalent world were Nicholas Bernard Valois Fitzgerald and his son-in-law, John Colgan Blanco. The first, who flourished in the 1730s, and died aged only 35 in 1741, was a brilliant meteor in the tinerfeño firmament. He had a library of 67 books and boasted a family tree, written in Latin on vellum, and enhanced by certificates of nobility and purity of blood issued in Waterford and La Orotava. His public benefactions included the supply of water to what is now the town of Puerto de la Cruz.

Colgan, who dominated the Irish community in the 1750s and 1760s, came near to dominating the entire island. His cartel of wine buyers outraged the indigenous aristocrats who grew the grapes. The Marquess of San Andrés accused him of "squeezing the land like a sponge, and draining its life-blood like a leech". For the Marquess of Villanueva del Prado of his day, he was a "mercantile despot". The Irish were acquiring something of the profile, and much of the resentment, that the Genoese had achieved in island society two centuries before.

It was perhaps Colgan's genius that found the solution to the problem of Tenerife's failing viticulture. The island had always produced a wine from second-class grapes, known as Vidueño, cheaply produced with indifferent results and reserved for the domestic and colonial trades. Whether or not it was Colgan who first had the idea of turning these wines into a sort of phoney Madeira to undercut the Portuguese suppliers, it was certainly he more than any other individual who dedicated himself, in the 1750s and 1760s, to the perfection and promotion of Tenerife's new wine.

Colgan saw to it that his product had the requisite body and colour; he offered it at competitive prices in pipes an eighth larger than those of Madeira. From 1766 he exported it to British East India, at £10 for a pipe to Madeira's £24 for a pipe. This "monstrous" difference, he hoped, would induce the East India Company "to send all their ships to this island, at least when the Gentlemen Directors are acquainted with its quality". As a promotional ploy, he held a tasting on a merchantman bound for Madras, "the quality whereof, the Captain and Gentlemen assured, pleased them as much and even better than any Madeira they have ever drank".

The fake Madeira helped to salvage Tenerife's economy. Its market penetration was never very strong within Europe, but in the English American colonies it enjoyed enormous popularity, which the American War of Independence could only boost. Colgan's efforts in East India were not unsuccessful. His "Madeira" had established itself as a sundowner's tipple—a cheap flavour of metropolitan life in distant colonies.

The material effects of the preservation of Tenerife's fragile 18th-century prosperity are still available for the visitor to see in the streets of the wine-rich Baroque towns, like Orotava in Tenerife and Los Llanos in La Palma. Even Santa Cruz de Tenerife, which was only a small port in the 18th century, has the sumptuous Casa de La Carta or de los Hamilton, with its glazed cloister intricately carved in *tea* wood.

Tenerife has the richest ensemble because it dominated the trade. Nearly 60 percent of Canarian wine came from the island in the 1770s, and the island always enjoyed the lion's share of concessions to trade with the New World. The regulations of 1718, for instance, allowed 600 metric tons to be exported to the Indies from Tenerife and only 150 from Gran Canaria.

When uninhibited trade was allowed to selected ports in 1778, Santa Cruz de Tenerife was the only Canarian outlet included on the list. In the 1770s Tenerife was producing over four times as much wine as any other island, over half as much corn and over three times as many potatoes. The population of the island was nearly 70,000—an increase of almost 60 percent over 100 years. According to the census of 1768, by comparison, Gran Canaria, Tenerife's rival to the east, had only just over 40,000 inhabitants.

Tenerife's industry created wealth, while the other islands provided her with manpower. No other island had a comparable intellectual life: the Casa Nava Grimón in La Laguna was the setting of a lively *salon*, from where figures of high esteem in mainland Spain proceeded: Tomás de Iriarte, for instance, who was the King of Spain's librarian, and José de Viera y Clavijo, one of the few Spanish historians of the age of Gibbon, both of whom dedicated their major work of research to the history of the Canaries.

In 1788 the Botanical Gardens of Orotava were founded. Meanwhile, it was in La Laguna that efforts to found a university were concentrated.

Left, a Spanish privateer protecting the wine-rich islands. Right, Nelson falls during the attack of 1797, in which he lost his arm.

However, these initial plans eventually foundered, and Viera y Clavijo himself recorded the apogee and incipient decline of Tenerife's trade. "Her glories," he wrote in 1776, "are passing into oblivion." He bemoaned the lack of ideas and of enlightened spirits; the remoteness of the court and the rule of indifferent bureaucrats from the peninsula; the shortage of rain; the exposure to southern winds, which brought the locusts, and northern winds, which brought the pirates. Above all, he noted, the demand for

Canarian wine was beginning to diminish.

Wine unwinds: For the rest of the century the trade was in a state of crisis. Disrupted by the American war, and ironically damaged by the much-vaunted trade decree of 1778, which in effect increased competition from peninsular wines, the situation was only temporarily restored by the peculiar conditions of the French Revolutionary and Napoleonic Wars.

In 1797, when Nelson's attack on Santa Cruz was beaten off, the citizens rowed out a present of wine to the defeated commander. It was a publicity gesture worthy of John Colgan, the former genius of the wine trade, himself. For a while the British navy consumed Tenerife's wine surplus during the blockade of the Atlantic against French shipping, but this unexpected reprieve was brought to an end by the peace of 1815. By then, revolutions in Spain's American colonies posed an even more severe threat to the Canarian economy. Previously the islands' generally adverse balance of trade had been made up by remittances from Canarian workers in the American colonies, but the disruption of their payments home caused by the war reduced their families to irremediable misery.

There was no substitute to hand for the declining wine trade. Sugar had never been entirely eradicated from La Palma; whereas the last sugar tithe was paid in Gran Canaria in 1648 and in Tenerife in 1718, La Palma still had a productive sugar mill in operation for most of the 19th century, although it had become a local industry.

Silk had made some contribution, also in La Palma. Mulberries had been introduced there as early as 1517 by Diego de Funes, a physician of Tenerife; by the mid-1770s there were 3,000 weavers. But the exports seem to have been directed to the same shrinking markets as the wines, and production figures plummeted in the 20 years after the Napoleonic Wars.

The visitor to Santa Cruz de Tenerife might easily be misled by the appearance of 19th-century prosperity. The Masonic eye that stares from the pediment of the temple in the Calle San Lúcas seems to glint with the unorthodox priorities of a radical bourgeois plutocracy; the ceramic-tiled fountains of the Parque Sanabria, the elegant villas that surround it, might have amused and housed the same class; in the high Victorian splendour of the interior of the Teatro Guimerá, the familiar ostentation of provincial *parvenues* is magnificently evoked.

Yet Santa Cruz is unrepresentative. From a modest 18th-century port it was transformed in the new century into the capital of the archipelago, where most of the institutions of government were concentrated. In any case, the town's monuments are mostly of the very late 19th or early 20th centuries, when, thanks to steamship navigation, the fortunes of the archipelago began to revive.

The main new product of the mid-century—cochineal, introduced from Mexico in 1825 and exported on a large scale in the third quarter of the century—was concentrated in the eastern islands; the policy-makers in Tenerife were not taken in by the "illusion of salvation" which cochineal represented. Even so, the arboriculturists of Orotava were aghast at the damage wrought by the cochineal craze to the native forest. The cochineal grubs formed and fed on a peculiar species of cactus, which, in some areas, displaced native pines or defunct vines and canes. Their ugly bulk, it was said, disfigured the landscape and threatened the rainfall levels when planted in place of trees. When the cochineal boom was destroyed by the swift rise of chemical dyes in the 1870s

and 1880s, the intelligentsia of the western islands accounted themselves lucky that Tenerife, relatively, and La Palma, Gomera and Hierro, largely, had escaped the scourge.

Hierro, though spared the effects of the reaction against cochineal, had nothing to substitute for it. As an English visitor of 1884 reported, "there is no sign of the island having benefitted by the sudden influx of wealth which cochineal brought generally to the archipelago. There are no public works half finished, and no large houses going to decay. All is poverty. The inhabitants are peasants, and the best of them are still but well-to-do peasants."

La Palma and Gomera, however, were beginning to reap the benefits of a well-run tobacco industry. Its leading figure was the homonymous creator of the Don Miguel brand, Don Miguel himself, who proudly showed foreign visitors round his manufactory in Tazacorte. But this sort of success was sporadic, and the structural problems of the economy remained unsolved.

Tax relief: Only a return to the free-trade regime of the early and mid-16th century could free the islands of dependence on vulnerable monocultures and structural trade-deficits. The dawn of the steamship age and the huge increase in European navigation to west Africa in the second half of the 19th century created a new opportunity.

In 1852, following the examples of the Portuguese in their Atlantic islands, the Spanish government granted free-port status to one port in each of the Canary Islands, except Tenerife, which was to have two, at Santa Cruz and what is now Puerto de la Cruz. In 1868 the entire archipelago was declared open to foreign shipping. In the eastern islands, cochineal and, in Tenerife, "invisible earnings" belatedly took the place of wine as the mainstays of the economy.

Left, a cochineal colony on a cactus; it proved a short-lived industry. Above, bananas lasted rather longer.

At first Tenerife was able to use its privileged status as the "capital" of the archipelago to channel new resources for her own benefit. Money was directed towards the painfully slow business of erecting an infrastructure for the internal development of the islands. In the 1860s Tenerife had the only first-class road in the archipelago, but it reached only as far as Orotava from Santa Cruz. It was not until 1876 that the highway south reached as far as Güimar.

Yet by the standards of the other islands this seemed spectacular. Gran Canaria, whose inhabitants felt starved of resources by tinerfeño greed, had barely ten miles of first-class road.

The resentment such disparities provoked helped to stimulate a political movement in Gran Canaria and, to a lesser extent, in the minor islands, to increase the autonomy of individual islands or to divide the archipelago into two provinces with a capital in Las Palmas as well as Santa Cruz.

Tenerife successfully resisted this initiative, but her economic supremacy was eroded by the development of Las Palmas as a harbour for steamships. In 1881 a harbour improvement scheme for Las Palmas was rushed through the government programme by the Canarian politician, Fernando León y Castillo, whose power base was in Gran Canaria. The effect was phenomenal.

By 1887 Las Palmas was carrying more traffic than Santa Cruz, and the huge foreign—and particularly British— investment of the 1890s in coaling, fruit production, hotels and financial services tended to benefit Gran Canaria first and foremost.

The western islands were not by-passed by the new prosperity, however. This was partly thanks to the continued importance, even in eclipse, of the port of Santa Cruz de Tenerife, but chiefly owing to the beginnings of mass cultivation of the banana in the 1880s.

Banana business: The commercially exploitable "Chinese" banana seems to have been introduced in 1855 by the French consul, Sabine Berthelot, who contributed so much to the study of the ethnology and natural history of the islands. The fruit had been known in other forms in the archipelago since the 16th century, when it was described by the English merchant Thomas Nichols as resembling a cucumber and "best eaten

FRANCO GOES TO WAR

The summer of 1936 was hot and sticky in the Canaries. Winds from the Sahara brought a constant succession of scorching winds and choking dust. A paunchy little man called Franco, once Commander-in-Chief of the Spanish Army, must have found his Canarian posting gruelling.

In March of that year Franco had been removed to Tenerife by the Republican government, fearful of his reputation as a soldier and of his right-wing sentiments—he was suspected of being involved in a series of plots aimed at setting up a dictatorship under a fellow officer, General Sanjurjo. While Sanjurjo was exiled to Portugal, Franco managed to wriggle out of charges of complicity.

In Sanjurjo's absence the military plotters were headed by General Mola. Just before he left for the Canaries, Franco, Mola, and another principal leader of the "Glorious Revolution" of 1936, General Goded, agreed at a secret meeting to back Sanjurjo, who was then in Germany seeking arms and ammunition.

In spite of this promise of support Franco refused to commit himself to any firm plan of action until barely a week before the rising. Nevertheless he joined the other discontented officers at their meetings in the woods of La Esperanza in Tenerife or in the English-owned hotel of Los Frailes on Gran Canaria.

Only the promise of command of Spain's best troops—her tough Moroccan mercenaries and her ruthless Foreign Legion—succeeded in bringing Franco into the plot. Within 48 hours a Dragon Rapide bi-plane had been chartered from the old Croydon aerodrome near London.

On 14 July 1936 the Rapide touched down at Gando, now Las Palmas airport and then the only one in the islands. On board was a select party of English tourists—a retired army major, Hugh Pollard, his daughter Diana, and her friend Dorothy Watson. The family went sightseeing. In Tenerife Pollard contacted one of Franco's officers and delivered his message—"*Galicia saluda a Francia*" (Galicia greets France).

On 16 July the ex-RAF pilot of the Dragon Rapide was warned to have his plane ready. On the same day, the commanding officer of the Las Palmas garrison, General Amadeo Balmes, died conveniently as he cleaned his pistol. By nightfall Franco had obtained the War Office's permission to travel over to his fellow-officer's funeral.

At midnight Franco, his wife and daughter boarded the little Clyde-built steamer, the *Viera y Clavijo*. Shortly after docking in Las Palmas, Franco found the North African garrisons had started the uprising prematurely. An arms search of the rebel HQ in Melilla on the Moroccan coastline had forced the plotters to strike early.

During that hot and hectic afternoon Franco left Las Palmas for the airport. Perhaps fearing an assassination attempt—he had survived three during his short spell on Tenerife—he commandeered "a scruffy tugboat" to get him there.

By the early hours of 18 July, Franco was in North Africa to broadcast his manifesto, promising "to make real in our homeland, for the first time and in this order, that trinity, Fraternity, Liberty and Equality."

The Canary Islands were in Franco's hands by 20 July. On the island of La Palma a false normality was maintained for a further eight sweltering days until the capital, Santa Cruz, was finally bombarded by a pro-Franco cruiser, and surrendered.

Within hours the repression began. Trade Unionists, teachers, left-wing or democratic politicians, and writers and artists were imprisoned or murdered.

Lieutenant Gonzalez Campos, the only officer in Tenerife to oppose the rising with arms, was given a summary court-martial, along with the civil governor and his staff, and shot. The governor's "crime" had been to shout, "Long live libertarian communism", though he was neither a libertine nor a communist, and independent witnesses had heard only the words "Long live the Republic".

Republican prisoners in Tenerife were herded into Fyffes' warehouse, near the present football ground in Santa Cruz. There they sweated it out, waiting to be shot in batches in the appropriately named Barranco del Infierno (Hell's Ravine) until the sport got tedious. The oil refinery now marks the spot.

black, when it is sweeter than any confection". A tinerfeño trader of English origin, Pedro Reid, launched the first exports from 1880; the firm of Wolfson and Fyffe followed, laying the basis of what was to become a virtual monopoly.

In the 1890s Elder and Dempster introduced refrigerated shipping, which made possible a further stage of growth. The Orotava Valley became carpeted with the thick frondure of banana plants that still cover much of the area. When the trade peaked in 1913, nearly three and a half million hands of bananas were exported from Tenerife, La Palma and Gran Canaria.

Yet the recurrent pattern of Canarian economic history could not be escaped. Just as the sugar trade had collapsed in the late 16th century, that of Malvasia in the early 18th, Vidueño wine in the early 19th and cochineal after only a generation's span of success, so banana exports were wrecked, after a scarcely longer supremacy, by World War I.

British control, of seaways and the internal economy alike, made Canarian involvement in the war more intense, and its effects more severe, than that of any other part of mainland Spain.

Employees of Fyffes banana company at a reception in Tenerife.

Between 1913 and 1917, banana exports fell by over 80 percent and the unit value by nearly as much. Emigration, especially to the New World, became a flood, and the main post office of Santa Cruz had special letterboxes for Cuba and Venezuela. The process of recovery was slow and imperfect, impeded by global depressions and recessions. Indeed, Santa Cruz did not again attain her pre-war levels of traffic until 1950.

Battered by economic ill fortune Tenerife seemed momentarily to lose heart in her struggle to retain political leadership over Gran Canaria. In 1927, the formal division of the archipelago into two provinces was meekly accepted. Santa Cruz became a provincial centre for the four western islands, (Tenerife, La Palma, Gomera and Hierro), consoling herself with the fact that of the two provinces, hers as a whole was much the bigger, richer and more populous, though Las Palmas excelled as a city by every standard of measurement.

The proclamation of the Spanish Second Republic, in 1931, excited new aspirations among tinerfeño politicians. It was hoped that the Canaries, like other historic communities within the Spanish state, might obtain federal or quasi-federal autonomy, with Santa Cruz as the capital.

Under the flamboyant dandy, Gil Roldán,

an assembly convened in Santa Cruz to demand this status. The representatives proclaimed "as a fundamental aspiration…that the Canarian archipelago, made up of free townships within each autonomous island, constitutes an unique natural region, endowed with a right to full autonomy, under the sovereign power of Spain." The status was not granted by the republic, and the programme was stultified by the advent of civil war in 1936, but the ultimate future of the islands was uncannily foreshadowed: under the devolved constitution of 1978, the Canaries are one of 14 autonomous regions, with a *cabildo* armed with island-wide authority in each island.

Prosperity under Franco: The outcome of the Spanish Civil War was, in a sense, a Canarian victory: not because Franco happened to launch his campaign from Tenerife when he flew from his command there on 18 July, 1936, to rally his African troops to the rebel cause; nor because Canarios had any particularly strong interest in or sympathy with nationalist politics. But the free-port privileges of the island became of even greater significance under a protectionist and, for a while, avowedly autarchic or despotic regime, which nevertheless allowed the islands to continue to enjoy the economic benefits of free trade.

It is fitting that many visitors who come by ship sail into Santa Cruz past the monument to Franco's victory and the dour mass of the *cabildo* building—a "fascist" pastiche with its vast art-deco tower and grim colonnade.

As in Spain generally, the Franco era brought long-deferred but ultimately spectacular prosperity. The basis of this recovery, in the western islands, was the continuing role of Santa Cruz as a staging-post for long-range shipping, with the growing diversity of the agrarian sector, now based on bananas, tomatoes, potatoes and tobacco large-scale commercial fishing and processing of foodstuffs.

In the 1960s, while agriculture continued to diversify further and new land came under cultivation on an unprecedented scale, the tourist boom wrought a revolution in the economy and society of the islands alike. At first, this was particularly characteristic of the eastern islands, which have most of the sandy beaches, but Tenerife, with Puerto de la Cruz and Los Cristianos as centres did not lag far behind.

The spectacular scenery of the western islands has enabled them to continue to profit from changes in taste. Saturation has not happened yet. Even today, the interior of Tenerife is largely unspoilt and the exploitation of Gomera, Hierro and La Palma, which have enormous tourist potential, has really only just begun.

Paradoxically, the picturesque features of traditional culture have fared better in the recent past than in the 19th and early 20th centuries. The demise of the cult of progress, the rise of a self-consciously Canarian autonomous government, the advent of a market for "local colour" have all helped to ensure the triumph of conservationist policies. By hydrofoil and modern road, it now takes only a couple of hours to get from Tenerife's airport, near the carbuncles of Los Cristianos, to the remote, reputedly "savage" village of Chipude in Gomera, where Guanchesque pottery is still made. This ease of communications, which seems a threat to traditional values, is probably the best guarantee of the survival of the community's character and of the potters' craft.

Left, a tourist, representing a new industry that has served to preserve some of the more attractive aspects of Canarian culture (right).

Legends Of The Isles

Quite who Canarios were and how they lived before the arrival of conquering mainland Europeans is still more a matter for supposition than of fact. But it seems appropriate that the islanders should have an insubstantiality about them; the island themselves have a shadowy form, figuring in various mythologies, some more modern than others, but none with any real founding in fact. Beyond the sphere of man's knowledge of the world until as recently as the 13th century, the Canaries feature in legend over and over again.

Atlantis: If you want to write a convincing history of a place that never existed, be sure to give it a good long, dry bibliography. J L Borges did this for his invented land of Uqbar, and Atlantis, an invention many centuries older than Uqbar, has its long, dry bibliography, too. "We can make the acquaintance of one 'eminent Atlantologist' after another in bulky works," as the Swedish archaeologist Carl Nylander put it. In other words, if a thing is written three times it becomes history.

But there are different kinds of bulky works. In the case of Atlantis, they are bulky works "of somewhat unnecessary learning, where references and footnote systems seem to have a decorative rather than clarifying effect." Like the literature of Uqbar, that of Atlantis is fundamentally fantasy and never really refers to reality in any of its varied and verbose passages.

Borges invented Uqbar, as Thomas Moore invented Utopia and Plato invented Atlantis—to make a point. All three existed only as metaphors for society, real or imagined, repressive or ideal.

The "historical" evidence for Atlantis is to be found in two of Plato's dialogues, *Timaeus* and *Critias*, which describe the visit of Solon, an Athenian scholar, to Egypt, which for contemporary Greeks was *the* cultural mecca. Solon made his trip around the beginning of the sixth century B.C. but, from an aged holy man in Sais, a city in the Nile Delta, he heard what was supposed to be the true history of the Greeks.

Left, myth and artistic licence combine in an intriguing play-ground figure in Gomera. Right, chieftain statue at Candelaria, perpetuating the islands' mythology.

Beyond the Pillars of Hercules, in the western ocean, had once lain Atlantis. Nine thousand years before Solon's time it had been the superpower of its day—wealthy, strong and ruled by the wisest of men. The capital of Atlantis was circular in plan, the centre being a huge pillar of gleaming bronze on which were inscribed the laws of Atlantis. Here, too, was the temple to Poseidon, God of the Ocean, and the palace. On one side was the Ocean and on the other the vast, well-ordered irrigated plain.

But power corrupts, and the rulers of Atlantis set out on a path of world domination. Only heroic little Athens stood up to Atlantis. And Athens won. The victory though was pyrrhic. A series of dreadful natural calamities destroyed Athens in 24 hours. Out in the west, Atlantis sank without trace to the bottom of Poseidon's ocean. Only Egypt came through the world-wide catastrophe, guardian of this ancient lore.

The Atlantis myth, if it reflects reality at all, is probably a dim memory of the destruction of the Minoan civilisation based in Crete. The location given by Plato—beyond the Pillars of Hercules, the Straits of Gibraltar—is little more than a literary convention; just as today we would place our imaginary societies in outer space. The Atlantis tale was the Star Trek of its day.

And the fall of Minoan Crete was in all probability as cataclysmic as the submersion of Atlantis. Nine centuries before Solon's trip to Egypt the volcanic island Thera, 70 miles (112 km) from Crete's northern coast, blew up. The Cretan civilisation ended with a horrendous bang.

Nevertheless, innumerable scholars have sought to locate Plato's Atlantis. Often the location of Atlantis coincides with the author's own country of origin—the Swede Olof Rudbeck placed its heartland in the Uppsala region, and there is a German work entitled *Atlantis, The Home of the Aryans.* The interests of more recent German anthropologists have focused more on the Guanches themselves.

The less patriotic, and the less xenophobic, have looked to the Atlantic Ocean, beyond the Straits of Gibraltar, and have lighted on the Canaries as the surviving mountain peaks of Atlantis. One Frenchman in the last century managed a marvellous reconstruction of the lost continent's outline—it took in the Azores, Madeira, the Canaries and the Cape Verde islands.

Of course, such suggestions take little notice of minor inconveniences like geography and geology. The Azores lie on the mid-Atlantic ridge, over 600 miles (1,000 km) from the Canaries, which are themselves loosely attached to Africa. The Cape Verdes are located approximately 1,300 miles (2,000 km) south of the Canaries.

And between the Azores and the Canaries are trenches reaching depths of four miles (seven km). Mount Teide on Tenerife would have been, by this reckoning, higher than Everest is today. Moreover, the forces involved in the feat of removing a block of land the size of the present European Community would have destroyed the rest of the world as well.

The Guanches: The "increasing flow of misguided learning, lack of critical discernment, or simply downright lunacy" that surrounds Atlantis has been transferred to Canarian prehistory at various times, creating the "mystery of the Guanches". Tall, blonde lost Vikings; primitive, club-swinging throwbacks; or last survivors of an Atlantean master-race—you pay your money and you take your pick, according to your particular prejudices. A lot of theories have popped out of the woodwork.

Almost as soon as Blumenback started his innocent collection of human skulls at Göttingen University in West Germany, the Canary Islands were seized on as a laboratory for the "proving" of racial theory. Towards the end of the last century, physical anthropologists, like the Frenchman René Verneau, began working on the islands, measuring and sizing up the skulls of the living and the dead.

According to theory, developed in the wake of Darwin's theory of evolution and the system used by Danish antiquarians to classify ancient finds, mankind passed through a series of developmental stages equated with present-day races. The differences between present-day human groups are more or less easy to define—though they depend more on dress, foods and social customs than on more fundamental distinctions. But bones are bones.

In those days, a system of classifying human skulls was worked out on the basis of the breadth and length of the skull. Verneau and the Harvard scholar, Hooton, were using the most sophisticated research technique they had. Later investigators were not.

Left, the Guanches—lost Vikings or survivors of an Atlantean master-race? Above, Guanche monument in Las Palmas.

Indeed, in 1941 Himmler asked the SS's *Ahnenerbe* (Cultural Division) to look for evidence to connect the Stone Age inhabitants of central Europe—the makers of the big-bottomed "Venus" figurines—with the Hottentots and Bushmen, whose womenfolk also have well-padded posteriors. Some of Himmler's ethnographers looked towards North Africa for the link.

A Franco regime in the Canaries, with its own obsessions with "purity of the blood", and the isolation of the islands in prehistory made the archipelago a favourite haunt of racial theorists.

On the basis of skull shape alone, a complex series of invasions was suggested; the more "primitive" inhabitants being driven further inland until they finally died out—the islands have very little inland areas to be driven into!

This was misguided learning—the same "frightening and pathetic muddle of ravished science" that produced the literature of Atlantisology.

However, even if the Guanches are not the lost tribe of Israel or shipwrecked Vikings, there are interesting questions to be asked about them.

Apparently the Guanches had no boats when the Europeans arrived. So were they either brought to the islands as prisoners by the Romans or the Carthaginians, or had they simply "forgotten" how to build boats? Only one European chronicler mentions a boat—a dug-out dragon-wood canoe with a matting sail—but he was writing his account a century after the conquest.

The earliest European chronicles describe the native islanders as "swimming" out to the ships, but off the coast of Morocco one-man reed-bundles served until very recently as inshore boats. They are used pretty much as a buoyancy aid. Much bigger craft are still used on Lake Chad, and Thor Heyerdahl has sailed one across the Atlantic, passing by the Canaries.

And in 1404 the French adventurer Jean de Béthencourt brought a slave from Gomera to act as an intermediary with the slave's "brother", the chief of Hierro. If there were no boats in pre-conquest times, how could the two men be related? From Hiero to Gomera is a very long swim.

San Borondón: Still, strange things do happen at sea. Islands come and go and even

COLUMBUS ON THE CANARIES

In 1415 man knew of the existence of Europe, North Africa, and the Near East; by 1550 world maps had been enlarged to incorporate North, Central and South America and the rest of Africa. The Canaries played a key strategic role in those discoveries, spearheaded by one man, Christopher Columbus.

Columbus is one of those almost mythical celebrities who almost every country claims a connection with, and the man himself was sufficiently stateless to be suitable material for a tug-of-war between nations. Honest readers may admit to having believed during early school days that Columbus was of their nationality, but if the Canary Islands and mainland Spain had their way you'd soon be brainwashed into believing that Cristobal Colón was a born-and-bred Spaniard, so heavily is supposed-Colombiana spread over places Spanish, not least the Canaries.

Mallorca claims to be the birthplace of the great man, and there are two supposed burial places on mainland Spain, one at Santo Domingo and one in Seville. In the Canaries there is hardly a town without a Calle Colón and the island of La Palma boasts a massive cement model of one of his ships, even though La Palma is about the only island that does not claim a direct connection with the navigator.

In fact Columbus was the son of an Italian cloth-weaver in the city of Genoa, then one of the world's greatest maritime cities. However it was the Spanish court, not the Italian, who eventually sponsored his expeditions. The extent of his brief flirtation with the Canaries has for a long time been the subject of much local discussion, fuelled by inter-island rivalry.

It was on his second voyage of 1492, a crucial journey that ended with the discovery of Cuba, that Columbus definitely stopped at the Canaries, putting in at Gomera. Quite why he chose the smallest island is a point of discussion: some suggest it was because he already knew and had been attracted to Beatriz de Bobadilla, the Countess of the island, and others say it was because Gomera, being the westernmost island, was the last stepping off point of the known world.

Gomera was by no means the best port in the islands, and Columbus evidently knew that, because when one of his fleet of three ships, the *Pinta*, broke a rudder in heavy weather, he left it to divert for repairs in Las Palmas on Gran Canaria while he hastened on to Gomera with the *Santa Maria* (his flagship) and the *Nina*.

Columbus himself described passing Tenerife (the last of the islands to be conquered, Tenerife was then still in Guanche hands, and staunchly resisting Spanish attacks) at an opportune moment, as he noted in his logbook: "As we were passing...we observed an eruption of the volcano. The smoke and flames, the glowing masses of lava, the muffled roaring from the earth's interior caused panic among the crew. They believed that the volcano had erupted because we had undertaken this voyage." Unfortunately Columbus's logbook does not go on to detail his movements through the islands on this and further journeys. Certainly the *Pinta* remained in Las Palmas for some time, and it is thought that Columbus went in search of it, although some local historians are adamant that he did not touch ground on Gran Canaria. Nevertheless Las Palmas leads the way in Colombiana, with a museum, a Casa Colón, a statue, and a church where he supposedly prayed before setting out for the New World, a claim also made of the church in San Sebastian de la Gomera.

The Las Palmas museum itself, although stimulating and atmospheric, has a collection of maps and objects relevant to Columbus's time, and includes an exhibition of South American objects of a similar period, but has none of Columbus's personal possessions.

Publications about the Canaries are divided about the course of the navigator. Some maintain that the only time Columbus did not make landfall in Las Palmas was during the second journey, when they acknowledge that he was clearly in Gomera. For the first, third and fourth journeys they say his resting place was Las Palmas. Others say that Columbus also stopped in Maspalomas on Gran Canaria and on the island of Hierro, and others still do not commit themselves at all.

move around. Beyond La Palma lies the island of San Borondón, though how far beyond is an open question. According to some Portuguese sailors who passed it in 1525, San Borondón is 220 sea miles nor'-nor'-west of La Palma; other 16th-century seamen put it another score of miles further off. One Renaissance geographer shifted it almost to the American coast.

No wonder, then, that two La Palma sea-captains, Hernando Troya and Hernando Alvares, could not find it in 1525, nor could their fellow-islander, de Villalobos, who set out in search of it 45 years later.

Others had more luck, they say—the Carthaginians and Caesar first, then Spaniards fleeing the Moorish invaders. By the 16th century the island was well-known to Portuguese, English and French pirates, who hid there safe in the knowledge that the strong currents around the island would keep pursuers at bay. How they got on with the archbishop, his six bishops and the inhabitants of San Borondón's seven cities has never been revealed.

The Italian military engineer Giovanni Torriani even went so far as to draw a map of the island, 264 miles (422 km) from north to south and 93 miles (148 km) from east to west, San Borondón is almost cut in two by major rivers. Torriani shows all seven cities on his map.

Above, the current around San Borondón supposedly prevented most ships from landing.

The Portuguese who landed in 1525 said it was full of tall trees. A Spanish nobleman turned pirate, Ceballos, confirmed that the forest came right down to the shore, and added that the woods were full of birds "so simple that they could be caught in the hand". There was a beautiful long sandy beach, but in the sand Ceballos had seen the footprints of a giant.

A French crew putting into La Palma after a storm, said they had left a wooden cross, a letter and some silver coins at the spot where they landed. Another ship-load of Portuguese saw oxen, goats, sheep and more giants' footprints in the sand. They had ended up leaving three of their crew there because of the strong current.

The power of that current was clearly shown in 1566 when Roque Nuñez, a Portuguese sea-dog, and Martín de Araña, a La Palma priest, set out for San Borondón. After only a day and a night at sea they saw land, but as they argued over which of them should land first the ferocious current drove them off the shore again.

The elusive San Borondón has not been picked up on any Satellite photo yet, but nevertheless some say you can see it, sometimes, from Tenerife and La Palma. The direction is right—nor'-nor'-west of La Palma—and about a couple of hundred sea-miles off. You can see its high peaks poking through the clouds; an optical illusion with its own mythical history, perhaps linked with the lost world of Atlantis.

Atlantis, the mystery of the Guanches, San Borondón—all are products of the Canaries' own history. Semi-mythical islands in the west, settled during the Renaissance when fantastic New and Old Worlds were being explored, the Canaries attracted their own mysteries.

Even in provable history, the history written down by the first European visitors, Stone Age tribesmen (the Guanches) kept the Spanish invaders at bay for nearly a century. The islanders had to be a little bit super-human to do that, and once you've begun to endow them with the strange origins of ancient mythology, then almost anything goes.

THE ISLANDER

Canarian tourism was never planned as such—planning anyway is neither a Canarian nor a Spanish characteristic—but you need never meet a Canario during a two-week sun-and-fun package holiday. Certainly not if you never venture out of the purpose-built (but not purpose-designed) resort centres.

On Lanzarote these days many waiters are beginning to forget what the words *café con leche* mean, and those foreigners familiar with the phrase learnt it during their first trip to Benidorm 20 years ago. Elsewhere, as most Canarios will tell you, the multi-lingual hotel receptionist is more likely to be a *godo*—a Goth, or peninsular Spaniard—than a Canario. Even many of the chambermaids, waiters and gardeners in the aptly-named tourists *apart hotels* are probably Andalusians and Galicians attracted by comparitively high wages.

So how do you find a Canary Islander? And how do you know you have found the real thing?

On the larger islands it is easier. Hire a car and head inland, or take a service bus to Las Palmas, Santa Cruz or Puerto Rosario. Or head west from Tenerife to one of the other islands—the German hippies on Gomera and the British and Swedish astronomers on La Palma are easily identified birds of passage. But if you are on Lanzarote the only way to find a Canario is to take the ferry from Playa Blanca to Fuerteventura.

Cartoon Canario: The caricature countryman is Cho' Juáa, who made his first appearance in 1944 in the *Diario de Las Palmas*. His expansive belly rests on the waistband of his sagging trousers. Somewhere around what would once have been waist level is a broad cloth belt out of which pokes the handle of his *naife* or Canarian knife. On his feet a pair of *closas*, over-sized down-at-heel boots, and on his head the black felt homburg that has seen better days—though when those days were is anybody's guess.

Over his well-filled shirt he wears a waistcoat, unfastened and unfastenable. And below his *bandido* moustache, a cigarette stub adheres to his lower lip—except on high days and holidays, when it is occasionally replaced by a cigar stub.

Cho' Juáa is no fool though. Like his more literary counterpart, Pepe Monagas who appears in several Canarian short stories by Pancho Guerra, he has an eye for a bargain—and for a mug. In his business dealings he is aided and abetted by Camildita, his shrewd and shrewish wife.

Preceding pages: young dancers; island punks. Left, traditional island costume. Right, two Camilditas—a dying breed.

Not that Cho' Juáa is really mean, he is just canny. And there is nothing he loves more than an opportunity to show off his largesse. What appear to be the verbal preliminaries to physical violence break out when two Canarios attempt to pay the same bill.

The Cho' Juáas and Camilditas of these islands are a dying breed. They can still be found on the smaller islands, or in villages like Teno Alto or Chinobre, on Tenerife, or Artenara and Tejeda in Gran Canaria. Occasionally they are to be seen in Las Palmas or Santa Cruz, but there is no place for their sharp negotiating skills—the market for three-legged goats was never large but in the cities it does not exist any longer.

A new breed: Cho' Juáa is now increasingly dependent on his city street-wise successors. Better-educated, taller and less corpulent, the new Canarios grew up with the tourist boom. They have all picked up a smattering of "Beach English" (often rude), and maybe a bit of Beach German, Beach Swedish and even Beach Finnish.

From Cho' Juáa they have inherited the ability to sell the same piece of useless *barranco* (ravine) slope twice over, and at varying market rates according to the buyer—double for Germans, a fifty percent mark-up for the Brits, the going rate to another Canario, and anything they can get away

with if the sale is to a *godo*. Nevertheless they will insist on taking you out to a slap-up dinner to seal the bargain.

In this respect Canarios are really no different from other Spaniards. They love the chance to take the leading role—no matter how insignificant the play, nor how small the audience. But five acts and a full house are preferred. Lines are never mumbled but projected across a crowded bar or bus, competing with all the other dramas being performed in the same small space.

Canarian restaurants at Sunday lunchtime are bedlam as three, or even four, generations compete for attention at the same table, and each table competes for the attention of the others. The waiters do deafening one-man shows in the midst of it all—the Canarian waiter is capable of bellowing an order across a rowdy restaurant like a parade-ground sergeant, but he keeps your attention at table by rattling off the menu in a low, almost inaudible, whisper. You must concentrate on him and him alone to find out what is on today—and, of course, *caballero*, he would never insult you by referring to the price of an individual item.

Like other Spaniards Canarios love a *fiesta*—anything from an *asadero* (a country barbecue) to a *verbena* (loosely translated as an all-night street party), or from a *trínqui* (drinks) to a *mogollón* (a much-longer-than-all-night street-party that grows out of *Carnaval*). An invitation to *tomar una copa* (to take a glass) really means to have several—so that tongues are loosened and stage-fright well and truly drowned. Should conversation flag then *arranques* (ones for the road) are ordered.

To keep in top conversational form a Canario, in the best Cho' Juáa or Pepe Monagas tradition, will pop into a bar for a rum at nine in the morning; for a *gin tónica* at eleven; and a bottle, or two, of *vino tinto* for lunch. But to stave off the tongue-tying effects of too much alcohol, it is taken with *tapas* or just a *bocata*—a *bocata* is literally a mouthful of food, a *tapa* slightly more.

Coffee, too, is an essential—small, strong and black (*café solo*); small and strong with a thick sludge of sickly condensed milk (*café cortado*); or a cup or glass of white coffee (*café con leche*). Coffee is invariably stiffened with liberal quantities of sugar. Even fresh orange juice, pressed out of little, sweet oranges, is heavily sugared by Canarios—a tradition derived from the Canaries' first export industry, sugar-cane growing.

Bad habits: If the sugar-industry, rum and *tapas* gave Cho' Juáa his sagging belly, it was one of the Canary Islands' other former staples—tobacco—that completed the caricature. Wherever Canarios congregate there is a fug of cigarette smoke—and the new anti-smoking legislation passed in the Madrid parliament is treated with the usual disdain reserved for any Madrid initiative.

This disregard for minor inconveniences—like "No Smoking" signs, parking restrictions, traffic lights, road signs and rubbish bins—is something else Canarios have in common with other Spaniards, though particularly in Las Palmas this has been developed into an art form. In Spanish this is called *individualismo* (individuality) when applied to yourself; *insolidaridad* (lack of social responsibility) when referring to others in general; and *barbaridad* (barbarism) when addressing the man who has just flicked his still-burning cigarette stub out of the bar door onto your brand new Lacoste sports shirt.

The Canario also shares mainland Spanish attitudes to women, children and the Church. He likes his women "*morena, bajita, gordita y con tetas grandes*" (dark, short, plump and well-endowed)—not that his preferences would check his interest in any other female shape, size or colouring. He has his *machismo* to maintain. Even Cho' Juáa is a Don Juan, and every woman is *guapa* (gorgeous).

Left, the wide hat and wide smile of a hunter. Above, old woman in Masca.

In Franco's time Canarian women could be divided into five types most of whom were dressed in black: children, expectant mothers, nursing mothers, nuns, or over-made-up characters from the last chapter of Orwell's *Animal Farm*. Since the demise of Franco there is, happily, a sixth type—curvaceous, vivacious, brightly and smartly dressed.

Whilst the average Canarian male is still ambivalent about the woman in his life—is she a whore or a Madonna?—both sexes absolutely adore children. As one Canarian teacher put it to me contentedly, pointing out a group of boisterous gum-chewing youths with attached ghetto-blasters: "these people, they are the future".

And nothing is too much for the future—private education for the uninterested, extra classes for the dull-witted, and presents for every child's birthday, saint's day, Christmas, Epiphany, first communion or just for the sake of giving. In the Canaries there is no segregation of the generations—even the smallest of children accompany their parents to *fiestas*, *verbenas*, political demonstrations, classical concerts, the cinema, and that other social attraction, church.

Even the most irreligious Canario goes to church several times a year—for baptisms, first communions, weddings and funerals of the various members of their extensive families. But services are not so much an act of worship as an act in the on-going drama. The priest plays to a full house, but the congregation is as uninterested in his performance as the audience in a northern Working Men's Club would be in Gregorian chant.

Lo nuestro: So what is it that makes Cho' Juáa and his heirs different—or, at least, see themselves as different—from other Spaniards?

Perhaps it is best summed up by the words *lo nuestro*—"our own". *Lo nuestro* is *gofio* and milk for breakfast; *Lo nuestro* is a distaste for bull-fighting, *godos*, and Canarios from any island except your own; it is a secret affection for cock-fights and dog-fighting, a love of Canarian wrestling, of Canarian music no matter how grating and of Canarian rum no matter how rasping; but above all it is distance and accent.

The Canary Islands are further from Madrid than they are from Dakar. From Fuerteventura you can see the coast of Morocco—and there is virtually no difference between Jandía (southern Fuerteventura) and the Sahara.

For Canarios geography outweighs all else. Even Canary Islanders with classic Latin features and Spanish surnames as far back as anyone can trace them will swear blind that they are the direct descendants of pure-bred Guanches. Most have a deep-rooted distrust of *godos*, and some have an even deeper loathing of the *metrópoli*—Madrid.

The *metrópoli*, especially during the various agricultural recessions of the last century and in the Franco years, was seen as stifling Canarian enterprise and imposing unwanted officials on the islanders. Sending Franco to the Canaries as military governor in 1936 was one such metropolitan infliction. Today, even with autonomous government taking over some aspects of regional administration, there is still considerable disgruntlement about the number of *godos* in high places and the need to seek the permission of central government for often minor changes. And bureaucrats in Madrid are renowned for their relaxed approach, treating the Canaries as a colony, in the opinion of some.

Alienation from the mainland is most obvious in the language. Canarians do not pronounce the letter "z" as a lisped "th", like the peninsulares, but as an "s", like the people of South and Central America.

Islanders will refer to "Lah Palmah" or "Ma'palomah" or "Santa Cru'" rather than Las Palmas, Maspalomas or Santa Cruz. Particularly on Gran Canaria consonants are clipped so sharply they cease to exist—so, for example, the name Juan becomes Juáa. Words are slurred together into a torrent which makes comprehension impossible on occasions—even among Canarios!

On some of the islands the local patois is less demanding, and on La Palma (beware the confusion with "Lah Palmah") the accent is particularly soft and clear, though still a South American Spanish. If you have picked up some peninsular Spanish, Canarios will either react blankly or with a campaign of re-education. Such lessons do not just concentrate on accent, they include vocabulary.

Words like *baifo*, a goat kid, is a Canarian peculiarity and comes from the native pre-Spanish language. Others like *naife*, *chóni* and *canbullonero* derive from the British commercial connection —*naife*, a Canarian knife; *chóni*, a foreigner, from the English "Johnny"; and a *canbullonero*, from the expression "can buy on", is a dock-side "fence" who buys stolen items of cargo from sailors in the port. Locally a cake is known as a *queque*, and a *yora* is a passenger from a Yeoward Line Ship.

But perhaps the most Canarian idiom of all is *Ustedes* as a plural form of "you" instead of the peninsular *vosotros*. On the mainland *Ustedes* is reserved for two or more people you have never met before or whose status is considerable—in the Canaries it is used amongst the closest of friends and family. *Vosotros* is thought of as almost an insult.

It is difficult to define *lo nuestro*. It is a weird mix of the Spanish *picaresco*, or roguishness; South American "magic realism"—Canarios are always a little larger than life; and that distinctively Canarian sentiment that *Canarias no es Europa, somos Africanos* (the Canaries aren't Europe, we are African).

Left, old or young, everyone loves a fiesta. Above, man alone; many Canarios feel alienation from Madrid.

La Plaza del Charco de los Camarones en 1828
Puerto de la Cruz

Pioneers and Parasols

The Canary Islands had to be discovered three times before they were truly on the world map.

Lost in antiquity and re-discovered in the middle ages, they descended into renewed obscurity in the early 19th century, when shrinking wine markets and revolts among Spain's American colonies seemed to make the archipelago economically redundant.

But it was the gloomiest era in the islands' economic history—the mid-19th century, when the wine trade had collapsed and only the short-lived cochineal industry offered any hope for the future—which saw the beginnings of what, in the long term, was to prove to be the Canaries' most exploitable industry: the interest of foreign visitors.

Scholastic attraction: The first re-discoverers of this period were scholars attracted by the islands' peculiar geology, climatology, botany and ethnography. They included Leopold von Buch, who made the first attempt to compile a systematic natural history of the island from observations made in person, and the German scientist Alexander von Humbolt. The most influential of these early observers, however, was Sabin Berthelot, a Frenchman and a diplomat who arrived from Paris in 1820, at the age of 26. His main interest was in the acclimatisation of tropical plants and fauna.

The Canaries had been selected as a place of experiment in this field in the reign of Charles III and, though the results had been disappointing, the Botanical Gardens of Orotava remained a magnet for an enterprising student of the subject. During a first stay of ten years, Berthelot became Director of the Botanical Gardens, played a major role in the acclimatisation of cochineal and developed a passionate interest in every aspect of Canariana, especially the archaeology and anthropology of the pre-Hispanic era.

In 1839 he published a miscellany of Canarian life and landscape, enlivened by engravings which introduced the Parisian public to the romantic scenery and dress of the archipelago. In 1842 *L'Ethnographie et les Annales de la conquête* followed. Eight further volumes, written with the collaboration of the English botanist, F B Webb, gradually completed his *Histoire naturelle des Iles Canaries*.

Preceding pages: 19th century painting of the Plaza in Puerto de la Cruz. Left, early visitors considered the islands romantic and stylish. Right, Sabine Berthelot.

After an absence of some years, Berthelot returned to the islands as French Consul in Santa Cruz de Tenerife. "My friends," he declared on disembarking, "I have come to die among you". The prophecy was true, if long delayed. He died on Tenerife in November, 1880, "an islander at heart", as he himself said. With his compelling enthusiasm he proved the most tireless and effective propagandist for the islands abroad.

In the 1850s the islands became newly accessible because of steamship navigation from Cadiz to Las Palmas and Santa Cruz de Tenerife. A public whose interest Berthelot had excited could now come to see the islands for themselves, and the Frenchman's friendships and collaboration with English scientists and artists helped to ensure the extension of the islands' appeal across the seas to England.

In the previous 300 years English residents had been well established in the Canaries, always as merchants or prisoners of the Inquisition: indeed, 80 percent of the penitents who passed before the tribunal of Las Palmas in the 18th century were English subjects. Few, however, had felt much love of or attraction to the islands.

Notable exceptions were Thomas Nichols, a 16th-century sugar merchant, who published *A Pleasant Description of the Fortunate Islands*—a work notable for containing the first description in English of the sensation of eating a banana—and George Glas, who in 1764 produced a somewhat capricious translation of a history of the islands originally written by a late 16th-century Franciscan. From the mid-19th century, however, a continuous tradition of English interest began.

Elizabeth Murray: The initiator of new English interest was a remarkable woman who arrived as the wife of a newly appointed British Consul in 1850. Elizabeth Murray was the daughter of a reputable portraitist who had been in Spain in 1812 to paint Wellington and his staff.

Born in 1815, Elizabeth was exhibiting at the Royal Academy from 1834. She had already visited Italy with her father, and had classes from Horace Vernet. When her father died in 1835 she was able to exploit the connections he had built up to pursue a surprisingly independent way of life. Having, as she said, "neither master nor money", she travelled in the Mediterranean and finished her artistic preparation in the most fashionable manner.

In 1835 she was commissioned to paint views of Malta for Queen Adelaide; from there she went to Constantinople at Sir Stratford Canning's invitation, and developed a talent for street-scenes with a romantic and exotic flavour. In Athens, she painted King Otto and his family. She found her ideal *milieu* in Morocco, where she spent nearly eight years from 1842, in observation, sketching and dalliance; in 1846 she married the British Consul, and it was his posting to Santa Cruz that removed her to the islands via Seville and Cadiz. She was received with enthusiasm by the intellectuals, led by Berthelot, and the artists, who had recently organised themselves as a Provincial Academy.

At first, Murray contributed mainly Greek and Moroccan views to their exhibitions, but the scenery of the islands had captured her from afar; from the ship that brought her to the Canaries, she declared the view of the islands "a spectacle which has nothing to match it in any other part of the world". She was indefatigable in seeking out subjects in the hinterland of Tenerife, accompanied only by a couple of servants, or staying with friends in the major settlements.

The fruit of her sketches and observations was the greater part (16 chapters out of 27) of *Sixteen Years of an Artist's Life in Morocco, Spain and the Canary Islands*, which appeared in 1859. The result in the islands was a sensation of a most unfortunate kind, for the Canarian intelligentsia, who had welcomed her so heartily, now felt betrayed. In the book, Mrs Murray declared Las Palmas "rather gloomy and uninteresting"; moreover Santa Cruz, she said, "does not contain anything which is of remarkable interest to the visitor".

She found Canarian religion distasteful, dress risible, architecture modest and mendicancy offensive. However lavish her praise for the islands' topographical beauty, Canarios found their own image was unflatteringly presented. They seemed to see themselves depicted as they feared they really were: coarse, brutish, backward, isolated and culturally impoverished—"like Blacks", a Las Palmas newspaper complained, "speaking in dialect and living in caves". The press, which had begun by publishing extracts from her work, soon suppressed it and began printing shocked denunciations of the authoress. It was fortunate that her husband was recalled in 1860.

Outside the Canaries, however, Mrs Murray's book was a positive influence, which helped to divulge an agreeable, and marketable, perception of the islands. What mattered were Mrs Murray's charming pictures, not her rather affected prose. The view of Orotova which forms the frontispiece of her second volume is typically enchanting. The steeply sloping city in the middle ground, with its Baroque towers and cloisters, and the gleaming pyramid of the Teide beyond, can still be appreciated as an almost unspoilt view by today's visitor.

Mrs Murray had a representative Victorian eye. She selected the romantic, the sentimental, the lavish, the exotic and the picturesque in her Canarian genre scenes and landscapes. Nor was she above heavy-handed social comment in her portraits of urchins, beggars and priests. Images which outraged the islanders were calculated to appeal to audiences abroad.

Paradise in paint: Elizabeth Murray never returned to the islands, but she influenced other image-makers of the Canaries, including Marianne North, the well-connected daughter of an MP. On a visit to Tenerife in 1875 to escape the English winter, she painted a large collection of oils of exotic plants, many sketched in the Botanical Gardens of Orotava, together with views showing the environment of the Canaries' unique native flora. She bequeathed her entire *oeuvre*, which included paintings made in the course of travel in six continents, to Kew Gardens, in London.

Left, Alexander Von Humboldt. Above, the harbour at Santa Cruz was transformed by the arrival of steamships.

Her written recollections of Tenerife, though not published until 1892, reached a wide readership. The Canaries were depicted as a sort of paradise, where climate and views were perfect, where roses never smelled so sweet and where, "I scarcely ever went out without finding some new wonder to paint, lived a life of the most perfect peace and happiness, and got strength every day with my kind friends."

Last, most influential and perhaps most formidable of the British Victorian viragos who travelled to the Canaries was Mrs Olivia Stone, who toured the islands in the winter and early spring of 1884. Mrs Stone was self-consciously a professional travel writer whose aim was to equip the tourist with a practical guide and to facilitate travel. Her aim was to establish "the best way of going round the islands in order to see the scenery". In a letter to *The Times*, her husband declared her findings, that the Canaries "require only to be known, to be much resorted to by the English." A prediction that has most certainly been proved correct.

Her husband, as her assistant, was able to make the first extensive photographic record of the islands on the course of the tour: on the basis of his work, her book appeared with lavish illustrations. Her inspection of the archipelago was exceptionally thorough. She was the first English writer to visit every island and claimed to be the first Englishwoman ever to have set foot on Hierro.

In some ways, Mrs Stone was an unlikely propagandist for the islands. She was a Protestant bigot who derided many Canarian customs. She flew the Union Jack from her tent, taught Canarian hoteliers to make plum pudding and argued that the islands would be better off under the British Empire than as part of Spain.

Paradise in print: The notes Olivia Stone wrote up daily on donkey-back yielded another Arcadian image for the readers of her book. It was a land where rainy mornings were so rare that people rose to look at them and where poor health could be transformed by exposure to a uniquely salubrious climate. The first edition of her *Tenerife and its Six Satellites* appeared in 1887. Mrs Stone could be pardoned for congratulating herself, by the time of the appearance of the 1889 edition, on the fact that "visitors have poured into the islands" as a result.

The most illustrious of these visitors was the Marquess of Bute, the most distinguished Scottish Catholic convert of the 19th century. He enjoyed wealth, leisure, a scholarly disposition and dazzling linguistic skill. In the 1870s he had devoted these gifts partly to civic and philanthropic works but particularly to travels in Italy and the Near East which produced an important series of academic and devotional translations, mainly from Latin, Hebrew, Arabic and Coptic. On Mrs Stone's advice he went to Tenerife to improve his health, with—temporarily, at least—satisfactory results. In consequence, the fashionable credentials of holidaying in the islands were established.

Guanche scholars: Bute became passionately interested in the archaeological and ethnographic remains of the Guanches. Since Berthelot's work on the subject, the field had largely been abandoned to local scholars, except for the efforts of René Verneau, who studied the physical anthropology of the Guanches in the 1870s and whose *Cinq annèes de séjour aux Iles Canaries* was an intriguing and popular record of his stay on the islands.

Bute's attempts to augment the literature on the islands were modest: he concentrated on the philological problems which lay in his own particular field, but his dissertation *On the Ancient Language of the Inhabitants of Tenerife* was an unprofitable work, devoted to demonstrating a fantastic connection between pre-conquest Canarian languages and those of some American Indians. Nevertheless, in his effort to compile materials he bought up almost the entire records of the early Canarian Inquisition, erroneously believing that they might contain some transcribed fragments of native speech.

He had these materials translated and then presented the originals to the Museo Canario of Las Palmas. As a result, the Canaries are the only province of Spain still to have their early Inquisitorial archives *in situ*. All others have been removed to Madrid.

The last figure in the great tradition of scientific curiosity among foreign visitors was Dominik Josef Wölfel, a Viennese anthropologist, who was fired with wonder about the pre-conquest islanders at a seminar in 1926, when he heard Eugen Fischer read a paper on the Guanches' fate.

Wölfel's many publications had slight influence on the image of the islands in the wider world because he almost always wrote in Spanish, but he founded an Institute in Vienna for the study of the subject. His transcriptions have now been superseded, and the ferocity of his partisanship on the Guanches' behalf is thought by many scholars to have distorted his judgement, but he remains a towering influence in Canarian studies and a striking example of how the islands have captivated their discoverers.

Right, the Marquess of Bute, here photographed in fancy dress.

EARLY TOURISM

The first tourists to the Canary Islands were an elegant lot. At the time I was a child on the islands and I have particularly vivid memories of the early years of tourism in Puerto de la Cruz.

The Grand Hotel Taoro, the largest hotel in Spain for many years, was not more than 100 yards from our house, *Miramar*, my birthplace. The hotel was built in 1892 upon a slag-heap-like mound of volcanic ash and rock called "The Mount of Misery", overlooking the small town of Puerto de la Cruz.

Around it barren fields of lava were converted into gardens for strolling, lawns for croquet or bowls, and 11 acres were transformed into a huge park of endemic and imported plants suitable for the international visitors. These included members of the Spanish Royal family, King Albert and King Leopold of the Belgians, the Duke of York (later King George VI of England), the Duke and Duchess of Kent, and the Prince of Savoy who became the last King of Italy.

The Grand, which cost £20,000 mainly raised by British investors, complemented the Marquesa, Monopole and Martianez Hotels in the town below.

Santa Cruz, the island's capital, then boasted two first class hotels, the Quisiana and the Pino de Oro, used as staging posts for travellers arriving and leaving by sea.

Any brave soul who ventured into any of the smaller towns might find a simple inn but certainly no real tourist accommodation. Such was the popularity of The Grand Hotel Taoro that on occasions male guests who had not taken the precaution of making reservations found themselves accommodated either upon or below the billiard tables, their rest perhaps disturbed by resounding dinner gongs, the thwack of wicker carpet beaters, or the rhythms of the orchestra from the Rococo bandstands in the gardens.

In 1929, when half the hotel building was destroyed by fire, guests tried to save their belongings by throwing them from the windows. I discovered collars, ties and socks amongst the garden shrubs. The fire proved disastrous; the damaged wing was not replaced and the hotel never recovered its former reputation. In 1975 it was reopened as the Casino Taoro and is today one of Spain's most successful gambling establishments, turning a fine profit for the Island Council which now owns it.

Preceding pages: a bullock cart provided by a hotel for its visitors. Left and right, transports of delight came in all shapes and sizes.

Early packages: Frequent sailings from Liverpool by fruit cargo ships of the Yeoward Line brought regular "trippers" or "Yeowardites" as they were rather disparagingly called by the resident British colony. The 16-day round-trip, calling at Lisbon, Madeira, Las Palmas and Tenerife, cost 10 guineas and was widely advertised.

The use of cruise clothes and leisure wear was unknown among these passengers. Tomato-red faced men, handkerchiefs knotted on their heads, accompanied by overdressed ladies were amusing sights to the locals as they were taxied about to see the places of interest in open Hudsons, Willys, Knights, Packards or Chryslers.

The real crunch for development came towards the end of the 1950s. Nothing had changed during the first half of the century.

Visitors were still arriving by sea, and air travel was tedious and involved a stop-over in Las Palmas.

When aeroplanes began to make direct, non-stop flights to Tenerife in 1959, all that changed. Sheer bedlam broke loose. "All Inclusive Winter Sunshine Holidays" began in earnest, causing a major impact on Puerto de la Cruz. Extensions to hotels were built on the strength of advance payments by tour operators, banana plantations were developed into hotels and gardens. The Golden Age had arrived.

It was at this stage of rapid expansion that many old and charming buildings were sacrificed, prompting press articles with headlines like "The Rape of the Hesperides" and "The Bedraggled Canaries".

The greatest and most insulting impact was the construction of the Belair tower block slap in the centre of town, with an apparently elastic permit to build eight floors, that somehow got stretched out to include 23. Since then the increase in numbers of tourists has been huge, as has been the infrastructure to cater for it.

That infrastructure includes the medical facilities set up to attend to the ever increasing number of elderly people who came on holiday to the island. In 1920 there were perhaps five or six doctors in the Orotava Valley, and there was no hospital, clinic or nursing home any closer than Santa Cruz—a lengthy 27 miles (44 kms) of dusty, winding road, two or more hours away from Puerto de la Cruz.

Doctor James Ingram, a physician from Edinburgh was one of the few doctors. He had arrived on this island several years before, having requalified in Spain so as to be able to practice medicine here. One of his patients developed para-typhoid and subsequently, meningitis after her fifth child. For many weeks a battle was fought for her life by Dr Ingram, two nurses and a middle-aged man with a small donkey; these last two made 24-hour round-trips to the ice cave 11,000 feet (5,350 metres) up on the slopes of Mount Teide—the only source then of coollants for fevered bodies. The eventual success of all their efforts enabled me to know my mother.

Today, as a direct consequence of tourism there are scores of doctors, dentists, nurses and specialists of all kinds in several medical centres and clinics—a far cry from the early days when visitors would come to the "new health resort of Tenerife" on account of the climate alone. The climate was eulogised in letters written to *The British Medical Journal* by its editor, Ernest Hart while on a "winter trip" to Tenerife in 1887 when he wrote "...the blue sky and all-pervading sun overhead, the delicious warmth but exquisite freshness of the air, all tell us that we have reached safely and happily the haven of our rest, and are safely lodged for this promising "winter holiday" in one of the choicest of the gardens of the earth—Puerto Orotava, the very pearl of the Fortunate Islands".

Over the years the pressure on the Puerto de la Cruz area to build more accommodation has been indirectly responsible for the developments in the south of Tenerife. Owners of banana plantations within the city limits—and there were many such plantations—were threatened with expropriation unless they made their land available for

tourist accommodation. Since many owned land in the south as well as in the north, their solution was to build terraces for plantations in the south and then transfer the earth and banana stumps to their new locations. Water was, of course, a vital consideration, but the same owners were able to switch their supplies to the south by direct piping.

Southern centres: As the number of visitors to Tenerife grew, so did the development in the south, first in the already settled communities of Los Cristianos, El Médano, Playa Santiago and Los Gigantes, and, later, to Playa de las Américas on the so-called "Costa de Silencio", named thus before the construction of the Reina Sofia airport.

Left, sunshine tours came to the right place. Above, "old fashioned" Puerto caters for all nationalities of new visitors.

On the southeastern side of Tenerife Güimar was an early health resort even before Puerto de la Cruz. A large private house was converted into the Hotel El Buen Retiro, situated in the upper part of the town, where it was a great success for some years. It had a resident doctor and was considered by Professor Thomas Huxley, visiting in 1889, to have the best climate in Tenerife.

On Gomera, La Palma and Hierro, the other three islands of the western group, there were no real tourists in the old days, but only seasoned or adventurous travellers who either had letters of introduction to local residents or were so hardened that they put up with the barest of comforts and, perhaps, fleas in the local *fondas* or inns.

On Gomera and La Palma accommodation is increasing and improving fast. Each of these islands has a good *Parador* (the government-run hotel group) and new hotels have recently been built. On Hierro there is a very attractive *Parador* where the food and service could improve, as well as the Boomerang Hotel started by a local who once emigrated to Australia and doesn't allow the island to forget it.

Thirty years on Puerto de la Cruz is a mass tourism mecca with the highest percentage of return visitors of any resort in the world, some coming back as often as fifty times and receiving gold medals from the local tourist moguls for their constancy.

Morals have changed from the days when my kindergarten teachers—two English spinsters—would separate the cockerel from the hens at sundown, to the present day when topless bathing is the norm and SAGA old people's holidays are known as "Sex and Games for the Aged". The Parish Priest will no longer refuse Communion to ladies in short sleeved dresses.

There is still an old fashioned air about the place, although you will not see English tourists being transported in hammocks, carried by bearers deliberately walking out of step to maintain a pleasant rhythm. In some ways the local is still out of step, and we count ourselves lucky to be somewhat "behind the times"—it's part of the charm.

EXPATRIATE LIFE

According to a recent survey by the *Jefatura Superior de Policía* (Police Headquarters), there were 23,224 foreigners officially resident in the province of Tenerife. A significant percentage when the region's total population amounts to some 700,000, especially when those figures only include members of the foreign community who are legally registered (many, probably several thousand, are not). Nor do they include the large numbers of semi-expatriates, those who traditionally—like migrating birds—flock to the Canary Islands between November and April.

The biggest group of foreign nationals living in the province of Tenerife is the British—7,000 officially registered with the British Consul, plus, he estimates, a similar number who are not registered (either because they are not required to because they are here for less than six months, or because their papers, if indeed they have any, are not in order).

The second group are the Germans, with some 6,000 officially registered with their Consul (the real number, again, is higher), followed by the Indian community, who are prominent in the commercial sector, owning many bazaars specialising in electrical goods and gifts. The Belgians are the fourth largest group, followed by Scandinavians, while the Honorary French Consul has 1,000 nationals on his books.

By far the lion's share of these expatriates live on Tenerife itself, generally in or close to Puerto de la Cruz, La Orotava, Santa Ursula, El Sauzal, Tacoronte, Mesa del Mar and Bajamar in the north; some live in Santa Cruz and nearby Radazul and Tabaiba; and in the south they concentrate around Los Cristianos, Playa de las Américas, the Costa del Silencio, Médano, Callao Salvaje, Marazul and Puerto Santiago-Los Gigantes. Additionally, there are small pioneering groups in the province's lesser islands of La Palma, Gomera and Hierro, most notably at Los Llanos de Aridane in La Palma, a wine-rich town which is becoming increasingly popular with Britons and Germans.

Preceding pages: British residents at home on Gran Canaria. Dogs galore...with British residents (left), and a German photographer (right).

Better health and tax: Of the legally-documented residents, irrespective of nationality, some 70 percent are retired. Mostly choosing to live here for the year-round mild climate, claimed to be particularly beneficial to those suffering from cardiac disease or respiratory conditions such as asthma. "I've known of individuals whose doctors have given them only a year or two to live in the UK," recalls the British Consul, Keith Hazell. "They come out here, and ten to 15 years later they're still going strong."

There are others who believe the Canaries are still the tax haven they once were. Generally, income tax is lower than in the UK and many European countries, but in recent years the islands have shown no reticence in introducing a range of taxes where once there were none. The hefty purchase tax on all private secondhand car sales imposed in 1987 is a typical example.

Then, as one would imagine, the region also attracts its share of tax evaders, swindlers, bankrupts and those wanted back home for tax fraud and so on. Generally, though, they aren't in the same league as John Palmer, the one-time jeweller implicated in the famous Brinks-Mat gold bullion robbery in the UK who, though deported in 1985, was later allowed back to Tenerife to attend his vast business concerns in the south of the island.

There are also, of course, important numbers of foreign residents working in the province and in possession of work permits of *cuenta propia* (self-employed) or *cuenta ajena* (employee) status. The range of occupations is wide, embracing, as one would expect, the tourist industry and the booming property market (15,000 Britons bought property here in 1985, 20,000 in 1986 and the trend continues), but also including the teaching profession; import and export; those working in bars, restaurants, specialist food shops, German and French *patissières*; publishing; even a British-owned donkey sanctuary. There is too, a sprinkling of German and British doctors and a few British dentists are beginning to arrive.

Permit problems: Paradoxically, however, as 1992 approaches (the year when Spain becomes a fully paid-up member of the European Community), it is becoming more and more difficult to obtain new work permits, while increasingly, even routine renewals are being turned down, as high unemployment among the local workforce (from qualified doctors to school-leavers) takes a firm and disquieting grip. For this reason, the authorities appear nervous about 1992, as the impending threat of an invasion of foreign, sometimes better-qualified workers looms on the not too distant horizon. The problem of umemployment is exacerbated by the presence of considerable numbers of illegal workers.

British Consular figures for December 1988 stated that there were 2,500 legally employed Britons in the province, but the actual number is far greater, with many working illegally, particularly for certain timeshare organisations. The risks for these clandestine workers (and their employers) are high, including fines, deportation and even prison. For the workers themselves, an accident or sudden illness may well prove frighteningly expensive (a typical four days' hospitalisation with no medical intervention is likely to cost more than £500) if they are not paying into the obligatory *seguridad social* system and, as is often the case, do not have any private medical insurance.

Inevitably, it's all a very far cry from the early expatriate days of the late 19th and early 20th centuries. The days when, as reported in Alexander Baillon's memoirs: "It was the custom for ladies to go about in

hammocks", so pot-holed and muddy were the streets, and when members of the newly-formed British Games Club (founded in 1903) objected to fellow members being allowed to play tennis on a Sunday afternoon, "although croquet parties on their own private lawns were given regularly…"

Distinguished Expatriates: Street names in Puerto de la Cruz and Santa Cruz de Tenerife pay tribute to the various distinguished European families who have contributed so richly to the island. Names like Valois (Walsh); Cologán (Colgan); Dr Ingram, the popular GP from Edinburgh; Blanco (White); Enrique Talg, whose family own the Hotel Tigaiga; Richard J Yeoward, of shipping line fame, though the family is involved in property development nowadays; Carlos J R Hamilton, the family of shipping agents; Buenaventura Bonet (a descendant is a well-known local dermatologist), and many more.

Other eminent families include the Reids, who served as Vice-Consuls in Puerto de la Cruz (from 1878 to 1973), and the Baillons, with several members of the family still living in the island to which Falklands-born Briton Alexander Baillon first came in 1906, to take on the then daunting task of managing Fyffes vast banana plantations near Adeje. Also worthy of mention is the Ahlers family, now in its fourth generation in Tenerife, and founding partners of one of the island's major companies, Ahlers y Rahn, which, among other things, imports Mercedes Benz cars direct from Germany.

In Puerto de la Cruz, the British Games Club offers bowls, tennis, croquet and badminton, as well as many less energetic pastimes, but it counts few younger residents among its membership of 220, a quarter of whom are in fact Spanish and English-speaking non-Britons. The Wednesday Group of English-speaking friends meets once a month for lunch and to organise various activities, while ESTA (the English-Speaking Theatre Association) usually puts on two different shows a year (one traditionally a pantomime), the proceeds of both going to charity.

Pillars of the community: The English Library at Parque Taoro boasts more than 3,000 titles, and close by is All Saints' Anglican Church, built in 1890. With a resident chaplain, the church provides regular services each Sunday and Wednesday, and is loaned frequently to the German, Swedish and Finnish communities. Also in Parque

Left, Swedish mother and twins on Lanzarote. Above, British tastes are catered for by British restaurants in Puerto de la Cruz.

Taoro is the British Yeoward School, founded in 1969, which offers a British curriculum to children from kindergarten age to 18, and recently a British Video Library has opened in nearby Santa Ursula, providing a much-needed service to the considerable numbers of British residents who are less than fluent in Spanish.

In Santa Cruz, there's St George's Anglican Church and—now legal in Spain—the island has its own, largely British Masonic Lodge, while there are Lions and Rotary Clubs in Puerto de la Cruz and Playa de las Américas, both with multi-national membership. The south also boasts the British Council-recognised British Wingate School

at Cabo Blanco, the newish Children's Centre at Guaza, and during the winter months, the Swallows Group meets twice weekly in Los Cristianos to exchange books and arrange outings and activities.

German-speaking expatriates are catered for by the Santa Cruz branch of the Altavista Club whose membership is also open to Spaniards, and there are regular church services weekly in Puerto de la Cruz and monthly in Santa Cruz. Also in the capital is a state-sponsored German school providing education to the age of 18, while there's a recently opened private German school on the outskirts of Playa de las Américas. For French-speakers, social life seems to revolve around the Alianza Francesa Club, opened 25 years ago in Santa Cruz, and the Union Française des Etrangers, which also operates its own video club.

Paradise Lost: Life in Tenerife isn't quite the utopia that many resident expatriates no doubt thought it would be. The climate, of course, is the reason why most people are here, but the cost of living—once cheap by northern European standards—is rising all the time. Strangely, while eating out needn't cost the earth, food is a major expense. Tobacco, wines, spirits, petrol and diesel are all cheaper than in Britain, as are *contribuciones urbanas* (rates) and one saves on central heating bills, but electricity and water tariffs are on the increase.

The cost of property is rising, and anyone moving here should be prepared for the fact that almost invariably it will grow more costly than it might at first have appeared. Compensations there are in large measure, but one needs patience and fortitude to accept philosophically the shortcomings of such as Telefónica (the telephone company) and UNELCO (the electricity generating board), both of whom fail dismally when it comes to meeting customer demand.

Hire a solicitor when buying property, choose an estate agent with a credible track-record and consult the Institute de Propietarios Extranjeros (Institute of Foreign Property Owners) before you sign anything. Make sure—if you're one of a couple—that you both want to settle in Tenerife: many a marriage has foundered when one has loved the island, while the other has found it impossible to adapt. Think of the future, too, as there is no safety net to provide long-term hospitalisation or residential care for the elderly, nor even a meals-on-wheels service.

No-one knows what 1992 will bring, but meanwhile, foreign residents will have the right to vote in the province's 1991 borough elections. A force to reckon with, the foreigners' main concerns include environmental issues and conservation, and incredibly, local politicians seem unaware of their considerable voting clout. The expat strength is probably sufficient, in some areas, to upset the municipal applecart.

Left, working residents...a British archaeologist, and (right) a jeweller on Lanzarote.

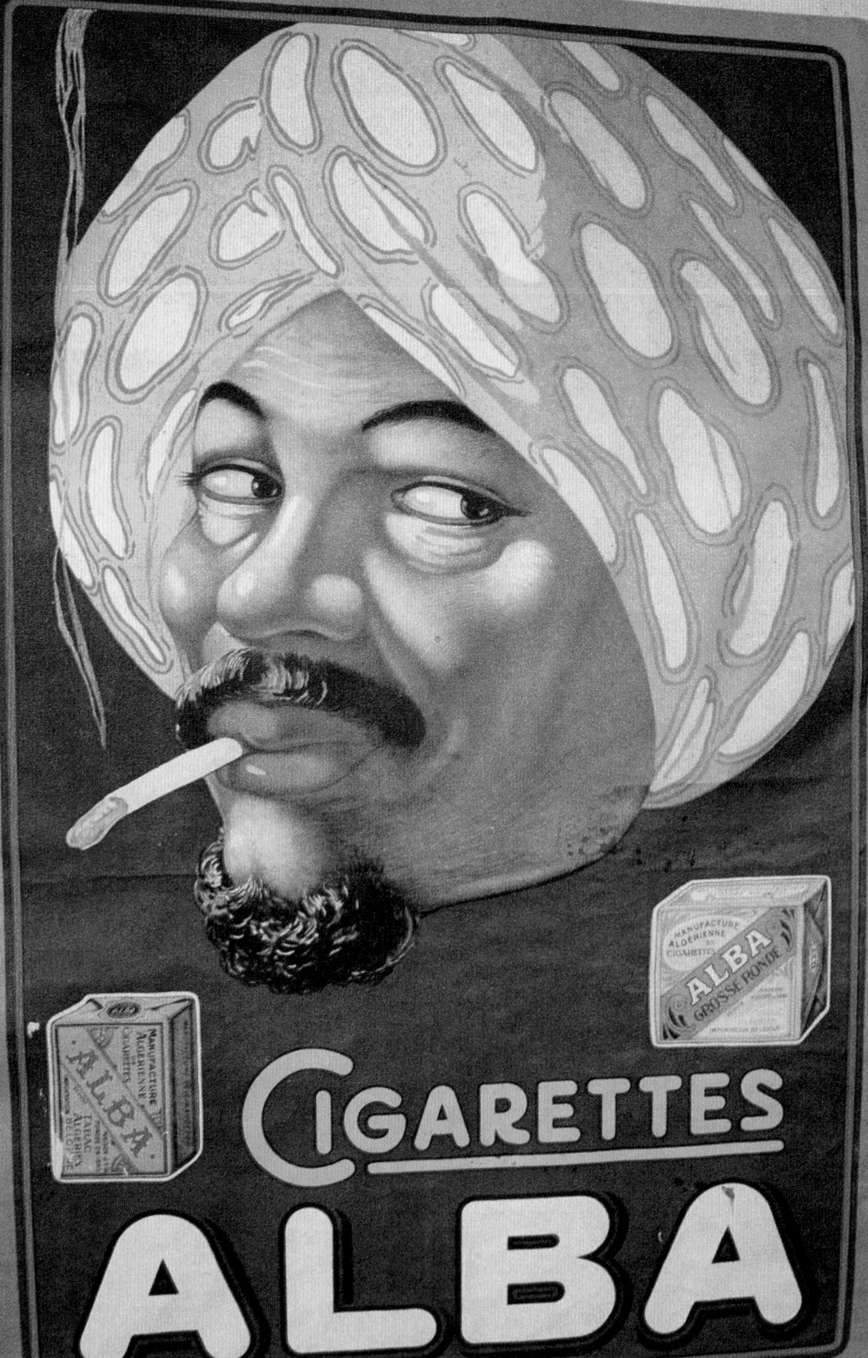
MANUFACTURE
ALGÉRIENNE
DE
CIGARETTES
ALBA
GROSSE RONDE
MANUFACTURE
ALGÉRIENNE
DE
CIGARETTES
ALBA
TABAC
CIGARETTES
ALBA
LES ATELIERS D'IMPRESSIONS D'ART O. DE RYCKER, BRUXELLES-FOREST.

Politics and Continents

When the first autonomous government came to power, some bright spark came up with the slogan "A Bridge between three Continents" as part of a campaign to widen the islands' economic base. As a piece of advertising hype it was convincing: geographically, the islands are stepping-stones between Europe, Africa and the Americas, and they have been so ever since Columbus sailed across the pond.

But the slogan ignored the stranglehold monopoly that Iberia and Trasmediterranea—the Spanish national air and sea carriers—have on communications to and from the islands, and even between them. As a result the Canaries are more of a cul-de-sac than a bridge.

The attempts made by the Canary Island autonomous government to foster South-South trade between Africa and South America have foundered on the rocks of these monopolies. Instead of being a three-way bridge the islands are the end of the line for charter flights or just refuelling stops. And yet the Canaries do still maintain links—often long-lasting—with all three continents.

The European connection: This is the most obvious of the continental bridges. The islands form two provinces and one autonomous region of modern Spain, and are part of the European Economic Community, though they enjoy a specially negotiated position within the Community which guarantees cheap booze and no VAT on goods on the islands. It also guarantees excessively high prices for Canarian farm produce compared with countries like Morocco and Israel. Belatedly the island government is trying to renegotiate before Canarian agriculture finally disappears under a thick layer of rotting tomatoes and bananas.

The European connection existed even before the conquest in the 15th century, but at the time it was limited to slaving and trading for dye-stuffs, animal fats and skins. Nevertheless some Europeans had mixed with the native population before and during the conquest; Mallorcan sailors may have introduced figs and architectural improvements and the Portuguese were once allied with the islanders against the Spanish.

The majority of the first European colonists were Spaniards from the frontier regions of Extremadura and Andalucia. Portuguese, Italian and even English merchants soon followed as the islands' first industry—sugar—began to develop.

Preceding pages: tourists, the biggest single influence. Left, Moroccan influence in the shops. Right, African dancers perform for holidaymakers.

Thomas Nichols, who wrote the first book in English on the Islands, came to the Canaries to trade cloth for sugar and wine. Others, like John Hill of Taunton, settled in the Canary Islands to farm land that "bringeth foorth all sortes of fruites"—Hill had the only vineyard on Hierro in Nichols' time.

But even before Tenerife and La Palma had been reduced by Spanish arms, the Spanish maritime empire had been born. Columbus and those that followed him used the Canary current to coast past the North African shore, through the islands and on westward to the Americas.

As ships began to move freely and confidently more Spaniards settled in the islands, whilst some of the descendants of the original islanders and the first European settlers moved on to the Americas. During the 16th and 17th centuries the Canary Islands were busy commercial centres through which passed much of Spain's American sea traffic. The ports of Las Palmas (Gran Canaria), Garachico (Tenerife) and Santa Cruz de La Palma (La Palma) flourished, until Garachico's harbour was destroyed overnight by a volcanic eruption in 1706.

However, the fortunes of the ports were so tied to the Spanish mainland that Las Palmas and the other ports stagnated, along with the Spanish empire and economy, during the 18th and early 19th centuries.

The essential elements of Canarian society had been welded together by the time Garachico was buried by boiling lava, and European and native were inextricably mixed.

African roots: On the lesser islands and in the mountainous interiors of the larger ones the native islanders survived in enclaves and lived almost as their Berber-speaking ancestors had done. But the power of the Inquisition—especially as the empire turned inwards during the 18th century—gradually imposed the trappings of Christianity on these African communities.

By 1800 the principal native pagan festivals had been taken over by the Catholic Church, and the heathen deities converted into various manifestations of the Virgin Mary. Over the course of the 18th century the "folk" costume of the Canary Islands took on its present form as the process of "civilising" the islanders went on.

Yet the North African roots of the islands' population never really died. They either went deeper underground—like the native martial arts, *juego del palo* and *lucha canaria*—or adapted to changed circumstances, as in the festival of the *Rama* in Agaete or Guía (Gran Canaria). Spanish became the accepted means of communication but it still contained a lot of Berberisms.

Almost from the earliest days of conquest native islanders joined their new masters first in attacks on the other islands and later in the destruction of the Aztec and Inca empires. Gran Canarians and Gomerans found themselves in the front line during the conquest of Tenerife. And before the 16th century was out Canarian wrestlers were putting on demonstrations of their prowess for the Spanish viceroy of Peru.

South American exodus: But it was the agricultural recessions of the last century that drove many islanders west to Argentina, Colombia, Venezuela and Cuba. And, like the Irish who emigrated to the States, these

Canarian migrants took with them their ill-defined ideas of liberty from foreign oppression and welded them into a coherent form in the Americas.

In 1810 Canarios had called for "a patriotec government, independent of that of the peninsula, to watch over all the Tribunals set up in the Province". In that same declaration, made as British and French forces slogged out the future of Europe on the Iberian peninsula, the Canarian Junta raised for the first time the Canarios' desire "to get rid of all the Spaniards now here and to put the people of this land in their place".

The same view was echoed in Spain's American colonies. Simón Bolívar, the liberator of most of Spanish America, referred to "Spaniards and Canarios" as quite different peoples. In some of Bolívar's decrees he even included the Canaries in his list of Spanish colonies to be freed.

In time the Spanish empire in America was whittled down to just Cuba and Puerto Rico, which many Canarios used as stepping-stones to continental America.

One of the most influential Canarian emigrants of the late 19th century, at least for Canarian politics, was Secindino Delgado, who at the age of 14 took advantage of a Spanish government offer of a free passage to the island of Cuba for anyone prepared to work for a year there. This offer was introduced in the same year that slavery was abolished by Spain in 1886, (over 80 years after it was abolished in Great Britain), and was designed to replace the lost cheap labour on the plantations.

Left, a quayside demonstration in Santa Cruz shows solidarity with Africa. Above, Castro lookalike in the Tenerife *Carnaval*.

Intimations of independence: In Havana Delgado lived "in the greatest harmony" with the Cubans, whose character contrasted with the pretentiousness of the *peninsulares*. There he met left-wing emigrés from the Canaries and mainland Spain and got to know members of the Cuban independence movement. During a trip to the United States he met the father of Cuban independence, José Martí (whose mother was a Canario); shortly afterwards he began to work for the Cuban freedom movement, writing for an anarchist paper *El Esclavo*.

Forced to flee Cuba in 1896 he returned for a short time to the Canaries where he developed his ideas about the future independence of the islands. The following year, in Venezuela, Delgado founded *El Guanche*, a newspaper devoted to promoting the cause of Canarian independence.

El Guanche seems to have been a short-lived venture, though it was re-established in 1924. Since then has been used as the title of the papers of the Canarian Nationalist Party, the Free Canary Islands Movement, the Seven Green Stars Movement and most recently by the Canarian Nationalist Congress. Delgado's paper had sufficient impact to spur a three-day battle for the control of La Laguna during a Canarian insurrection in 1909.

Delgado's main aim was that the islands should gain a degree of autonomy from Madrid so as to run their own affairs directly, though some of the successor parties that have used the *El Guanche* title have had more extreme aims.

One strange aspect of Canarian nationalism is the view—proposed with varying degrees of seriousness—that the Canaries would have been much better off if the Tenerife militia had let Nelson take Santa Cruz in 1797.

British and American interest: The reasoning behind this curious notion is that the British, who invested heavily in bunkering facilities in the Canaries during Delgado's lifetime (1872 to 1912), were better administrators than the Spanish. The British built, as Canarios will proudly tell, most of the roads on the islands, set up the first public utility companies and they created *Ciudad Jardín* (Garden City), the only pleasant part of Las Palmas (Gran Canaria). They also built up Canarian agriculture, growing bananas, tomatoes and early potatoes, and they expanded the port of Las Palmas at a time when Canarian farmers had just gone through their worst crisis.

Indeed at one stage the possibility of annexation by Great Britain was taken so seriously that the Commander-in-Chief of the Spanish garrison in the islands informed Madrid, in 1873, that a separatist group "was proposing to take advantage of the right moment for England to annexe the islands".

The British were not the only ones interested in the rump of Spain's overseas possessions. The United States eyed the islands after throwing Spain out of the Philippines, Cuba and Puerto Rico in 1898, and Hitler had plans drawn up to take the Canaries over from France during World War II.

British military intelligence also had contacts with Canarian independence groups during the War, and it was probably the now infamous double-agent Kim Philby, former head of the Iberia section, who finally severed the connection.

The islands' strategic importance is now well understood by both NATO and the Warsaw Pact—the Canaries lie across the main shipping lanes from Europe to South America and the southern USA, as well as the routes from Europe to West and South Africa and beyond.

With Franco in charge, the Canary Islanders became loyal Spaniards, and the propaganda seems to have worked—the most Spanish Canarios are those aged between 35 and 60; those younger or older are Canarios first and Spaniards second, if they think of themselves as Spanish at all.

Banned by Franco and spurned by Republicans in exile, the Canarian independence movement languished during the 1950s and early 1960s. But even before Franco and his regime showed signs of fading, MPAIAC (pronounced *emy-pie-ac*) was founded by Antonio Cubillo in 1963. MPAIAC's manifesto stated that, "opposition to Spain exists in our country not only because of historical reasons but also through ethnic, political, economic, geographic and cultural differences that make Canarios a self-contained unity distinct from Spaniards".

Tactics of terror: In 1976 and 1977, as Franco slipped into history, MPAIAC turned to terrorism, launching over a hundred bomb attacks against peninsula-based companies, military targets and, in an expression of solidarity with the Africans, the South African airline offices on the islands.

It was an MPAIAC bomb scare at Las Palmas airport which led to the world's worst air disaster in March 1977, when two jumbo jets were diverted to the inadequate Los Rodeos (now Tenerife North) airport where they collided. Street disturbances in the late 1970s were put down rigorously by the Spanish government; during a demonstration in December 1977 a student was killed, and after the funeral riot police from the peninsula ran amok.

election. But that does not mean that Canarios are disinterested in the independence issue—more moderate parties like AIC (a confederation of island parties) which was until November 1988 a major partner in a coalition regional government, take about 30 percent of the vote.

Unhappily for good government AIC is now dominated by ATI (the Tenerife island party) which has led to accusations of preferential treatment for Tenerife at the expense of the other islands. This has opened up the old wound of the *pleito insular*—is Tenerife or Gran Canaria to be the final seat of regional power?

The rivalry between the two islands—

Cubillo was eventually expelled and found temporary refuge in Algeria. Spanish political pressure and an assassination attempt, which left him unable to walk, curbed his influence at the UN and the OAU where he had managed to gain some acceptance of the Canarian case.

Since the return to democratic government, Cubillo has been able to return, and he now heads the Canarian Nationalist Congress party. The CNC gained a mere 1.3 percent of the vote at the last, and its first,

Left, Franco, on a rare visit to the islands. Above, moving bridges...frequent, but not cheap.

between the *canariones* of Gran Canaria and the *chicharreros* of Tenerife—makes a nonsense of regional government. There are two parliament buildings and two sets of offices. Government departments are split between the two islands, and if you want to find a particular official the chances are that he will be on the other island.

The marketing man might have liked the Canaries to a bridge between three continents and three cultures, but Canarios would sooner be at least two bridges—better still, seven independent ones—and Iberia and Trasmediterranean continue to ensure that the tolls on any bridge are exorbitant.

S. BENITO
ELPRIX

ÑADA
CA 2200

PLACES

The western province of the autonomous region of the Canary Islands comprises the islands of Tenerife, La Palma, Gomera and Hierro. Tenerife, shaped like a ham, is the most populous island, the cultural centre of the archipelago, the centre of learning and academia and, until comparatively recently, also the centre of island government. Tenerife's Mount Teide was once the Everest of Europe, helping to put the island on the map, and it was to Tenerife that the first tourists came.

Life in the Anaga mountains of the north and the Teno *massif* of the southwest has not changed greatly in the past few centuries, with some families still living in cave houses. Elsewhere the arrival of tourism has had its impact: foreign urbanisations around Puerto de la Cruz, the foremost tourist town, have devoured most of the banana plantations of the northern shore. In the south, developments such as Los Cristianos and Playa de las Américas crowd a once-deserted shoreline; before the tourists came, there was simply not enough fresh water in that region to make it of any interest to the agriculturally motivated tinerfeños.

The island of Gomera, shaped like a cow-pat, is no more than 20 miles (32 km) distant from Tenerife, yet is almost untouched by

Preceding pages: Casa de los Balcones in Orotava; fishermen on the north coast of Tenerife; La Laguna, intellectual centre of the province; the road to Mount Teide.

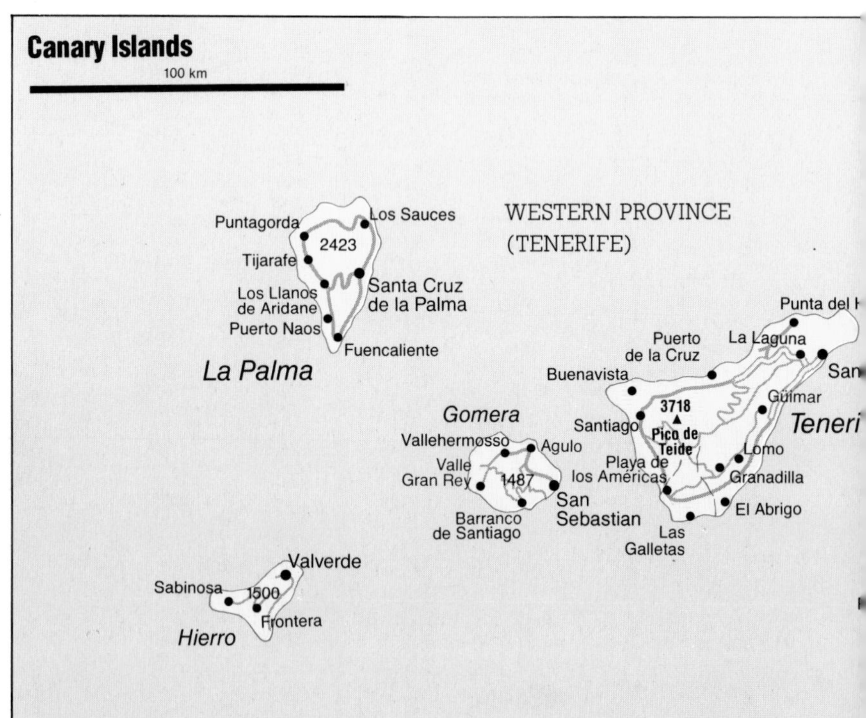

tourism. Rising steeply to a point at Mount Garajonay, the island's centre is covered with the protected forest of the Garajonay National Park, laced with very good walking tracks. The six major valleys of Gomera are steep and heavily terraced, although much of the terracing is now abandoned following the island's depopulation.

Hierro, shaped like the axe-head of an aboriginal tool, is the most backward of the islands, although it produces the best local wine. The tablelands at its centre are reminiscent of pastures of northern Europe; the massive bay of El Golfo is probably part of the largest volcanic crater in the world, and Hierro also boasts the world's smallest hotel, with just four rooms.

La Palma, shaped like a molar, is the greenest of the islands. It too is remarkably high for its size, and on its highest point, the Roque de los Muchachos, is a multi-national observatory. Santa Cruz de la Palma, the port and capital, is one of the prettiest towns in the archipelago, with elegant balconies and squares. Around the southern shores are beaches of black sand, and in the north, in the top of the molar, is the Caldera de Taburiente, a vast and forested volcanic cavity with the status of a national park.

Between them, these smaller islands could pretend to the title of European Bali; craggy *campesinos*, brilliant sunshine, weird and wonderful fiestas, deep and ancient forest and precipitous roads with death-defying driving. They are the landscapes of the independent traveller, undiscovered, diverse and intriguing.

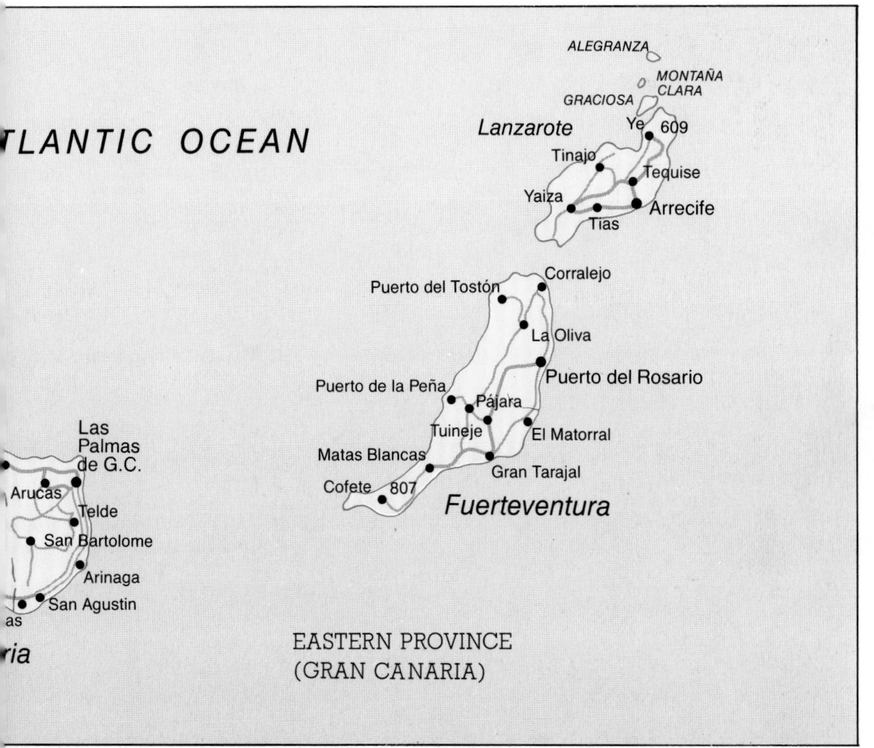

Tenerife

15 km

ATLANTIC OCEAN

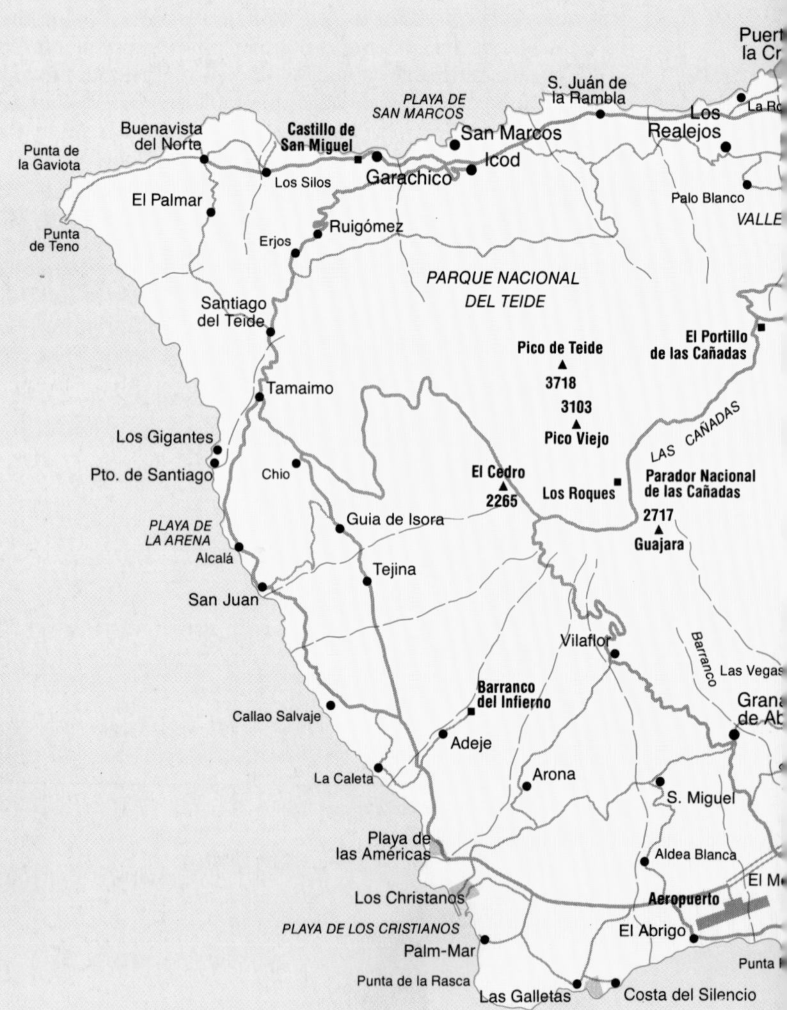

Roque de Fuera
Roque de Tierra
Punta del Hidalgo
PLAYA DEL ROQUE
Punta del Hidalgo
Bajamar
Taganana
MONTE DE
LAS MERCEDES
Tejina
Tegueste
Mirador Cruz
del Carmen
Igueste
Las Mercedes
PLAYA DE
LAS TERESITAS
Mesa del Mar
S. Andrés
La Laguna
Sauzal
Tacoronte
Aeropuerto
de los Rodeos
Matanza
Acentejo
Santa Cruz
de Tenerife
Taco
La Esperanza
Sobradillo
S. Maria del Mar
Santa Ursula
Tabaiba
Barranco
Hondo
Las Arenitas
Candelaria
Arafo
Güimar
Pto. de Güimar
Mirador de
Don Martin
El Escobonal
PLAYA DE LA MARGALLERA
Zarza
Fasnia
PLAYA DE TOPUERQUE
Icor
Arico Nuevo
Poris de
Abona
Punta de Abona
ATLANTIC OCEAN

TENERIFE: THE NORTHERN TIP

Tiene mi santacrucera
de nieve y rosas la cara;
la nieve se la dio el Teide,
y las rosas, la Orotava.
My Santa Cruz lady has
a face of snow and roses;
Teide gave her the snow
and La Orotava the roses.

"OK, Santa Cruz mightn't be a beautiful city like, say, Seville but the people here are *really* lovely." Relaxing with a *ronmiel* liqueur in the Cafetería Olimpo, a British businessman summed up his feelings about his adopted home. You'd have to travel far afield to discover the equals of the Santacruceros, who endow their birthplace with a warm and friendly feeling that earns it the soubriquet *Capital de la Amabilidad* (Capital of Kindliness).

Left, Santa Cruz. Right, statue in Sanabria park.

The capital of Tenerife is a commercial and administrative centre, with one of Spain's busiest ports. Precisely because visitors haven't overrun the place, the Parisian enjoying a beer in the Bar Atlántico or the Berliner buying a camera in the Maya department store will both find themselves treated with a kindness and courtesy that, regrettably, mass tourism has diluted elsewhere. Despite its being a major port, street crime remains a rare occurrence.

During the city's pre-Lenten *Carnival*, the whole central area is turned into an enormous party for two weeks. According to the *Guinness Book of Records*, Santa Cruz was the site of the world's biggest-ever dance. On 3 March 1987, an astounding total of 240,000 people boogeyed the night away to the music of Spanish superstar Celia Cruz and the Orchestra of the Caracas Boys.

Violent origins: But life in Santa Cruz hasn't always been one long party. The city's history can be traced back to 1464 when Spain's Sancho de Herrera landed in the Guanche area known as Añaza. With the agreement of the friendly natives he proceeded to build a fortified tower but soon provoked an unnecessary crisis by garotting five Guanches who had the temerity to redesign a Spanish soldier's face with their fists. Thereupon the local chief, the Mencey of Anaga, attacked the fort with 1,000 men and Herrera was compelled to make a high-speed exit in his boat.

The next European of note to make an appearance was the Andalusian aristocrat Don Alonso Fernández de Lugo who arrived in 1494 with a force of over 1,000 men. To mark his safe journey, he raised up a wooden cross on the shore around which Mass was celebrated. When houses were built on that spot, the settlement adopted the name of Santa Cruz (Holy Cross).

Lugo went on to conquer the Guanches and, because its bay provided a fine anchorage, Santa Cruz quickly developed as a port. However its economic success made it a target for seaborne raiders, including that master of marine warfare, Admiral Nelson. In 1797, commanding a fleet of eight men o'war, he decided to chance his arm in battle—and promptly lost it! During an exchange of fire with shore batteries a grapeshot shattered his right elbow forcing him to withdraw and have the arm amputated.

So Santa Cruz was left to continue its steady development into an economic powerhouse, with the ultimate accolade coming in 1822 when it was named capital of the whole Canaries. That title was maintained until 1927 when the islands were split into the twin provinces of Santa Cruz de Tenerife and Las Palmas de Gran Canaria.

Town centre: Nowadays Santa Cruz has a population of almost 225,000 and they all seem to drive through the **Plaza de España** during the rush hour. Situated beside the port, this imposing square's centrepiece is a towering monument to the dead of the Spanish Civil War. From the floor of the monument the northern skyline is filled with the serrated Anaga Mountains while on the south side of the square is seen the head post office and Palacio Insular, seat of the island's administration and local tourist office.

Adjoining the Plaza de España is the **Plaza de la Candelaria**, a pedestrian precinct and public meeting place. At one end a white Carrara marble statue, dating from 1778, depicts the local legend of the *Triunfo de la Candelaria* (Triumph of the Virgin of Candelaria), as the Virgin, on top of a four-sided column, makes her appearance before the four Guanche chiefs who stand around the base.

At one corner of the plaza is the **Casino de Tenerife**, founded in 1840 and now the oldest private club on the island and a mecca for bridge players.

Further up the hill is the **Palacio Carta** (Carta Palace), built in 1742 and an outstanding example of a traditional Canarian building. The Banco Español de Crédito has its office here but you don't need an account to go inside and discover how banking can be elevated into an aesthetic experience. Change a

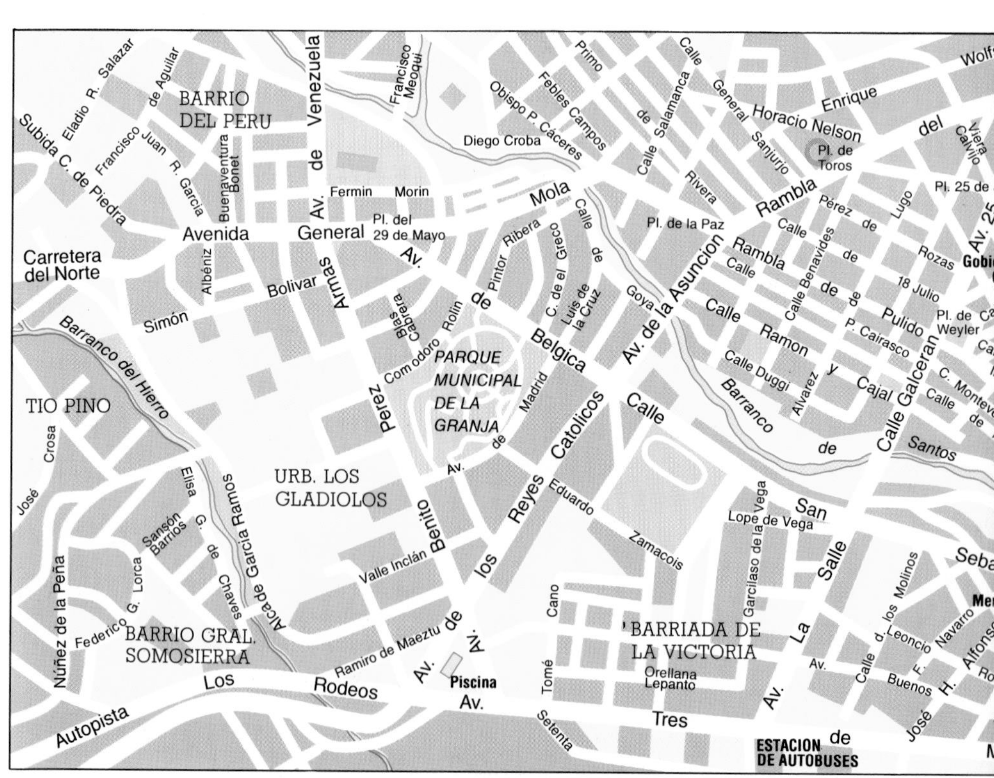

traveller's cheque whilst marvelling at the delectable *patio*.

Above this courtyard, in the opening on to the sky, huge awnings are rolled up ready to be drawn across to shade clerks and cashiers from the midday sun. It's almost enough to make paying bills a pleasure.

Opposite the Palacio Carta is **Mr Smile's** hamburger bar. Pop inside for a hot dog when they're busy—really busy—and you'll discover the true meaning of fast-food.

Leading out of the Plaza de la Candelaria is the **Calle de Castillo**, Santa Cruz's principal shopping thoroughfare, which testifies to the truth of Robert Louis Stevenson's dictum "Everyone lives by selling something." Here is the best of the world's merchandise, from Spanish leather goods to Scotch whisky to Japanese audio equipment, at the keenest of prices.

A haven of peace in this trading quarter is the **Círculo de Bellas Artes de Tenerife** (Fine Arts Circle of Tenerife) whose cool, white marble salon provides a showcase for painting and sculpture.

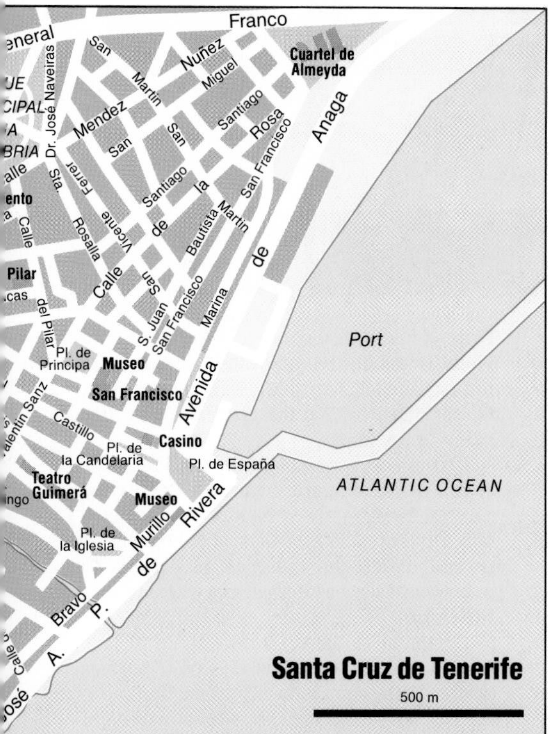

Culture: The outstanding display of Guanche relics at the **Museo Arqueológico**, located in the Palacio Insular, includes skulls, pottery, necklaces, pine lances and, most interesting of all, mummies which were wrapped in animal skins. There are also full-size models, providing a modern-day impression of what Tenerife's first inhabitants looked like.

A short walk from the museum is Santa Cruz's most important church, the **Iglesia de Nuestra Señora de la Concepción**, whose six-tier belfry has long been a city landmark. Originally constructed in 1502, it was ravaged by fire in 1642 and had to undergo extensive rebuilding work.

The brightly illuminated nave is flanked by twin aisles and a series of side altars, while a statue of the Virgin Mary by the famous 18th century sculptor José Luján Pérez adorns the high altar. The church is also a repository for British flags seized during Nelson's attack and the Cruz de la Conquista (Cross of the Conquest) which Lugo was said to have planted on disembarking at Santa Cruz.

The **Barranco de Santos** divides the Iglesia from the **Mercado de Nuestra Señora de Africa**, a food emporium that reveals just how bountiful Mother Nature is on this island. Inside an arcaded courtyard, open only during the morning, dozens of stalls sell an amazing array of fruit, flowers, vegetables, fish and meat. Treat yourself to a *chirimoya* (custard apple) with its strange perfumed flesh. Note too how neat and tidy market traders keep the place, with not a shred of litter in sight.

On the edge of the city centre, the **Parque Municipal García Sanabria** is an oasis of greenery amid apartment blocks and offices. This pleasantly shaded area, named after a mayor, was laid down in the 1920s and supplied the setting for an international exhibition of sculpture in 1973. Some of the exhibits remain, intriguing the casual observer

Santa Cruz de Tenerife

Cruising The Nightlife Circuit

Most people who visit Tenerife stay in or around the three holiday centres of Playa de las Américas, Los Cristianos and Puerto de la Cruz. In these towns it is often easy to forget that there is a large population of Spaniards totally unconnected to the tourist industry, living and working on the island.

Santa Cruz, the capital, is a busy port with a population of around 200,000, but it does not cater for tourists. Accordingly, fun-seeking visitors may find the nightlife during the week a little dull in comparison to Playa de las Américas, where the bars and discos are full of tourists every night. The simple reason for this is that during the week locals have to be at work at 9 o'clock in the morning, and office hours do not allow for late nights.

Friday and Saturday nights are a different story altogether. Because, in general, there are no official closing times for bars, clubs and discos, people tend to go out late and stay out until the early morning. By 11 p.m. most of the popular bars in Santa Cruz are populated by crowds of the under 20s who are often given a midnight curfew by their parents. The Paris discotheque or the El Tropa in the Rambla General Franco are the favourites with this age group.

Older people therefore arrange to meet later, normally between 11 p.m. and midnight. The usual routine is to meet your friends in a particular bar and then move around a circuit of well-recognised nightspots as the day grows older. In general people do not invite each other home, probably because most people live in extended family situations and relaxed socialising is not possible in a domestic environment. Central meeting places are therefore used.

There are two main meeting areas in Santa Cruz. Bars on the Calle Ramon y Cajal, particularly the Cervezeria Rhin Barril, a German beer cellar at the top end of the street, are always crowded between 11 and 12.30. The Residencia Anaga is also a popular meeting point, particularly the bar Tormantene.

If you lack transport and decide to stay in Santa Cruz then there are a few possibilities close to these meeting points. The Daida disco, also in the Residencia Anaga, is probably the most popular in Santa Cruz. Others are the El Tropa and Chic in the Rambla.

To enter a discotheque in Tenerife you quite often do not have to pay, and if you do, your entry ticket will entitle you to a free drink.

Alternatively you could go to the bars situated behind the bull-ring, where Espacio 41 is favoured by Santa Cruz punks and "gothics"; La Calle bar in front is decorated to resemble a street with mock shop fronts, and around the corner El Cactus and El Saxo are also popular. The music in these bars is loud, so if you prefer a quieter drink then all the bars along the Avenida Anaga are popular until about 4 a.m., when most people begin to drift home to sleep.

Shortly after midnight people with transport travel six miles (10 km) up the hill to La Laguna, the university town. La Laguna City Council has placed a curfew of 3 a.m. on bars and discos in the town because of noise nuisance to the residents, but until this time the bars are crowded, mostly with students. El Sur and El Boar are favourite bars as well as Morapeos and the disco-bar Twitters. During the academic year the disco Sketch is always crowded.

At 3 a.m., if you decide to continue, the next venue is onward via the autoroute to Puerto de la Cruz. A favourite disco here is El Coto, below the Hotel Botanico, but it is often so crowded with tourists and locals that it is difficult to get in. The Guitar disco around the corner is also used by many of the locals.

If your stamina lasts till the end you still have to face the 40 minute drive back to Santa Cruz. Be careful, because this stretch of road is noted for speed and breathaliser traps, and there have been several late-night fatalities involving young people on their way home from just such a nightlife circuit.

Breakfast in Santa Cruz consists of *churros* (sweet cakes) covered in chocolate and strong coffee. In the summer a nap on the beach is often the best way to recuperate, after a hard night out on the tiles.

and providing climbing frames for energetic children.

The **port** of Santa Cruz is well worth a visit. Contrary to what applies in many other parts of the world, the public is allowed full access to the cargo-laden quays—yet another pointer to the basic honest nature of the Santacrucero. The extensive outer sea walls are topped off with a promenade which makes a popular rendezvous for anglers and a perfect viewing gallery.

Prominent among the boats are Soviet trawlers for whom this remains a favourite port of call because of the shopping facilities. Crews are able to stock up with radios and cassette players for the folks back home in Leningrad or Tallin before sailing to the rich fishing grounds off the coast of Africa.

If because you're in part of Spain you'd like to watch a bullfight, forget it. A **Plaza de Toros** does exist on the Rambla del General Franco but it's no longer used as such because of the prohibitive cost of mounting *corridas*. However, the aficionado's loss has proved the rock fan's gain. The bullring has now become an atmospheric venue for gigs by such a pop luminary as the Godfather of Soul, James Brown.

University town: With a population of 120,000, **La Laguna** is the next most important town on Tenerife after Santa Cruz. Situated in the middle of the semi-tropical **Aguere Valley**, it lies just five miles (eight kms) from the centre of the capital, with the outskirts of both merging along the La Cuesta highway. Because of the altitude (1,805 ft/550 metres), La Laguna enjoys a cooler climate than coastal areas, which helps contribute to the attractions of living in this historic place.

La Laguna means pond or small lake and it was probably because of this feature that the conquistador, Alonso Fernández de Lugo, founded the settlement and made it capital of the Canaries in 1496. The archipelago's only university was opened here in 1701 and during term time the presence of so many students imbues shops, bars

he port of
anta Cruz.

and restaurants with a youthful, exuberant air.

In the historic quarter the original layout of rectangular blocks remains so there are narrow streets running between ancient mansions that enclose plant-bedecked *patios*. Because it has managed to retain its essentially Spanish character, La Laguna reveals how towns on the island looked before modern developers moved in.

The town's cathedral, **Santa Iglesia**, was founded in 1515 although the present edifice, crowned with a dome and twin towers, was erected between 1904 and 1915 after the previous one had fallen into ruin. Quixotically, the outside has been painted pink and this bizarre choice of colour might explain why graffiti vandals have turned their attention to its external walls.

Inside, the arched nave is illuminated by beautiful stained glass windows while in one corner the gilt-encrusted Capilla de la Virgen de los Remedios (Chapel of the Virgin of the Remedies) flames forth with its message of hope for a steady stream of supplicants. Behind the high altar lies the simple tomb of Lugo, "Conquistador de Tenerife y La Palma, fundador de La Laguna" (Conqueror of Tenerife and La Palma, founder of La Laguna).

From the cathedral, the **Calle Obispo Rey Redondo** leads past the **Teatro Leal**, where plays and concerts are performed in a triple-tiered hall, to the town's oldest church, the **Iglesia de Nuestra Señora de la Concepción**. This was constructed in 1502 although the tower is the third on the site, having been built around 1701, and major renovation was carried out as recently as 1974. Its interior is noteworthy for a 15th-century baptismal font, which was used to baptise Guanche leaders, and the deftly carved wood of the ceiling, pulpit and choir stalls.

While the Iglesia de la Concepción stands at one end of the Calle Obispo Rey Redondo, the other end runs into the **Plaza del Adelantado** (Governor's Square), where the **Ayuntamiento** (Town Hall) is situated. This handsome

The ceiling of the Iglesia de la Concepción

elbows its way into the **Monte de las Mercedes**, a dense forest of laurel trees, regarded as the most beautiful on the island. In reality it is a remnant of the primitive woodlands which during the earth's tertiary era stretched up and around the Mediterranean as far as Asia.

The first opportunity to escape the forest comes after five miles (eight km) at the **Mirador del Valle de Aguere**, which overlooks La Laguna. Beyond the town haughty Teide lauds over the skyline.

A few minutes' drive further on is **Cruz del Carmen**, with a chapel and statue of Nuestra Señora de las Mercedes. At a height of 3,018 ft (920 metres), this *mirador*, surrounded by verdant woodland, is a popular area for picnics and barbecues.

It's a short walk to **Taborno**, the highest peak in the Anaga. Members of the public aren't allowed on the actual summit (3,360 ft, 1,024 metres) because aircraft navigation beacons have been installed there. Nevertheless there are dizzying views of the

Coastline near San Andrés.

example of neo-classical architecture contains the flag which Lugo planted on Tenerife to claim the island for Spain.

From the Ayuntamiento there's a short walk down the **Calle Nava y Grimón** to the **Santuario del Cristo**, home of the Canaries' most revered statue of Jesus, which was brought to Tenerife by Lugo. Every September this becomes the object of devotion for thousands of pilgrims who arrive from all parts of insular and peninsular Spain.

On the southern outskirts of La Laguna, on a bridge over the Autopista del Norte, stands a statue depicting Friar José de Anchieta, who was born in the city in 1533. After going to Brazil as a missionary, he was said to have converted the miraculous total of two million Indians to Christianity. The statue was a gift from Brazil.

Los Rodeos airport, a few minutes along the motorway, is used mainly for domestic flights and was the scene of the world's worst aircraft disaster in 1977 when Boeing 747s belonging to KLM and Pan Am collided on the runway, killing 582 people.

The Anaga: La Laguna is the gateway to the **Anaga Mountains**, a sweeping rampart of volcanic peaks that fills the north-east corner of Tenerife. The principal route into this thinly populated area runs northwards out of the town along the spinal cord of the Anaga and is punctuated by a succession of stunning viewpoints.

Soon after La Laguna, the tree-lined carriageway reaches the village of Las Canteras where a side road turns off the ridge route to **Punta del Hidalgo** (10 miles, 16 km). This quiet town at the north-west corner of the Anaga peninsula rests in the shadow of the Siamese twin peaks of Dos Hermanos (Two Brothers) which rise up to 1,128 ft (344 metres) and 1,010 ft (308 metres) respectively.

Popular with German tourists, the resort area has two sea-water bathing pools. Local people maintain that sunsets here are the most spectacular on Tenerife, fit to ravish the most jaundiced retina.

Beyond Las Canteras, the Anaga road

surrounding countryside.

The next stop on the road is the **Mirador del Pico del Inglés**, a truly spectacular balcony, 3,149 ft (960 metres) up in the air, from which to gaze in awe at the island below. Its name is said to derive from the days when English buccaneers who roamed neighbouring seas had a spy at this spot to signal whenever a vessel was nearby.

From here the road follows the Anaga's spine for six miles (10 km) to the **Mirador del Bailadero** (Bailadero Viewpoint), whose name is a corruption of *baladero*, or bleating place. This indicated a spot where, in the event of drought or shortage of grazing for animals, Guanches would separate sheep and goats from their young so the mothers' bleating would appease the gods and make them send rain.

Possibly as a result of this belief, El Bailadero has long been regarded as a meeting place for witches although nowadays its most sinister visitors are thirsty families who drive up to two bars that cling grimly to the precipices.

After El Bailadero there are three routes available, with the first crawling uneasily along a knife-edge of rocks to **Chinobre**, another superb viewpoint encompassing the whole of the north of the island. In due course the road arrives at the safe haven of **Chamorga** (six miles, 10 km), a scattering of white farmhouses amongst steep hillsides etched with terraces by what seems a giant's hand. In the village centre a pretty little chapel is dedicated to a local man who died in the mountains.

The second possibility, a heady, ear-popping descent to the white village of **Taganana** and on to **Almaciga**, four miles (six km) away on the northern coast, entails passing through a black tunnel that burrows from one side of the summit ridge to the other, with El Bailadero bars perched up above. At Almaciga there are a couple of restful beaches with magnificent views of Mount Teide.

The third route is down a serpentine road to the coastal town of **San Andrés**, whose houses appear to be clambering over each other up the sheer hillside. Alongside this town is the artificial beach of **Las Teresitas**, built in 1975 by Santa Cruz municipal council. A total of four million sacks of sand were shipped from the Spanish Sahara to create the biggest man-made beach in the world and a favourite bathing spot for Santacruceros.

However, if you want to get away from crowds of sun-worshippers, around the next headland a steep track leads down to the secluded beach of **Las Gaviotas**. This curve of brown sand, aptly named after the seagulls that circle its high cliffs, has a couple of bars and remains quiet enough to attract pneumatic nudists. At one end the Punta de los Organos is a strange cliff with rocks shaped like organ pipes.

The coastal road from Santa Cruz, which passes through San Andrés, terminates at the hideaway village of **Igueste**, straddling a fertile *barranco* and boasting a pretty church dedicated to Saint Peter. From here a drive of 13 miles (21 km) via Santa Cruz brings you back to your starting point at La Laguna.

Left, village in the Anaga Mountains. Right, Las Teresitas beach.

SevenUp

WALKING THE ANAGA MOUNTAIN TRAILS

Even in the bustling streets of Santa Cruz you can't fail to be aware of the jagged mountains to the north. Look across the Plaza de España and there they are, fangs of rock against the blue flesh of the sky. The torn curtain of stone is framed in the entrance arch of the market.

The Anaga Mountains form a dramatic backcloth to the capital—and visitors to Santa Cruz would be shortsighted to even think about ignoring them, those summits seem so distant, untouchable, even forbidding, particularly when clouds boil around the peaks.

Yet cars and buses can traverse the range quite easily along a road from La Laguna. That ridgeway is the key to a superb network of *senderos turísticos* (tourist paths) that lead through dense woods and deep gorges to hidden villages, lost valleys and secret beaches—the Anaga that few people ever see.

Would-be explorers should observe some commonsense guidelines. Obviously you'll need strong footwear, warm, waterproof clothing and a good supply of food and drink. But in addition:

1. Use a good map. Spain's Servicio Geográfico del Ejército (Army Ordnance Survey) publishes a large-scale map of the Anaga. ICONA, the national conservation service, and the island's government have also combined to produce a free map of the *senderos turísticos*, Tenerife: Anaga, Zona 1, but unfortunately not many tourist offices seem to stock it. If you can get hold of one, use it with the military map as the latter doesn't show all the latest paths and roads.

2. Go with at least one companion.

3. Take a compass to confirm your direction of travel, particularly when cloud cover comes down, and have a whistle to attract attention.

4. Keep strictly to the signposted routes. After heavy rain, if the path has been washed away or blocked by a landslide DO NOT try to continue.

5. Leave a note with a friend or acquaintance or the reception desk of your hotel detailing your proposed route.

The choice of outings is endless, from gentle strolls of a couple of hundred yards to demanding expeditions that can last from dawn to dusk—or weeks if you like camping. If you're tempted to see the real Anaga, here are two walks, one hard, one easy, that can be thoroughly recommended.

In the far northeast, the Faro de Anaga (Anaga Lighthouse) warns away ships sailing around this wild corner of the island. But for any intrepid walker, that beacon acts as a beckoning finger.

The starting point of this walk comes at the end of the road that plummets from El Bailadero, through picturesque Taganana and Almaciga, to the slumbering coastal village of Benijo. From here take the dirt track snaking around the cliffs, with superb views of the twin Anaga Rocks.

The Roque de Dentro (Inner Rock) rears out of the waves like a giant tooth to a height of 584 ft (178 metres) whereas the flatter Roque de Fuera (Outer Rock) reaches just 210 ft (64 metres). Looking back, the vista extends almost to Punta del Hidalgo while the skyline is pierced by Tenerife's own Matterhorn, the pyramidal Roque de Taborno, 2,315 ft (706 metres) high.

After 30 minutes, you come to El Draguillo, a cluster of white farmhouses set among a veritable plethora of prickly pears. Its name derives from "drago", or dragon tree, because several of these grow hereabouts. Now the dirt track ends, replaced by a sinuous path that leads into a shady *barranco* offering welcome relief from the sun.

Up the other side, the path crosses broad rivers of scree. Here, from this perch above the Atlantic, you can appreciate the vivid imagery of Canarian writer Victor Zurita, who saw Tenerife as a concubine sleeping in the arms of the sea, which in turns caresses and violates her; any reasonably strong wind soon creates a battleground between sea and land with this path providing an airy grandstand. Beyond the scree lies Las Palmas, a settlement of half a dozen farms.

The next landmark is an enormous volcanic boulder embedded in the mountainside below which a stone house has been built by some enterprising islander, using the boulder as its roof. From here it's only a matter of minutes to your destination. The path crosses grassy slopes and suddenly, after two and a half hours and four miles (six km), the Anaga Lighthouse stands before you. This guardian of seafarers, 656 ft (200 metres) above sea-level, is manned by three keepers who live with their wives and children inside the building. All necessities have to be carried in from the village of Chamorga, one and a half miles away at the head of the deep Barranco de Roque Bermejo. The kids also have to make the steep climb up there to school and, so their parents say, always hurry back to life on the edge of the world.

Because of the tumbling jumble of its terrain, the Anaga has long concealed villages which could only be reached from the outside world along narrow and vertiginous paths. But in recent years rivulets of asphalt have slowly trickled down the sides of *barrancos* to join these outlying settlements to the roads.

Nonetheless, a couple of remote communities survive with absolutely no road link. One such place is Chinamada, 2,033 ft (620 metres) up in the mountains, where the people still live in caves just as the Guanches did. This easy, mile-and-a-half walk to Tenerife's Shangri-la should not be missed by any reasonably active visitor.

It begins in the quiet village of Las Carboneras, reached by a spiralling road that descends northwards from the main ridgeway from La Laguna, between the *miradores* of Cruz del Carmen and Pico del Inglés. In the village, this road ends at the pretty little Plaza de San Isidro, with a church of that name at one end.From here the serpentine path, with steps cut into steeper points, leads beneath towering cliffs and above yawning chasms. At first, the terraces zig-zagging down the hillsides appear well tended; but, further along, they become more neglected and overgrown, testimony to chronic depopulation.

The panorama is dominated by monumental Roque de Taborno (2,315 ft, 706 metres), a basalt bullet aimed at the azure sky. However, don't confuse this with the Anaga's highest point, Taborno, further inland.

The path skirts a rock face and there they are—the first white houses of Chinamada, squatting on ledges above the sheer *barranco*. To all intents and purposes they look just the same as other farms in the Anaga. Only when you get closer does it become obvious the doors and windows are set in the rock wall with the living quarters extending into caves in the mountainside.

Their basic design consists of three areas—living room, bedroom and kitchen, complete with a chimney through the rock to allow cooking smoke to escape. Smaller caves a short distance away provide storage space, animal quarters, guest bedrooms—and the lavatory.

Electricity hasn't been discovered up here, and villagers rely on gas bottles for cooking and batteries for their radios. One or two high-flyers even possess battery-powered TV sets.

Any items this community of 30 requires from the known world, be they wardrobes or window panes, have to be carried in on their broad backs from Las Carboneras but nearly all daily needs can be met by the fertile land. Along with staple foods of potatoes (two crops a year), wheat and maize, they grow lettuces, peppers, cauliflowers, figs, tomatoes, lemons, oranges, apples, pears, avocadoes, apricots and cherries. They also make their own potent wine and aromatic goats' cheese, hunt rabbits and partridge and eat strong-tasting goat meat.

If old Antonio isn't busy down on the terraces he might invite you in for a *taza* of strong black coffee—to the accompaniment of loud Spanish music from his Stone Age gramophone. Should the rest of the universe disappear tomorrow, Chinamada would survive.

Far inland across the wild, impassable *barrancos*, a huddle of tiny farmhouses represents the high-tech village of Batán which rejoices in electricity, telephones, a road, and those outlandish creatures, tourists. To the west Punta del Hidalgo's high-rise hotels are visible beside the sea. From there buses can be caught to the rest of the island but that entails an hour's steady walk down to the coast—and a two-hour slog back.

As you leave the village to return to Las Carboneras, you'll notice a little saddle of flat land—the only level area around, half the size of a tennis court—on which a tiny chapel is being built. The villagers are carrying in all the material along their pathway from civilization in a moving expression of hope for the future of Chinamada.

HONDURAS
TE 1 2908

PUERTO AND THE NORTH COAST

For hundreds of thousands of tourists, **Puerto de la Cruz** is the sophisticated holiday town that introduced them to the delights of Tenerife. It's true that in recent years a brash newcomer, Playa de las Américas, has thrust ahead in the popularity stakes, but Puerto knows its market. The town is quite glad to see Southern Tenerife siphoning off younger, more raucous holidaymakers. As one restaurant owner put it: "We prefer the beer and hamburger brigade to go somewhere else."

As the principal town on the northern coast of the island, with a population of 40,000, Puerto occupies a favoured situation where the fertile Orotava Valley runs into the rocky shore of the Atlantic. It has been a destination for travellers and holidaymakers since the 19th century.

However, its importance as a commercial and trading centre extends way back. For in 1706 a disaster happened 16 miles (26 km) west of the town that was to have lasting effects. A volcanic eruption from Teide devastated Tenerife's main port, Garachico, and Puerto de la Cruz (then called Puerto de la Orotava) became overnight the principal outlet for local produce, particularly the island's wine.

Rest and recreation: The next development to have profound repercussions was the arrival of well-heeled Victorian tourists from England in the last decades of the 19th century. Puerto also acted as a sanatorium for those recovering from ailments prevalent in industrial cities and became a rest and recuperation centre for British empire-builders on the long voyage home from Africa and Asia.

Since that first influx of tourists, who stayed in such hotels as the Monopol and Taoro (now the casino), the total of visitors to Puerto has increased steadily. Today 900,000 arrive each year, with the Spanish, British and Germans leading the throng. February's spectacular *Carnaval* does bring in extra visitors and August attracts Spaniards fleeing from the mainland's summer oven.

The full name of the town's main square and focus of its social life is **Plaza del Charco de los Camarones**, or Square of the Shrimp Pool, so called because local people used to catch shrimps there in a tidal pond.

Shaded by palms and laurel trees, which were brought from Cuba in 1852, it contains an animated children's play area and a stage on which bands perform occasionally in the open air. Chess is sometimes played with giant pieces on the pavement in one corner, watched by a thoughtful, knowledgeable audience. The square is also the site of Puerto's biggest and busiest taxi rank.

A short distance through the northeast corner of the Plaza along the **Calle de María** is the **Puerto Pesquero**, or fishing port, a tiny, stony beach which in the 18th century offered the island's main outlet for exports. Nowadays local fishermen berth their boats here. At its eastern side is a white and black building with a wooden cross

Preceding pages: Puerto de la Cruz. Left, in the fishing harbour. Right, the lido.

on the wall. This is the **Casa de la Real Aduana** (Royal Customs House), the oldest building in Puerto, which dates back to 1620 and was occupied by Customs officers until 1833. The ground floor is now a shop selling fine embroidery and craftwork while the upper floors form a private residence. However the lovely *patio*, full of antique furniture and interesting artefacts, is open to the public, courtesy of its British owner.

The entrance to the Royal Customs House lies in the cobble-stoned **Calle de las Lonjas** which leads past fishmongers' shops and a club for fishermen to the **Mercado** (Market). This somewhat shabby collection of stalls is reminiscent of an African bazaar and with single-minded bargaining any resolute tourist can expect some good buys in Canarian embroidery, jewellery and leatherwear.

Beyond stands the **Ayuntamiento** (Town Hall), built in 1973 and headquarters of the municipal police. Across the road the traditional 18th century **Casa de Miranda** belonged to the family of Francisco Miranda, a hero of Venezuelan independence.

From here, the steps of the **Calle Punto Fijo** lead to the **Iglesia de Nuestra Señora de la Peña de Francia** (Church of Our Lady of the Rock of France), Puerto's main church, which was built between 1684 and 1697, although the tower came as a later addition in 1898. The dark interior acts as a gloomy frame for the magnificent high altar, while the organ was brought from London in 1814 by Bernardo de Cologán, an islander of Irish descent. In a room at the back there's a fleet of massive carts which are pulled through the streets during religious processions.

Across the square is the local tourist information centre. The square itself features a statue of the famous engineer Agustín de Betancourt who was born in Puerto in 1758 and died in St Petersburg in 1824. He had an illustrious career as a builder of roads and canals and founded a school of bridge and road building for Tsar Alexander I.

In the **Calle de Quintana** beside the square, the **Monopol** is one of Puerto's oldest hotels, with a beautiful *patio* and newly installed Canarian balconies. At the end of this street is the **Punta del Viento** (Windy Point), a terrace overlooking the rocky shore and **Costa de Martiánez** complex of swimming pools. Beneath is a restaurant on an open balcony in the cliff face.

The promenade, **Calle de San Telmo**, runs from the Punta, alongside foaming Atlantic breakers to the brilliant white **Iglesia de San Telmo**, looking for all the world as if it's been carved out of icing sugar. This chapel is dedicated to the patron saint of sailors, invoked on countless occasions by seafarers negotiating Puerto's perilous coast. Mass is celebrated in German here and buried under the floor are victims of a flood caused by a great storm in 1826.

Beyond San Telmo, the **Plaza de los Reyes Católicos** (Square of the Catholic Kings) is adorned with a bust of Francisco Miranda, the Venezuelan national hero whose family home was mentioned earlier.

Puerto's seaside promenade.

Classy botany: The **Avenida de Colón** is a pleasant boulevard lined by stalls displaying jewellery, clothes and souvenirs. Seated at their easels, artists vie with each other to do high-speed portraits, either representational or comical, of willing sitters.

Along the seaward side of the Avenida de Colón, behind the stalls, gardens are laid out from where a close-up view can be enjoyed of the beautiful **Costa de Martiánez** development, set amid palms and lawns. At the end of the Avenida is the distinctive **Café Columbus**, shaped like a Spanish galleon, from where coaches leave for various tourist attractions. From here it's a taxi ride to the famous **Jardín Botánico** (Botanical Garden), a few minutes from central Puerto. Choose one of the hottest days to go as this explosion of tropical vegetation forms a refreshing, relaxing haven. The garden was founded in 1788 by King Carlos III of Spain as a half-way house for exotic plants from America, Africa and Asia en route for Spain. Hence the official name of Jardín de Aclimatación (acclimatization garden) de la Orotava.

Unfortunately the transfer of many new species to Spain didn't prove a success but this botanical El Dorado, home of 4,000 trees, bushes and plants, remains as a living legacy of glorious failure. Among the enormous variety of palms is the colossal Coussapoa Dealbata, a Gothic horror story of a tree from the South American jungles, which hasn't even been blessed with the civilizing accolade of an English name. This 200-year-old tangle of trunks and roots, branches and bark, seems to be biding its time until nightfall. Then, so they whisper, it snakes out those wooden tentacles to gorge on tourists locked inside the garden.

In a lighter vein there's the Palo Borracho (Drunken Log), also from South America, a bloated, swaying apparition that appears to have been watered too liberally with barrels of the island's knockout Guajiro rum.

There's a free bus service from the Café Columbus to the **Loro Parque**

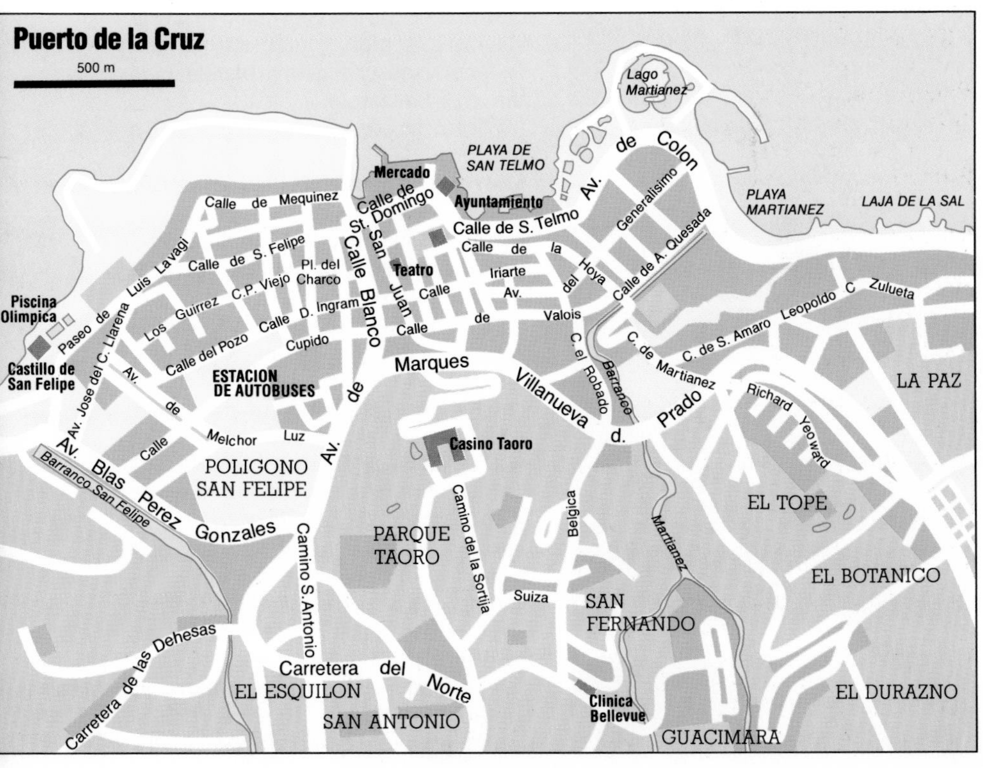

(Parrot Park) in the Punta Brava district. On view here in cages are more than 200 species of these iridescent birds in what is said to be the biggest collection in the world, although Miami's Parrot Park does cover a wider area. Visitors can see some 1,500 birds on display but behind the scenes there are at least 2,500 more.

As well as an indoor show of tricks by performing parrots, there's an outdoor flying demonstration by trained birds who delight in rearranging the hair partings of members of the audience. Lorovision, an 180-degree cinema, gives a stomach-churning idea of what it's like to be able to fly—and also to drive a fire engine or sports car at breakneck speed. A recent addition to the park's attractions and well worth the entire entrance fee is Europe's largest dolphinarium.

High-rolling: Even if you're not the least bit interested in gambling, the **Casino Taoro**, once the biggest hotel in Spain, can be an rivetting experience—particularly when a Spanish croupier attempts to explain in English the rules of French roulette to an ecstatic Italian tourist who believes he's just hit the biggest jackpot this side of Las Vegas. Punters need their passports to gain entry because reception runs a computer check on everyone who goes in, making sure their credentials, and credit, are OK. If you do forget your passport, they'll even pay for a taxi back to the hotel to collect it. Gamblers here run the gamut from wide-eyed innocents abroad who thought chips came with fish to battle-hardened high-rollers who've spent far too many sleepless nights. As a backcloth to all the wheeling and dealing, through the curtain windows there's a magnificent view of the coast below and the Orotava Valley above, with house lights looking like so many diamonds scattered across a cloak of black velvet.

Parrots in the Loro Parque.

If, after a hard night's gambling, you fancy recuperating with a mixture of exercise and relaxation, then the **Complejo Turístico Municipal Costa de Martiánez** (Martiánez Coast Municipal Tourist Complex) fits the bill perfectly. This eye-catching series of eight swimming pools, also known as the Lido San Telmo, was designed by César Manrique, sculptor, architect, painter, designer, landscaper, town planner, and native of Lanzarote.

Within the complex, on an island in a huge artificial lake, is the subterranean **Andromeda** nightclub, unique in so far as it's been constructed below sea-level. A black and silver amphitheatre, topped off with a restaurant, provides the setting for a good floor show.

The **Casa Iriarte**, one of the town's best preserved 18th-century buildings, with carved Canarian balconies and a verdant *patio*, is situated on the corner of Calle Iriarte and Calle San Juan. The writer Tomás de Iriarte y Nieves-Ravelo was born here in 1750 but now the house contains shops selling craftwork. Upstairs there's a naval museum and display of old photos and posters, including one advertising sailings from Liverpool to Santa Cruz de Tenerife for the princely sum of six guineas.

A free bus serves the **Bananera el Guanche** (Guanche Banana Plantation), a privately-owned garden where you can watch a video film on the banana plant—despite the size, it's not a tree—and then stroll along waymarked paths looking at a wide variety of exotic fruit. Here are papaya, mango, pineapple, lychee, pomegranate, kiwi, grapefruit, custard apple and the perverse medlar, similar to a crab-apple, which can only be eaten when decaying. In addition, there are plants that yield other crops such as coffee, peanuts, sugar cane, tobacco, ginseng and sapodilla (chicle), whose milky sap is used to make chewing gum. There's also a cactus garden, containing 400 varieties.

Nearby towns: Within easy reach of Puerto by car or local bus are a number of historic and beautiful towns. Top of the list must come **La Orotava**, situated 1,100 ft (335 metres) up in the fecund valley of the same name, some two and a half miles (four km) away.

Before the Spanish conquest the town formed part of Taoro, the richest of the nine Guanche kingdoms, and in 1594 Fray Alonso de Espinosa enthused: "Around La Orotava is a league of the finest, most fertile land in these islands, and even in the whole of Spain, because on it can be grown and bred everything you may desire."

The township developed around the original **Iglesia de Nuestra Señora de la Concepción**, built in the 16th century and destroyed by earthquakes in 1704 and 1705. Many of Orotava's narrow, cobbled streets and fine stone mansions have been preserved.

The present church is an outstanding example of Baroque architecture and was declared a national historical and artistic monument in 1948. It dates back to the late 18th century although the marble high altar by the Italian sculptor Gagini was rescued from the remains of the first church. Above the dark interior a halo of blue hovers around the dome, irradiating the finely-carved choir stalls and a beautiful statue of Saint John by master craftsman Luján Pérez.

The neo-classical style **Palacio Municipal** overlooks the **Plaza de Franco**. Here, to celebrate Corpus Christi in June, local people create

lowercarpet n La rotava.

KING OF THE DRAGONS

Cuando la sangre del drago salta,
Llegar la desdicha nunca falta.
When the dragon tree's blood spurts out,
There will always be calamity about.

Although the bizarre outburst of foliage that is the dragon tree may be found throughout the Canaries, its grandest and oldest specimen has taken root in Icod de los Vinos where, with a height of nearly 56 ft (17 metres) and a trunk 20 ft (six metres) round, it justifiably attracts thousands of visitors every year.

In Spanish its name is *Drago Milenario* (1,000-year-old Dragon Tree) and healthy controversy surrounds its age. Unfortunately this genus of tree, *Dracaena draco*, does not form annual rings so the method of dating relies on counting branches—and that's where the experts start tearing their hair out. Because, annoyingly, the dragon tree's system of branching does not follow a definite pattern but rather occurs in an irregular, random manner. So it's a matter of earnest opinion where one branch ends and another begins. This might explain why, when the celebrated German scientist Alexander von Humboldt visited Tenerife in 1799, he succeeded in dating one specimen at an incredible 6,000 years old, making it the oldest living thing in the world! However the Icod giant is now thought to be between 2,000 and 3,000 years old although, whisper it under your breath—and never, but never, in Icod—some botanists insist on an age of less than 500 years.

But among historians there is no disagreement that the dragon tree has played a significant role in Tenerife's history. The Guanches regarded it as a symbol of fertility and wisdom, carrying out sacred ceremonies in places such as the Orotava Valley where it flourished. In fact one colossus they venerated there attained a height of 60 ft (18 metres) before it was blown down in 1867.

Guanches went to war bearing shields made from its bark. It had medicinal qualities too, since the resin, known as dragon's blood because it turns red on contact with air, was applied to their bodies as a healing ointment, and used to embalm their dead. In 1633 the herbalist John Gerarde said it was recommended for treating "overmuch flowing of the courses, in fluxes, dysenteries, spitting of blood and fastening loose teeth."

Its cosmetic properties were much appreciated too by wealthy noblewomen in Venice who used it as an ingredient in a dye to make their hair golden. As for Florentine masons, they poured liquid dragon's blood over heated pieces of marble to stain it red while 17th century violin-makers, in Italy again, esteemed it as a rich varnish for their instruments. In addition to its medicinal qualities, the carmine resin was believed in ancient times to have supernatural powers and could be burnt as an incense to thwart witches and sorcerers. The tree itself was also thought to be able to foretell events; a fine blossom foretells a good harvest.

The tree's curative characteristics haven't been forgotten by healers who practise a special ritual for treating hernias. This entails taking the patient before dawn to a tree at a crossroads. There, as day breaks, they lift him—or her—so he can place the bare soles of his feet flat on the trunk. Their outline is then cut in the bark with a knife. Tradition maintains that, if these cuts close up, the hernia will be cured within a year. But if the outline doesn't disappear, the ritual has to be repeated the following year, until when the hernia sufferer has to grin and bear his discomfort—and avoid lifting heavy bunches of bananas.

Surprisingly the Spanish name for this tree, *drago*, does not mean dragon (that's the same as in English, *dragón*). The 19th-century writer, Olivia Stone, defended the appropriateness of the name: "Did it not bleed thick, red blood, did it not bristle with swords, and was not its abode on those isles of the Blest, far beyond the Gates of Gades, in the veritable Garden of Hesperides?"

For all its healing gifts, nowadays the Icod Dragon Tree cannot itself claim to be in the rudest of health. Its trunk has been shored up with concrete against storms. The road immediately alongside has also posed problems, although plans do exist to re-route it and leave the dragon in peace.

ephemeral religious pictures of quite staggering beauty on the paving stones, using volcanic cinders, sand and earth from Las Cañadas. If you can't be around for the actual festival, shops sell postcards of these extraordinary works of religious faith.

From the plaza, go around the corner to the **Calle San Francisco**, site of the **Casas de los Balcones** (Houses of the Balconies), 17th century mansions with two tiers of exquisitely carved pinewood balconies. A craft shop occupies one of the houses and permits visitors to view the palm-shaded *patio* within.

Further up the street is the **Hospital de la Santísima Trinidad** (Holy Trinity Hospital) with a revolving drum in its main door which was used as a receptacle for abandoned babies. The terrace outside provides a glorious vantage point from which to gaze at the luscious **Orotava Valley.**

East of Puerto de la Cruz, the Autopista del Norte sweeps past the twin towns of **La Victoria de Acentejo** (The Victory of Acentejo) and **La Matanza de Acentejo** (The Massacre of Acentejo). The latter gets its name from the site in a gorge where in 1494 Guanche warriors inflicted a disastrous defeat on the Spanish invaders, led by Alonso Fernández de Lugo. In fact he was only able to escape by giving his red cloak to a soldier whom the Guanches killed.

he Iglesia e Santiago, os Realejos.

So Lugo was able to resume his campaign the following year. This time, after five hours of bloody battle on open land nearby, the Guanches were defeated—they were said to have had nearly 2,000 dead, the Spanish just 64—and "Victoria!" was proclaimed.

Beyond La Matanza, the town of **Tacoronte**, 12 miles (19 km) from Puerto de la Cruz, is the centre of a wine-growing area and, because of this, offers a selection of fine restaurants. The spicy *conejo en salmorejo* (rabbit in hot sauce) is especially recommended.

To the west of Puerto, a good road leads after three miles (five km) to another historical site, **Los Realejos**, where Guanche chiefs finally surrendered to the Spanish in 1496. The **Iglesia de Santiago**, built in 1498, is Tenerife's oldest.

Beyond San Juan de la Rambla, with its Canarian houses, the road slices through banana plantations to the town of **Icod de los Vinos**, 12 miles (19 km) from Puerto. The name derives from the Guanche word "Benicod", meaning "beautiful place", and the Spanish "de los Vinos" (of the wines) because this is another region of vineyards. The white wine here has been adjudged by some connoisseurs to be the island's best.

According to Guanche legend, Icod was the sacred place where the gods, the Son and the Great One, joined together to create their race. Today, the town's principal attraction and objective of daily coach parties is the theatrically flamboyant **Dragon Tree**, the finest example in the Canaries and estimated to be up to 3,000 years old. If you'd like to grow one of your own, seeds are available in shops close by—but you'll have to wait a couple of thousand years to see it in its prime.

Three miles (five km) past Icod is the immaculate little town of **Garachico**,

THE CURSE OF GARACHICO

Standing in the little Plaza de Juan González de la Torre in that gem of a town Garachico, you'd be hard pressed to imagine a more peaceful, relaxing spot on the fair isle of Tenerife. Yet to be at this very place less than three centuries ago would have meant instant cremation. For in 1706 the good people of this prosperous town had to flee for their lives in a catastrophe that was a distant echo of the birth of the universe.

Mount Teide erupted, sending a relentless river of flaming lava down to the northern coast where Garachico lay directly in its path. Streets, squares and houses were metamorphosed into a frightening battlefield of the elements, and the town, Tenerife's premier port, was never to recover.

In the years after the Spanish conquest, Garachico's natural harbour was quickly recognised as a perfect anchorage for the loading and unloading of vessels. Once Alonso Fernández de Lugo had completed his military campaigns, the bay was endowed with port facilities and became the island's chief commercial centre.

Wealthy families in Genoa arrived on the scene to exploit the myriad trading opportunities of the island. In deference to them, Garachico became locally known as the Rado del Genovés (the Genoese Road).

During the 17th century the town's growth continued because of increasing demand in Europe, especially England, for the island's Malvasía (Malmsey) wine. The strength of the port was such that it managed to shrug off the effects of one natural calamity: on 11 December 1645, heavy rains in the mountains above started a landslide which killed more than 100 people and buried 40 ships beneath stones and mud in part of the harbour.

But on 5 May 1706, a greater disaster, which thankfully claimed no lives, spelled the end of an era for Garachico. One of the Narices del Teide (Nostrils of Teide) flared open, sending forth a torrent of molten mayhem. Fortunately the speed of the flow was such that the populace, men, women and children, rich and poor, had time to flee on foot and on horseback.

Behind them, Teide's volcanic outburst had already divided into twin rivers of destruction. One of these proceeded to engage in a titanic battle with the Atlantic, hissing its way into the harbour's boiling waters. Meanwhile the other river had embarked on the ruination of the town, burying or burning most of it, including the parish church, monastery of Santa Clara and palaces and warehouses of prosperous merchants.

The devastation was almost total, with homes and harbour lost beneath solid rock and a huge swathe of land, where valuable vineyards and pine forests had stood, turned overnight into a stony desert. Many traders refused to tempt providence again, moving instead to Puerto de la Orotava (now Puerto de la Cruz) and Santa Cruz.

Rumours spread about the reason for the disaster: an evil monk. At that time it was the custom for powerful landowners to have a personal chaplain resident in their mansions. One such domestic priest, a Franciscan, enjoyed so much influence that in due course he became a veritable tyrant to an aristocratic household, dictating to his lord and master and dominating the family.

Such a state of affairs could not be allowed to continue and eventually the nobleman plucked up courage to tell this father confessor that his presence could no longer be tolerated in what was previously a happy home. The monk had no alternative but to remove himself from the house, filled with most unchristian thoughts about the grandee. But equally he felt intense hatred towards the townspeople who all knew about his humiliation.

As he trudged angrily from the town, he stopped at the last turning overlooking it. There he uttered the fateful words that were to seal Garachico's fate:

Garachico, pueblo rico,
Gastadero de dinero,
Mal risco te caiga encima!
Garachico, rich town,
Waster of wealth,
Let an evil rock fall on you!

And thus it was that a few days later the wrath of a vengeful priest brought havoc to Garachico, from which it never recovered.

Tenerife's most important port until a volcanic eruption in 1706 laid it waste and filled in the harbour. One building to survive this disaster was the **Castillo de San Miguel** from whose roof you can clearly see, solidified on the hillside, the two rivers of lava.

The **Convento de San Francisco** was also untouched and now fulfills the role of a cultural centre and library where visitors can admire the serene cloisters. Outside, in a little square, a statue of the South American liberator Simón Boliívar celebrates the fact his mother was born here.

For a modern-day representation of the town's catastrophe, pop into the **Isla Baja** restaurant. It features a model the size of a dining table, illustrating exactly what happened on that fateful day in 1706 and providing an excellent talking point as tourists tuck into their *gambas a la plancha* (grilled prawns).

One result of the disaster was that the residents of Garachico became eager customers of a revolutionary new business called house insurance. On some homes can be seen the original fire plates, dating from the 1720s, which proved those properties were insured with London companies.

After Garachico the road turns its back on the sea and moves inland to **Los Silos**, named after Guanche granary stores. Along the way look out for the roadside ovens, used in the 19th century to roast the cochineal beetle into a powder which was then exported to Europe for use as a dye.

Tenerife's most westerly town, **Buenavista**, lies six miles (10 km) from Garachico on a coastal plain between the deep-blue sea and the dark cliffs of the **Macizo de Teno** (Teno *Massif*). Here the main road comes to an end but a little used stretch of asphalt and then a dirt track carries on for seven miles (11 km) to the lighthouse at **Punta de Teno**. This western tip of the island was regarded by the Guanches as the end of the world. From here the island of Gomera can be seen across the water, often with its mountains shouldering their way through a layer of cloud.

The lighthouse on Punta de Teno.

Parque Nacional del Teide

Presented with a new guest, Tenerife's foreign residents often find themselves arguing over the most pleasurable way by which the uninitiated should approach Teide. Traditionalists favour the old route up through the Orotava Valley, a symphonic progress from the lush to the lava-strewn, well-trodden by former sulphur and pumice miners and the *neveros* bringing *hielo* down to make ice-cream..More popular with tinerfeños is the long dorsal road up from **La Esperanza**, which affords tantalising glimpses of Teide itself through cool forests of eucalyptus and Canary pine.

At weekends many drive up from La Laguna and Santa Cruz to enjoy its walks and picnic areas, in winter continuing to the Parque Nacional and the novelty of snow. Snow sometimes blocks this road, built by the military in the 1940s, but for most of the year it is a beautiful drive along the mountainous spine of the island, offering clear views to both north and south, the bright light revealing the hidden colours of rock, bark and heather.

It was among these impressive pines that officers of the Tenerife garrison demonstrated their solidarity with Franco, then Captain-General of the Canaries, at **Las Raices** (The Roots) on 17 June 1936. A monument stands near the spot where more than 100 soldiers sat down to an *alfresco* lunch, all ranks eating paella. A photograph hanging in the Museo Militar in Santa Cruz captures the jovial atmosphere of the time, only a month before the outbreak of the Spanish Civil War.

Star attraction: The majestic scale of Teide becomes clear as the *carretera dorsal* emerges from the trees to join the road from La Orotava at **El Portillo**, the entrance to the **Parque Nacional del Teide**. To the east lie several white towers set atop the Montaña de Izaña, gleaming in the sun like giant origami: the telescopes of the **Observatorio Astronomico del Teide.**

Begun in 1965, the Observatory originally studied the night sky from the two smaller, silver-domed towers, but the development of Puerto de la Cruz and Reina Sofia airport has now corrupted the atmosphere to a prohibitive degree. Stellar observation transferred to La Palma where the light is now protected, and today the Izaña site is an international solar observatory. The larger white towers used for studying the sun owe their futuristic appearance to the need to isolate the instruments from the distorting turbulence caused as the surrounding land heats up.

Connoisseurs of the melancholic may prefer to approach Teide from the southwest, taking the increasingly deserted road winding up from **Chio**. Here a land rich with figs and almonds succumbs to terraces overrun by sprawling prickly pear and euphorbia, in turn giving way to ranks of gold-green pines that gradually thin to a deathly wilderness of lava. A straight road leads into the Parque with superb views back over the sea to the cloud-rimmed islands of

'receding ages: eide in inter. eft, nusual ocks in as añadas. ight, a aditional ethod of ansport.

Hierro, Gomera and La Palma.

Ahead one can clearly differentiate between the older peak of Chahorro or Pico Viejo (10,279 ft, 3,134 metres) and behind it the larger cone of Teide (12,402 ft, 3,718 metres).

Ugly shoulder: The nearby Mirador de Chio is a gloriously dismal stop, a chance to catch Teide in its darkest garb: a spent, ashen landscape where arrogant ravens rule. Like a baby eating chocolate, Teide leaves its mess for all to see: disgorged lava spills down its cindery slopes, creation petrified. Among these black lavaslides lies the gory wound of **Las Narices del Teide** (Teide's Nostrils), the Parque's most recent eruption in 1798.

The most popular route to Teide, up via **Vilaflor**, is perhaps the most dramatic. In 90 minutes you can climb from sea to snow, from semi-desert to lava-desert, passing in and out of elegant pine forests, rising above the tree-line, above the clouds, into the badlands of Teide where the burnt rubble lies scattered like the debris of an Almighty row. You can even call in at the Moon, for just east of Vilaflor lies the **Paisaje Lunar** where the erosion of pyroclastic fragments has created a coffee-and-cream wonderland of sandstone cones (turn right soon after the **Mirador de los Pinos:** expect an hour's drive and half an hour's scramble).

The thrill of this approach is that the road must scale the jagged crater walls lining the whole southern side of the Parque Nacional before you drop into the mysterious world of **Las Cañadas**, the interior crater.

Within the rim: The **Circo** or interior rim of the crater provides the best clues to how the present **caldera**, 10 miles (16 km) wide, was formed some three million years ago. There are two theories: the first suggests a greater part of the Parque was originally covered by a huge volcano as high as 16,000 ft (4,880 metres), the dome of which collapsed to leave a giant crater of which only the southern walls remained visible after the formation of **Pico Viejo** and **El Teide** two million years later. The sec-

Architectur[al] landscape around Vilaflor.

ond suggests that two craters existed before Teide's emergence, the dividing line between the two circles being what is now known as the **Roques de García.**

The route to the Roques cuts across dark lava, seemingly fresh as the day it was thrown down, that spreads towards a former lake, Llano de Ucanca, and forms the first of the seven *cañadas* (small sandy plateaux) that give the Parque its name. Closer to the Roques some parts of the stone are tinged jade green from copper oxide, known locally as **Los Azulejos**.

The Roques are undoubtedly the most photographed lumps of rock in the Canaries; up to a million people come every year to enjoy the anthropomorphic shapes of their eroded strata. Perpetually swarming with bright anoraks, their popularity is curious: perhaps it's the sweeping view over the despondent Llano de Ucanca, or the good base they offer for snaps of Teide's stony vomit, or maybe its just the most convenient place for coaches to park.

Across the road is a small Ermita, **Nuestra Señora de las Nieves**, and the somewhat neglected **Parador de Turismo**, the only accommodation available in Las Cañadas. During the day its toilets are a popular stop for coach parties, but those staying overnight discover a more profound call of nature: an eternal glow as the sunset burnishes the yellow rocks of **Los Caprichos**, the dark nocturnal silence of the *caldera* domed with stars, the morning sun unveiling a new, pink Teide.

Walking in the Parque: For a taste of the Parque's tranquillity take the track south of the Ermita that leads east towards the Guajara mountain, a level walk that curls through the Cañadas to El Portillo (four hours). At its head is the **Guajara Pass**, named after a Guanche princess, which formed the summit of the old **Camino Chasna**, the original link for travellers moving between the Orotava Valley and Chasna (Vilaflor).

Along here the well-camouflaged stone huts of the Guanches still stand from the days when sheep and goats were brought up to graze in the summer

he road uts rough va rmations.

months. The Guanches buried their dead in remote caves up in the walls of the Circo, where mummified corpses are still discovered by archaeologists, most recently in 1988.

Anyone who walks in the Parque Nacional and encounters its unique flora soon realises that it's not one park but many, according to the time of year you visit. In winter snow decorates Teide like icing on a bun and only the bright faces of the Teide daisy and the stubborn carcasses of drooping *taginaste* (viper's bugloss) punctuate the ghostly Cañadas.

To return in May when the omnipresent broom *retama del pico* blooms pink and white and the *tajinaste* bursts red is to discover a new, technicolour world. Extremes of temperature and wind have produced a spectacular flora that blossoms briefly but brightly, giving birth to endemic species like the Teide violet and the tenacious *cedro canario*.

In 1956, two years after the Parque was formed, experiments began to introduce conifers to Las Cañadas, and Moroccan cedars now surround the new **Visitors Centre** at El Portillo (open 9 a.m.- 4 p.m.). This provides videos and information about the Parque and has details of the excellent signposted and guided walks available. A second Centre will soon open near the *Parador*.

Between here and Teide lie three *montañas*, Las Mostazas (The Mustards) and two domed volcanoes **Rajadas** and **Blanca**. The first two are surrounded by a rich Nescafé-coloured lava, often capped by the shiny black of obsidian, used by the Guanches to make *tabonas* (cutting-stones). Close to the road lies the **Arenas Blancas**, a pleasant stop where everyone picnics on dunes of pumice that bear an unfortunate resemblance to cat litter.

To the peak: Montaña Blanca is still "of smooth surface and light-yellow colour" as Charles Piazzi Smyth found it in 1856, "which every here and there has exudations of yellow and red lava which have half-stretched, half-slobbered, down the sides like so much treacle or hasty pudding." Destined to

Evening lig[ht] in the Cañadas.

become Royal Astronomer, Piazzi Smyth scrambled up here with his Sheepshanks Equatorial to watch the Great Bear sink behind Teide. He spent two months observing the Canary sky, discovering the astronomical advantages of "a residence above the clouds" and inspiring the establishment of observatories in the Canary Islands.

Montaña Blanca is also the starting point for those wishing to climb Teide on foot. The construction of a Teléferico or cable car in 1971 (up cars run 9 a.m.- 4 p.m., last down 5 p.m., closed if windy) fortunately makes the ascent easier for the 300,000 people who climb Teide every year. The 3,936-ft (1,200-metre) climb takes only eight minutes, but expect to queue at least an hour before you get a ride.

As you wait, comfort yourself with thoughts of the arduous efforts Victorian climbers of the peak faced. A day trip then began well before dawn from La Orotava, riding on horseback by the light of the moon and pine-torches. Eight hours later travellers reached the Estancia de los Ingleses on Montaña Blanca, where they cooled themselves with barrels of ice from the nearby Cueva de Hielo and took fortifying draughts of quinine prior to the steep ascent by mule to the Altavista. There the ladies and children rested in what little shade was available while the gentlemen struggled to the summit.

The descent was equally hazardous: "rather anxious work", as Lady Brassey noted in her journal of 1876, wearily recording how she got lost on the mountain and that it was some 29 hours before her party finally returned to their yacht for supper and champagne.

Modern adventurers stepping off the cable car at **La Rambleta** now find themselves part of a designer climb as busy as the escalators in a Harrods' sale. The fluorescent ski-wear and goggles favoured by the newly-chic Spanish are not essential, but neither is it wise to adopt the shorts and lager- can bravura of British youth. Settle for sunglasses, hat and strong-soled shoes, and make regular stops to catch your breath: at this height the air is rare and progress slow—anyone with heart or respiratory problems should not attempt the climb. Those in need of urgent acclimatisation will find a bar dispenses a welcome hot chocolate and brandy to the needy.

Alternatively one can explore two short signposted paths that curl round to either side of Teide. The first leads west past sulphurous fumaroles for a fine view of Pico Viejo's crater, 2,624 ft (800 metres) in diameter. The second runs east to the **Mirador La Fortaleza**, across the *bloques* (jagged blocks) and *pahoehoe* (ropey cords) formed by the last lava flows of Teide.

Keen visitors should get up early to get the best from Teide, catching the first car up before crowds and clouds diminish the awaiting spectacle. The best rewards rightly go to those who slog up by foot from the base, overnighting at the Altavista to catch the dawn and Teide's triangular shadow spread across orange-tinted clouds.

Effort well spent: However you get there, it is still worth every sigh and groan and the choking stench of sulphur: Teide impresses all-comers who make it to the iron cross marking its summit. It is not simply the views over Tenerife: the dense line of pine winding along the dorsal ridge to Anaga, the spotty white houses of Puerto and the north coast, the dark circumference of Las Cañadas, the way the lava stops short at the rugged upper cut of Teno.

There's also the sight of the other islands floating in the clouds like apparitions: La Palma, Gomera, Hierro behind, Gran Canaria to the east. After all, you're not only on top of the highest mountain in Spain, but on top of El Teide—a symbol of power that today adorns everything from cement to telephones, a cloudy pillar mighty enough to uphold the classical heavens, a force that Columbus saw erupting, that brought fear to the Guanches who believed a Devil lived in its bowels and would one day rise up and steal the sun forever. Moreover there's an impossible but tangible feeling the whole thing might just blow up beneath your feet, blasting you and everyone's video camera to a far, far nothing.

TE-1-3893
Onda

TE-1-3824

SOUTH TENERIFE

"What are we going to do?" pipe the children of holidaymakers stepping off their planes at Tenerife South airport. "There's nothing here!"

At first glance, southern Tenerife does seem little more than an overgrown quarry with a bad rash of building sites. In 1965, when Los Cristianos had but one *hostal* and a cinema, when Playa de las Américas was still the dream of a Catalan detergent manufacturer, there really was nothing here. But now these resorts are the centre of the biggest tourist development in Spain, and every year 1.25 million people find something to do after all.

Concrete skirt: It is an achievement to make so much out of arid nothing, while keeping the truly beautiful parts of the island unspoilt. Drive 10 minutes into the hills behind the resorts and everything changes. The south's very first *mirador* **El Roque de la Centinela** west of San Miguel, looks suspiciously like it was built (in 1953) for developers to stand on as they carved up their kingdoms below, but it also shows how little land the *cuidades touristicas* (tourist towns) actually occupy, clinging to the sea's skirt like timid children.

A crazy paving of plastic greenhouses and water reservoirs marches ubiquitously to the coast, proof that not all farmers are seduced by the sweeter fruits of tourism. The banana may no longer be king, but it still holds a distant sway over the land, while glassy fields of flowers and salad crops grow up beside the airport.

From the *mirador*, a white ribbon of houses is visible winding high through Teide's foothills, a legacy of the island's aboriginal inhabitants who didn't share our current obsession with the seaside. The Guanches couldn't even swim, living inland in the natural caves formed amongst the *barrancos* that serrate the southern and western slopes of Tenerife.

Their villages survived the impact of the Spanish conquest, which came slowly to the south: few colonisers ventured further than the Güimar Valley, and those that did were driven to build their fortified settlements inland by the frequent attacks of pirates on a lawless coastline. A century ago families were still living in caves near **Fasnia**, and a census in 1930 found nearly all the south's 45,000 inhabitants living in a band of villages two to four miles (3.2 to 6.4 km) from the coast.

Agriculture still shapes these inland towns, strung along the high road winding from Cristianos to Güimar and thence to Santa Cruz. Some like **San Miguel** and **Granadilla** developed as collection points for the fruit and tomatoes grown on the laboriously-constructed terracing; many still have a road that trickles down to the sea and a small port from where fruit-boats took the produce to Santa Cruz.

Others grew up as homes for the unskilled labourers who in 1941 earned 10 pesetas a day. There was only one escape route then, and some bars still have posters urging you to *"reservar su*

'receding ages: Los :ristianos. eft, beach ursuits. ₹ight, old griculture nd new ourism in nusual ombination.

pasaje para Venezuela". Tourism has brought a softer option, and many now commute to the resorts below. "My father worked hard growing tomatoes—no way do I want that!" a bar owner declares. "He prayed for rain, now I pray for a decent waiter." For some, the goal is a modern apartment in Las Américas, others like to return to the hills where their communities remain intact despite the changes.

Up here, cinemas may close while video shops open but continuity remains, epitomised by the immaculate white church in every village, set without fail in an empty plaza where typical laurel trees tower high above, old man on a bench below. Perhaps a bell-tower has been added by a prosperous landowner, or a dragon tree planted by a grateful son. Of particular delight is the *parroquia* or village church of San Juan Batista at **Lomo de Arico**, its interior enlivened by bold painted panels.

Unless you have need of rotavator parts, it is unlikely you'll be detained in such towns for long. Many have sprawling outskirts in dire need of a "*Pinta tu pueblo de blanco*" scheme, a campaign that sporadically appears throughout the Canaries in an attempt to get householders to paint their unfinished breezeblock walls white. As one doesn't pay taxes on a building until it's complete, such schemes are always a failure.

Ridge and plain: Further north the **Mirador Don Martin** has been hijacked by a hotel, but is still the best place to contemplate the **Güimar Valley** far below. Formed by faulting, its rich plain is punctuated by the clear outline of the Güimar volcano, protected since 1979. A Guanche capital, Güimar formed a secret alliance with the Spanish invaders and has never looked back since. The continuity of its prosperity is reflected in the 18th-century **Iglesia de San Pedro Apóstol**, adorned inside by carved wooden apses added in 1930.

For a sense of old Güimar, walk east to the white houses and cobbled streets near the **Dominican convent** (now the Ayuntamiento) where a plaque commemorates Isidro Quintero Acosta, a

The pace o[f] life is slow above the resorts.

local boy who introduced the cultivation of cochineal to the island. On the eastwards exit from town look out for the headquarters of the Guardia Civil, its battlements and turrets the acme of toytown grandeur.

On the hill the village of **Arafo** is quieter and prettier, the scene of a popular *romería* (pilgrimage) on the last Saturday in August. The Bar El Frances beside the neat church offers a pleasant stop among cats and vines. From here a little-used road winds up to the dorsal ridge, with good views back.

Potent virgin: Down on the coast the peeling paint and BMXs of **Candeleria** give little indication that an imposing basilica, **Nuestra Señora de la Candelaria**, dominates the seafront at its western end. Completed in 1959, the church is the current resting place for a Virgin whose miraculous and itinerant career began in 1392, when two Guanche shepherds discovered her Holy Image among the rocks of Playa del Socorro, holding a naked child in her right arm and a candle in the other.

Venerated as "Chaxiraxi" by the pagan Guanches, the statue was later stolen by a noble from Fuerteventura, where an outbreak of plague inspired its prompt return. Enshrined in the Cave de San Blas (further along the seafront) it came into the care of Dominican monks, who converted both icon and island to Christianity. Rescued from a church fire in 1789, the Virgin made a tempestuous exit in 1826 when a tidal wave broke into the new church and swept her out to sea.

A copy of Our Lady now stands above the altar like a fairy princess, the power of her sanctity manifest by the generous array of flowers placed at her feet and the devout who repeatedly crawl towards the altar on their knees. A door to the right leads to the cliff wall where worshippers light candles.

Outside, 10 sturdy-thighed Guanche chiefs also pay suppliant attention from the sea-wall (although Chief Pelinor on the far left has a distinct interest in the Bar Plaza). Every 14-15 August the plaza fills with pilgrims come to honour

andelaria, ith sturdy uanche hiefs in tone.

BEACHMAKING

"Vamos a la playa!" a Spanish pop song recently urged, a big hit in the beach bars and kiosks of Tenerife. Tourist maps pick up the tune, throwing *la playa* around the coast as a bank-robber splashes gold on the neck of his missus.

Hire cars search out these beaches, quickly discovering how all that's not *punta* can be *playa*; in fact Tenerife's natural beaches are poor by Mediterranean standards, and invariably comprise a short, pebbly shoreline with a snatch of overpopulated grey or dirty-yellow sand. "How on earth," wonders the aspirant sunbather, "did they get away with a tourist miracle built on "sun and sea" holidays?"

The answer lies in the ingenuity of Tenerife's developers, who over the past 25 years have created artificial beaches and swimming pools out of rocks and bays all around the island. Originally the strength of the currents along the coast was considered the main problem: while these make the water clear and the waves fun they can also make swimming unsafe. One solution was to create seawater pools, using rocks and concrete to corner off part of the shore—one of the first swimming pools in Playa de las Américas was like this, still in use in front of the Hotel Europe. A superlative example of this principle is at Puerto de la Cruz, where César Manrique's lido Lago de Martianez, built on reclaimed land, questions the very need for beaches.

A further problem was a shortage of sand: along the north coast the beaches are relatively young, and whatever black sand is formed from the basaltic lava is often washed away to leave a pebbly shingle. In the south, strong winds blow the sand inland, and while pumice lightens its colour the absence of quartz and shells prevents it from being classically "golden".

The most spectacular response to such deficiencies was made in 1970 with the construction of Las Teresitas beach to the north of Santa Cruz. Here the local pebbled beach was dramatically transformed by dumping 3.5 million cubic feet (98,000 cu metres) of Saharan sand on top. The archetypically golden sand was extracted and shipped over using equipment from the phosphate mines of the Spanish Sahara, and a breakwater of rocks built across the bay to prevent the tide taking it straight back.

Costs prevented a repeat of this littoral translation, but a subtler initiative was also under way. Holiday brochures set about wooing foreign holidaymakers away from the conventional image of the golden sandy beach, suggesting how they could happily lie in mud-grey sand and watch the kids roll about like gulls in an oil slick. Copywriters stressed how black sand was "unusual" and "volcanic" (hence dramatic), how its iron and radioactive content had therapeutic benefits, how black sand retained the sun's warmth for longer (and so burns your feet quicker). Now the beaches in the north are so busy you're lucky if you can find some "novel" black sand to lie on.

In fact, these days people will lie anywhere so long as it is in the sun. Sunbathers happily lie on beaches before they're finished, snoozing in the rubble as the bulldozers approach. Privacy often appears more important than comfort: the extravagant efforts of Tenerife's developers to provide beaches are being ironically countered by the growing desire to find undeveloped beaches on the island. Tourists risk life and limb to get to idyllic little pebble beaches, whole families scramble out to remote coves, scaring the pants off nudists and hippies.

In the meantime, the *playas* grow. Las Teresitas is to be revamped, a new lido is planned for Santa Cruz. A Dutch machine has now arrived in the islands that can suck sand up from the sea-bed, depositing instant *playa* on the shore.

But most beachmakers have returned to a more artful and well-established method: the building of *barras* or breakwaters out into the ocean. You spot them everywhere, dog-legs of boulders branching out into the water, positioned by engineers between the currents and shore so that sand will naturally accumulate in each sheltered corner. The rocks, or *escollera*, are brought down from the hills, often in boulders big enough to fill a whole truck, and cranes lift them into the sea. Before long the sand and then the bathers begin to gather round.

the shrine of Our Lady of Candelaria, since 1867 the patron saint of all the Canary Islands. Candles also burn throughout South America, where her name graces towns and squares from Texas to Argentina.

On the road to beauty: Far less sublime is the new *autopista* that runs south from Santa Cruz, which few modern pilgrims escape. Those unexcited by its hoardings and candelabra cacti might savour its authentic dreariness, for a new *Programa de Embellecimiento de Carreteras* will one day beautify its length with trees and flowers. The south is moving upmarket now, to five-star hotels, golf courses and marinas, to fewer people but more money. "We must preserve the island's quality," say the poolside pundits.

Anyone tempted to sneak off to the quiet ports below the *autopista* will find them busy with hire cars who are also finding nothing there. Construction work currently mars Puerto de Güimar, where a new *playa* and Club Nautico promise better days. **Poris de Abona** has some quiet fish restaurants and a sheltered sandy beach down a track towards the lighthouse.

Further south the clear line of Montaña Roja dominates blonde beaches at **El Médano** and **Playa de la Tejita**. Winds here can be very strong, to the joy of windsurfers who dance on the surf like brightly coloured butterflies. International competitions take place here.

The exhibition of esoteric propellers on a nearby hill is the Parque Eolico, an experimental project that hopes to use windpower as an alternative source to the imported fuels currently keeping the bright lights of the resorts burning.

El Abrigo has excellent fish restaurants overlooking its tiny anchorage: they fill up quickly at lunchtime, but those at the top of the town are equally good and a bit cheaper. Further west two new golf courses green the desert as you near the Costa del Silencio, graced by one of the first and most enduring of *urbanizacions* **Tenbel** (built with Belgian investment), its neighbour **El**

Windsurfers by the resort of Tenbel.

Fantasy Island

"Are you sexy?" ask the machines at the disco door. "Hello flowers, are you happy?" quip the timeshare boys. "Join us," call the girls on the Jolly Roger Fun Cruise. From the Costa Silencio to Los Gigantes, from "The Foaming Quart" to "Ye Olde Tea Shoppe", a bright neon grin runs round the south coast of Tenerife, a Smiley badge of pure tourism.

Its heart is a promenade of chauvinistic bars and discos between the now inseparable resorts of Los Cristianos and Playa de las Américas, a patriotic bunting strung from "The Old Bill" to the "Fawlty Towers Pub", a distillation of one face of British culture.

Here the seaside holiday lives on in gaudy success. For most, the pursuit of happiness lasts only a fortnight: a last fling for adolescents, a well-deserved rest for Mum, a knees-up for the old 'uns. Today the traditional pleasures of staying up late and drinking too much are laced with a new affluence—watersports and duty-free, a chance to joyride in Suzuki Santanas, to dance in the sun till the pop videos turn real. Families maraud by day, the yobs let rip at night—next year they'll be back with the wife, then the kids, slowly metamorphosing into snobs.

The British rule this party, even though all Europe and Scandinavia attends, apart from the French, who sit disdainfully up on a hill at the Club Marazul. Internationalism is limited to the common goal of sun, sea and sex. Flags may meet on menus and multilingual compères tell bad jokes in bad languages, but every night the bars and cafés subdivide into foreign enclaves.

For a lucky few, happiness is more than a one-night stand: ways are found to stay in the fun, maybe running a bar, a video shop, hiring out cars. A place for nobodies to be something, for a fresh start, somewhere to forget crimes, conduct crimes: a fast-buck world where the successful get marbled villas in the hills and the failures get deported (about 70 a year).

Property makes the big dreams come true. For the OPCs (Off Property Contacts) touting timeshare it is a chance for £30 on every "send-up" to the luxury show flats. For the couples sent up it's a chance for £25 cash and a bottle of bubbly. Everywhere estate agents chase clients, investors trail tycoons, owners go for resale. And everyone buys: £6,000 for a lifetime of fortnights back at the party, £60,000 for a two-bedroom view over it, £600,000 for a security villa far away from it.

The pace of change shocks everyone. "Guaranteed Sea-views" disappear quickly. Conflict grows between holidaymakers out for two weeks' fun and long-term residents who want to sit on the balcony discussing the price of Larios gin and listening to the BBC's World Service. Consistently good weather forces the English to find new topics of conversation, such as the *gamberros ingleses*, English hooligans, whose hell-raising invigorates what would otherwise be a vast retirement home.

As any bar manager will tell you, the English don't have a monopoly over this unpleasant export: "It's Germans, Dutch, Italians, Spaniards, Swedes. The young, they don't care." The girls are just as wild as the boys, ask any tour rep. Nor is it solely the young, as those who oversee the apartments know: "Policemen, dentists, solicitors—the nicest of people go mad out here." Even the retired get carried away, splashing out a lifetime's savings on dream properties of which not a brick has been laid.

The tinerfeños have their own lunacies too, well-established and officially sanctioned. The local calendar blooms bright with fiestas, when Canarian music keeps both yobs and snobs awake and early bathers find drunken porters by the pool. Local revenge is sweetest at the best of these, *Nuestra Señora del Carmen* (first week in September) in Los Cristianos, when the *jovenes* run fully-dressed from swimming pool to swimming pool, dragging everyone with them.

Everyone blames this madness on each other, until finally they point their fingers to the sky. "It's the sun, I tell you..." Here its bewitching rays, sweetened by cheap drink and an infectious holiday atmosphere, inspire a golden delirium where for a fortnight or more life can be magically different. Fantasy Island, in fact.

Chapparal, and the growing fishing port of **Las Galletas**, one of the few places you can still buy the daily catch.

Urban shore: Tenerife's southern corner is ruled by the Montaña de Guaza, a volcanic cone no doubt as uninterested in the developers from Los Cristianos now gnawing its western flanks as it was when Spanish conquistadors landed here five centuries ago to accept the surrender of Pelinor, Chief of Adeje.

Once used to export tomatoes from Arona, the harbour at **Los Cristianos** keeps itself busy with fishing and the thrice-daily ferry is packed to Gomera, 90 minutes away. In November it packs with yachts waiting for the trade winds that will carry them to the Caribbean.

The harbour also gives Los Cristianos a salty realism its wholly artificial neighbour **Playa de las Américas** can never attain, despite the expensive cocktail of gin palaces in its new marina, **Puerto Colon**. Unburdened by historical monuments (apart from the World War II pill-box on the beach) Las Américas flaunts its modernity without shame, most boldly in the vulgar blue of its new five-star **Grand Hotel Mediterranean Palace Luxe**, an overdue departure from traditionally white battery-apartments.

The message from the discos is blunter: "Trauma", "Vertigo", "Bananas". One might despair at such willful tackiness but for the waggish self-mockery—"Billy Bunter Sangria", "Topless Boxing (England v Sweden!!!)"—that keeps the frivolity flying. Playa de las Américas at midnight is no place for the serious (unless you're a serious drinker), its only task is FUN, and fun it has.

Cutting straight through its centre is the *barranco* Troya, beside the Hotel Troya, the dividing line between **Arona** and **Adeje**, the two Ayuntamientos in control of what appears to casual visitors as a developer's free-for-all. In fact building controls remain strict—"There are two mountains in Tenerife, one's Teide and the other's paper," quip the property boys, whingeing how all along the coast property giants lie tied

he urban hore, not ll sand nd sun.

by the strings of Spanish bureaucracy like Gulliver on the beaches of Lilliput.

High and mighty: Arona and Adeje sit high in the hills, at suitably aloof distances from the boom towns they oversee. Both try to maintain the quiet atmosphere of hacienda days, even though their fate was sealed long ago by the arrogance of their Guanche chiefs who refused all those years ago to join Bencomo's alliance against the Spanish invaders. Arona has a new prison now, where delinquent tourists are jeeped up by the Guardia Civil, drunkenly proclaiming their innocence: "All I done was kick a taxi."

Expats now own many of its white *casas*. In the surrounding hills successful Canarios and foreigners are building themselves villas, unable to live with the monster they've created.

On the other side of the 3,283 ft (1,000 metres) Roque del Conde Mountain, Adeje sustains a more distinguished air. A fine avenue of laurels leads to the 16th-century church of **Santa Ursula**, which boasts some casually hung Gobelins tapestries. The town was the former seat of the Guanche court from which the island was ruled. Later the Counts of Gomera took over.

The **Casa Fuerte** at the top of the town is now only a faint echo of the fortified mansion which the Counts built in 1556. Sacked by English pirates 30 years later, it was all but destroyed by fire in the 19th century. A cannon stands outside the gates of the present building, in which three families still live. In one house a set of wooden stocks hang on the wall, a grim souvenir of the days when slave-traders used the southern coast of Tenerife to corral their human cargo prior to the voyage to America.

Barriers of stone: Further up the hill is the entrance to the **Barranco del Infierno** (Hell's Gorge), the deepest ravine in the Canaries. Allow a good two hours for the walk, which becomes something of a scramble as steep gorge walls narrow to a verdant V and the path crisscrosses a stream thick with willow and eucalyptus. The summer heat can be hellish, but the flora has a paradisical

Guia de Isora.

abundance. At its green heart lie towers of babbling waterfalls that will soothe many a soul.

Barrancos have eroded deep into the the arid slopes of the western coast, segregating the small villages along the new road to **Guia de Isora**. The pines here once descended as far as 1,000 ft (305 metres), but today the land is given over to well-tended tomatoes and the massed ranks of banana that peep at the traffic from breezeblock pens.

Today cranes tower ominously over the port of **San Juan**, ready to pluck bananas and plant swimming pools, and galleons touting Dolphin Cruises moor beside its bright fishing boats. Soon its church, now so full on Sundays that the congregation stands outside, will have to be knocked down like that of Los Cristianos and replaced by a larger edifice worthy of a new prosperity. But tourism has also revived the local fishing industry and San Juan's a great spot for a swim and a long fish lunch served in the Canarian style with *papas arrugadas* and *mojo* sauce.

Further north the small port of **Alcalá** is undeveloped and significantly lacks interest. Perhaps it is being kept as a control by which we may judge the frenzy that has grown up at **Puerto de Santiago** and beyond. Visitors overwhelmed by the intensity of white boxes scaling the cliffs for a view of Gomera may repair to the good sandy beach at **Playa de la Arena**, recently awarded an EEC "Bandera Azul" (blue ribbon) for cleanliness.

The resort of **Los Gigantes** next door enjoys an upmarket image, its playboy tone set by a private marina bedecked with speedboats.

Rough corner: A boat trip gives the best view of the precipitous cliffs (Acantilados) marking the southern edge of the **Masizo de Teno**, a peninsula of old basaltic lava-flows now sliced deep into valleys and jagged ridges by erosion. With the exception of its northern coast, Teno, like Anaga at the opposite end of the island, resisted the advances of later lava-flows and may yet halt the tide of *urbanizacion*

implicity t hand: in e Teno *assif.*

flowing up the west coast.

Los Gigantes was also the outlet for the agricultural produce grown in the fertile terraces that climb up to **Tamaimo**, still rich with bananas, vines and potatoes. Piles of bright tomatoes often lie beside the road, rejected by exporters for their small size but a welcome find for passers-by. Further inland is the relaxed village of **Santiago del Teide**, where cacti line the roofs and Canary balconies grace even the newest *casas*. Its small church has a gently domed roof—at Christmas the interior is decorated with poinsettias and oranges, incense burns and loudspeakers broadcast carols to the cows.

From here a road runs north along the edge of Teno, climbing from vines and potatoes to bramble and broom and the unfamiliar sight of grass. At its peak are small pastoral plateaux and a sign at **Erjos del Teide**, 3,664 ft (1,117 metres), marking the traditional mountain pass leading to the north coast.

Santiago can also be reached by a higher road from **Chio**, passing through the small town of **Arguayo** and almond groves that are amass with blossom in late January. This route allows inspection of the volcanic debris emitted by Montaña de Chinyero, Tenerife's most recent eruption. During 10 days in 1909 it blew ash and cinders into the sky with a noise that could be heard in Orotava. Stones flew up to 2,000 ft (610 metres) and a stream of lava rolled towards Santiago del Teide at two ft (61 cm) per minute, dividing at Montaña Bilma and leaving a trail three miles long by *half* a mile wide (4.8 km by 0.8 km).

Secret village: A hidden Shangri-la that was until recently one of Tenerife's best kept secrets, is the village of **Masca**, tucked deep in Teno's folds. For many years the precariously steep descent was only feasible by mule, but now a series of hairpin bends of intestinal intensity join this tiny village to the outside world. A small private **Museo** (walk down from the road) houses an idiosyncratic collection of Mascan *objêts trouvés*. Sitting on the bougainvillea-covered terrace of the La Pimentera da Salvatore restaurant (at La Vica) romantics may feel the valley's isolation should have been preserved.

Wild lavender, marigold and oxyalis illumine the roadside northwards, offering comfort to petrified passengers proceeding in cars up from the valley floor. A small *mirador* waits at the top of the ridge, where the land fans wide into the well-cultivated fields around **El Palmar**. The town is dominated by a dark red cone of volcanic scoria from which sections have been quarried, cut like slices from a pie to help build the neighbouring houses. Twenty years ago their windows were lit by oil lamps and candles.

At the foot of the valley lies the coastal town of **Buenavista**, but seekers of solitude should first explore the road out to the small village of **Teno Alto**. Here several tracks offer good walks amongst the windy wheat fields and stone shepherd's huts. From this ancient headland one can look back to the distant towers of Playa de las Américas, or out to the lighthouse of **Punta de Teno** and the shimmering Atlantic.

Left, keeping wilderness at bay in Masca. Right, a Masca man

LA GOMERA

The other islanders are not kind about the Gomerans: they make jokes about them in the mould of the British jokes about the Irish or the European jokes about the Belgians: "Why does a Gomeran keep an empty bottle in his fridge?" "For his friends who don't drink."

The jokes are not really fair. Like the other smaller islands Gomera has suffered extensively as a result of the fluctuating economic fortunes of the Canaries, although it is more fortunate than, say, Fuerteventura simply by dint of being enormously more fertile. However, staple industries such as vineyards, banana, tomato and potato growing are only just staple, and large numbers of Gomera's interior villages are all but deserted, with the remaining villagers rather poor.

Today there are 20,000 people on an island of 146 sq miles (378 sq km), 10,000 less than in 1940. As a rule, it is the brighter, more ambitious people who emigrate leaving the slower and more traditional behind, thus the jokes.

Officials in the island *cabildo* (local government) say that the island population is presently stable, but Gomera's fortunes are not improving: the fishing industry on the south of the island has failed, and tourism has yet to step into the breach. Roughly 15,000 tourists visit the island every year; next door Tenerife receives an average of two million a year, but very few bother to cross the short stretch of water (20 miles, 32 km) between the two islands. Nevertheless tourism has had its impact, with large numbers of Gomerans leaving to work in Tenerife's hotels.

From the air Gomera looks like a cow-pat. It is high, reaching 4,879 ft, (1,487 metres) at its highest point, which is almost in the centre of the island. From here, the land falls away in six main steep-sided *barrancos* (ravines) to the sea. As with the other islands, its southern shores are warm and dry and its northern shores are cooller and wetter; accordingly, southern slopes are considerably more barren than northern, but a major feature of the islandscape is the Garajonay National Park, a large area of largely untouched moss-cloaked ancient forest that covers the central high ground of the island.

Gomera's main claim to fame is that it was from here that Columbus set off on his America-finding trip, the second of his voyages. Quite why he chose Gomera is a debating point. There are those who say that he was attracted by the island's countess, Beatriz de Bobadilla, who was something of a medieval nymphomaniac and had disgraced herself in the Spanish court; others believe it was simply because Gomera was the very last known stepping-off point for the unknown West.

Barren doorstep: The port of **San Sebastian**, the main town on the island, hasn't altered much in size since Columbus's day and Beatriz's tower, the Torre del Conde, looks as if it was built yesterday. The town is situated in what is probably the most barren region of the island, and makes a depressing intro-

receding ages: eldscape round pina; oodland in arajonay ark. Left, alle Gran ey. Right, inbow over e *arrancos.*

duction to Gomera; the rest of the island only begins to become interesting at road distances of about 10 miles (16 km) from the town.

The three-times-a-day ferry from Los Cristianos, southern Tenerife, sets the pulse of San Sebastian: two heart beats when it arrives and one when it leaves. The double heartbeat of the arrival of the *MV Benchijigua* is powerful enough to send waves of traffic round the veins of the island—the island's buses, day-tripping tourists over from Tenerife, beer, post and newspapers, warming the hearts of the islanders as if San Sebastian had just imbibed a slug of Venezuelan rum, which is drunk here in large quantities at breakfast-time. The island's principle buses (to Santiago, Vallehermoso and Valle Gran Rey) time their departures to co-ordinate with the three ferry sailings.

San Sebastian's 7,000 residents live in rather ugly buildings behind the black strand, a stretch of unused beach that is the equal of any on the island; elsewhere only the main street, the **Calle del Medio**, has much distinction.

The town proper begins at the **Plaza Calvo Sotelo**, a cracked square with laurel trees sprouting through the concrete, which was once probably quite distinguished, but which has been ruined by an ugly kiosk bar where the bandstand should be. At the northern corner is the proposed site of the tourist office, to be completed when the contracted builder has finished his other work, but for the present the only person responsible for tourism is a secretary in the town hall who speaks some English.

Between the port and the Plaza are a couple of grand buildings in the colonial Canary style containing the library and some administrative offices; the *cabildo* itself is housed in a smaller, less distinguished building a third of the way up Calle del Medio, and marked principally by flagpoles on the exterior.

The **Torre del Conde**, which stands in isolation behind the beach, was built in 1450 by Fernan Peraza the Elder, largely for protection against the marauding islanders, who were still far

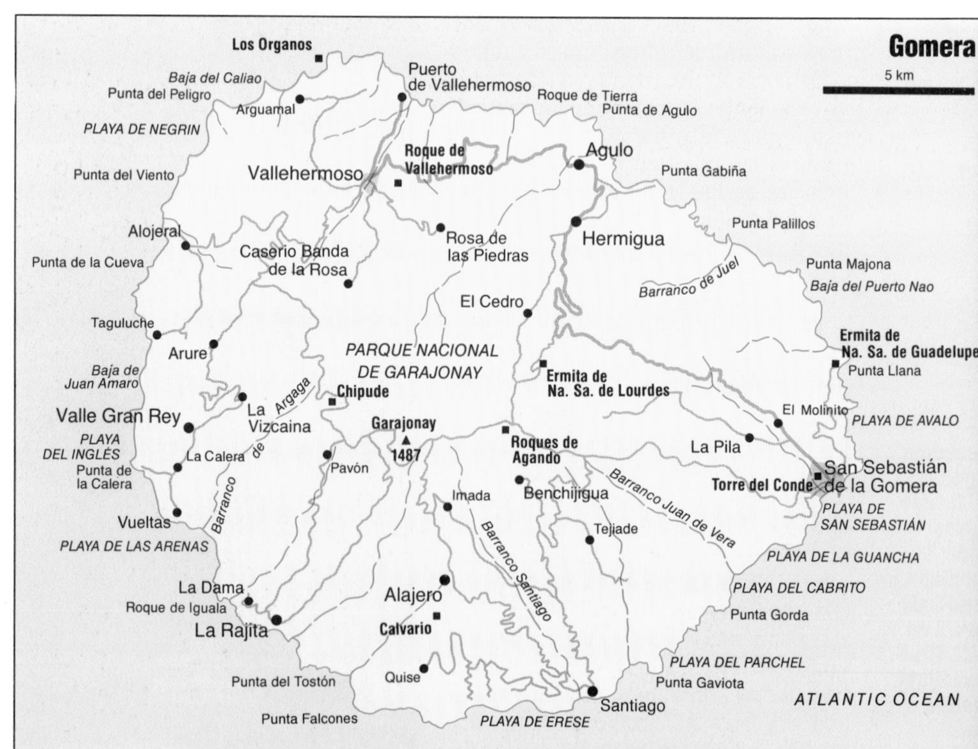

from happy at their colonisation by the Spanish. It was Peraza's son, Fernan Peraza the Younger, who married Beatriz, and the two of them were apparently well-matched in sexual appetite: Peraza conceived a passion for a young Guanche princess, Iballa, and it was while hastening to meet her in a convenient cave up in the island's high ground near the Roques of Agando, Zarzita and Ojila that he was ambushed by two Guanche chiefs and thrown off the mountain; the place is still called the **Degollada de Peraza**.

As for the tower, it looks as if it was built yesterday. It contains a small museum of South American history but has been padlocked for some years, and the well outside it is full of old washing-up liquid bottles. The small industrial estate nearby is the island's electricity generating plant, which thunders away day and night.

Hidden from sight off the Calle del Medio are several excellent *patios* (interior courtyards), one belonging to the Gomera *hostal*, another to the Gomera Garden bar. In the evenings the light spills out of these doorways and the town, which seems comatose through much of the rest of the day, is remarkably alive. Out of a considerable selection of eating places the **El Pejin** fish restaurant (it looks like a bar from the outside) is the most popular.

Half-way up the street is the **Iglesia de la Asuncion** (built 1490 - 1510), where Columbus supposedly prayed for the last time before setting off on his journey. The overall style is Gothic, but the construction is half-brick, half-lime, giving a piebald effect on the outside. On the wall inside is a series of elegant altar pieces and an ancient and much faded mural (dated 1760) by Jose Mesa, a Gomeran artist, of the English naval attack on the island.

A little further up the street is the Casa de Colón, which is supposedly where Columbus stayed in Gomera, when he wasn't in the tower with Beatriz. The unexceptional building has been bought and restored by the island *cabildo*, and now houses exhibitions. Beyond is the

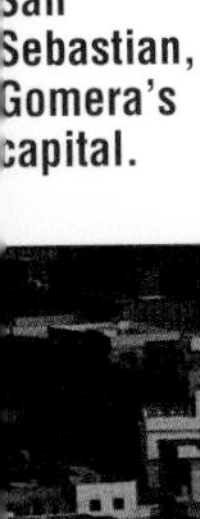

San Sebastian, Gomera's capital.

Ermitage de San Sebastian, the oldest building in the town, long and dark and reminiscent of early primitive mission churches in the United States.

Whistling gardeners: Directly above the quay on a small hill called Lomo de la Horca (literally "ridge of the gallows") stands San Sebastian's **Parador** (state-owned hotel), on the former site of a small church. The *Parador* has the deserved reputation of being one of the best hotels on the Canaries and is consequently full most of the time. Built in island-colonial style in 1976, it has a deliberate air of antiquity created by extensive use of elegant dark wood and much of the island's history is on its walls. The gardens (unfortunately largely gravel underfoot) contain examples of many Canarian shrubs.

Some of the *Parador*'s gardeners are accomplished in the art of *silbo*, a whistling language that was once widespread on the island, allowing Gomerans to communicate complicated messages at great distances across the *barrancos*. *Silbo* is one of the many mysteries of the Canaries, being a language entirely in its own right unrelated to Spanish and of unknown origin; it was probably developed to overcome the difficulties of communication caused by Gomera's steep terrain, although there is a theory that the original Guanches developed the language after their tongues had been cut off by the Spanish conquistadores, to stop them from plotting against the invaders. The language is fast dying out, and without tourism it probably would not have survived until now.

Beyond the *Parador* the road runs through unpleasant suburbs, past the lighthouse and becomes a track to the Playa de Avalo, a pebbly beach on the end of a now-deserted valley which is used as a rough campsite and a nudist beach. The track winds further round the headland, past the city rubbish tip, to the **Ermitage of Nuestra Señora de Guadalupe**, a lonely building on a low promontory surrounded by sea that houses the Virgin of Guadalupe, who is brought by boat around to San Sebas-

Garrison building in San Sebastian.

tian every year to be the focus of Gomera's principal fiesta.

Northern route: The sun comes late and departs early from the valley of **Hermigua** (2,656 inhabitants), which has the rarefied atmosphere of a Himalayan village. The 1,476-ft (450-metre) tunnel which separates the two valleys also separates two worlds: where the San Sebastian valley is barren and hot its neighbour is sleepy, damp and largely overgrown.

The floor of Hermigua valley is swimming in banana plantations, and trellised vines cling like cobwebs into the crevises in the hillsides. The town itself spreads into two distinct sections, upper and lower. In the upper part, where houses pile on top of each other up the hillside in an attempt to scramble into the sun, are the **Los Telares** apartments (the only accommodation on the northern side of the island) and the Los Telares craft centre, with local blankets and pottery for sale. Here also is the Santo Domingo convent, which contains some fine Moorish woodwork.

The lower part of the town is the commercial centre with the banana cooperative, the principal church and shops. The beach is unattractive. It was here that Fernan Peraza the Younger supposedly killed Juan Rejon, the Spanish hero and founder of Las Palmas on Gran Canaria. This deed was unproven, but it nevertheless earned Peraza much disgrace with the Spanish court.

Around the headland the village of **Agulo** is also in two clusters on adjacent small hills, set in a bowl of basalt. In the upper village an unusual big Moorish domed church dominates Plaza Leoncio Bento, but what distinguishes the town is its location; one side of the basalt bowl has dropped away into the sea, giving way to impressive much-photographed views of Agulo with Tenerife and Mount Teide in the background, and this is why the town is remembered.

The forest: A left turn inland just before the village of Las Rosas leads to the **Juego de Bolas visitors' centre** for the **Garajonay National Park** (3,984 hec-

Gomerans are the butt of unfair local jokes.

tares), one of nine parks in the whole of Spain. The centre (closed on Tuesdays) is adminstered by ICONA, Spain's nature conservation institute, who are also responsible for the forest walks.

It has a wealth of information on flora and fauna, models and displays, a small museum with a cut-away Gomeran house (the village houses have not changed much even today) and pottery, basketwork and weaving demonstrations, although the latter only function with the arrival of coach parties. The ancient moss-cloaked laurisilva and cedar forest of Garajonay, a surviving shred of similar forests that once covered the subtropical world, was declared a heritage of mankind by UNESCO in 1986.

The centre also retails ICONA's own guide to the park, with tracks and paths marked, and just how necessary this is you will appreciate if you try to drive from the centre through **Acevinos** to **El Cedro**, a route well worth the expedition. On the tourist map of the island (the map produced locally is up-to-date; avoid all others) this route is marked as being of equal quality to the neighbouring metalled road to Laguna Grande, but in truth it is the kind of rough track that you wouldn't dream of tackling in anything but walking boots, let alone a hired car.

The cedar tree after which El Cedro is named has long since gone. The straggling village survives on agriculture. In the woods above the village clearing is the **Ermitage of Nuestra Señora de Lourdes**, erected, as it says on the chapel, in 1964 as a result of the donation of Florence Parry, an Englishwoman. The chapel, with its tiny altar and wooden benches, is the focus for an annual pilgrimage through the dark forest on the last Sunday in August.

A track cuts up from the chapel to the main road near **Laguna Grande**, a forest clearing where there was once a lake (these days only a big puddle even after long rain) and which acts as a pivotal point for a lot of walkers on the island. If you can't get a walking map from the Juego de Bolas visitors' centre, copy the

The chapel at El Cedro.

plan on the noticeboard here.

The Laguna Grande restaurant is reminiscent of an alpine log cabin, complete with roaring fire, and an understandably good place to finish a long walk. An hour or so on foot from here is **Mount Garajonay** itself (4,878 ft, 1,487 metres), supposedly named after Gomera's Romeo and Juliet, Jonay and Gara, who committed suicide together on the peak rather than be separated forever by their parents, who opposed their marriage.

In the winter these woods are often dripping with mist, but in the summer forest fires are a major problem. Twenty-one people, including a newly-elected mayor from Tenerife, were trapped and killed by a fire in 1984 when the wind changed direction.

Youth centres: Despite the new roads, travelling across the island is still a time-consuming business, and it is for this reason that many of Gomera's schoolchildren are boarders. The innovative playground on the outskirts of **Vallehermoso** (4,516 inhabitants) testifies to the volume of children who attend the town's schools. Vallehermoso, a substantial, compact town, is important as an administrative and commercial centre, but has little for tourists. Towering above it is the **Roque de Cano**, which like the three Roques near Garajonay, is made out of solidified lava, the snout of a volcano left behind after the volcano walls have eroded.

Also much damaged by time is the old port of Vallehermoso, which has not stood up to the heavy surf on the beach for long. Around the coast to the west are **Los Organos**, cliffs dramatically weathered into the shapes of organ pipes, which can be visited by boat from Valle Gran Rey.

On the southern route out of Vallehermoso there was once a telling bit of graffiti: "Vallehermoso welcomes tempting fine figure of a woman...for lustful time, orgy time, God too." In other words, the artist wanted a piece of the action he believed was going on down the road.

"Down the road" is **Valle Gran Rey**,

[H]ippy [a]bout to [e]mbark for [V]alle Gran [R]ey.

where large numbers of houses are rented out on a semi-permanent basis to hundreds of young Europeans, principally Germans, who have many of the trappings of hippies. This steep-sided lush valley has been styled as an earthly paradise, dripping with foliage and running water, but its visitors are not the soft, melodious, odorous, willowy, sleepy, smiley people that hippies properly are; more often they are intellectual, severe-faced greens in colourful clothes who have made personal ideological decisions and are now setting rigorously about pursuing them, with no real outward sign of enjoyment, barely a whiff of marijuana on the breeze, and little hope for the man in Vallehermoso. The valley population swelled enormously after the Chernobyl disaster.

The road starts down Valle Gran Rey from the village of **Arure**, distinguished principally by a stunning viewpoint (**Mirador Ermita El Santo**, down a track to the right of the road under a small bridge) over Taguluche and the western coast, with La Palma in the distance on a clear day.

Where the long, intensely cultivated (bananas, mangoes and avocadoes) valley of Valle Gran Rey opens up to front the sea is the small village of **La Calera**, on the hill to the right. A flower-covered jumble of houses crawling over each other up the hill, La Calera is Gomera's equivalent of Montmartre, with small boutique-type shops and restaurants and roadside canals of abundant running water. House prices here are the highest on the island. Many of the food shops advertise "Miel de Palma", palm honey, which has been made locally; the date palm trees are tapped almost daily, and the *guarapo* or sap which is collected from their tops is boiled until it forms a thick syrup. Working palms are distinguised by tin collars on their trunks which keep the ants away from the sweet liquid.

Valle Gran Rey's shore towns, one at either end of the beach, have been developed with the new tourism in mind and are less attractive. **La Playa Calera**

Local potters at work in El Cercado.

is a poor substitute for Playa del Inglés, which is a small but clean beach of black sand around the coast to the west. **Vueltas** is a fishing port of no particular distinction, apart from the fact that it accommodates numbers of tourists, has plenty of bars and restaurants, and is the departure point for the *M V Alcatraz*, a motorboat which runs along the coast to San Sebastian.

Centres of industry: The new road from Valle Gran Rey to San Sebastian runs cleanly down the centre of the island through a spine of forest; parallel with it is the old road, which winds through the villages of El Cercado and Chipude to the south, perched between the untoucheable woods and the unfarmable barren southern slopes.

El Cercado, which as its name suggests is built around a loop in the road, is the home of traditional pottery (*Alfareria*), unusual in that it is made entirely with the hands without the assistance of a potter's wheel. The town has a couple of pleasant bars which serve good, if basic, local food, and is a good place to aim at at the end of a walk through the national park.

he port of
antiago.

Beyond Chipude a road dives to the sea again down over barren slopes to **Playa de Santiago**, the sunniest place on the island and accordingly the only place where tourism on a par with that on the major islands has taken root: the **Hotel Tecina** is an upmarket resort hotel with 330 rooms, a very extensive facility for such a small island.

The Tecina is the creation of the Norwegian shipping family Fred Olsen, long-time unofficial lords of the isle, who run the ferry, help the banana industry and own all of the extensive *barranco* **Benchijigua** (thus the ferry name), and without whom, as they say in the Oscar ceremonies, not a lot would have been possible.

The Olsens also used to run a small fish-processing industry in the village, and even though that has since closed fishing is still crucial to the settlement; when the boats come in so also do the lorries, and the scavenging skate as big as barn doors come flapping along the bottom of the fishing harbour.

While the Hotel Tecina looks like a brand new island village from a distance, there is no disguising the sad decay that the once significant village of Benchijigua itself has fallen into, now largely abandoned. It is superbly sited at the foot of the **Roques Agando**, **Zarzita** and **Ojila**, which like the Roque de Cano are lava snouts which have lost their volcanic casings.

The Santiago road rejoins the dorsal road at the point where Peraza the younger met his end, and from here it is a long descent towards San Sebastian. For the last few miles the harbour and ferry station are clearly visible; so much the more irritating for you, if you are visiting for the day and miscalculate your return, arriving at the top of the hill in time to see the boat disengage itself tantalisingly slowly from the quay.

The best thing to do in these circumstances is to divert to the monument of Sagrado Corazon de Jesus, a 23-ft (seven-metre) figure of Christ overlooking the ferry, the sea, Tenerife and everything else, and watch the sun set.

La Palma

Once the northeast trade winds brought galleons from the Spanish peninsula to the island of San Miguel de la Palma on their way to South America, but now the winds bring only rain and mist to the northern slopes of the island, to the endless delight of La Palma's visitors and residents. The winds are the reason for the luxuriant vegetation which gives La Palma its soubriquet of La Isla Verde, the Green Island. By contrast with its drier neighbours, some of which see virtually no rain, this is a farmer's paradise.

La Palma—it is known by the short form of its name except on very formal occasions—was conquered for the Spanish Crown of Castille in 1492 by Alonso Fernández de Lugo, although thereafter it languished in rural isolation from the time of the Civil War until the death of Franco.

Since then it has continued to resist the tourist development of some of the rest of the Canary Islands, and is governed with a concern for ecology. Here are few concrete apartments and no billboards outside the confines of the airport. There is even a law preserving the night from pollution by artificial lights: La Palma has stewardship of the darkest, clearest sky in Europe, and from the observatory on the mountains, astronomers from several European nations view the universe.

The Palmeros love the beauty of their home, its green forests, its year-round flowers and its spectacular scenery. Tourist facilities are, frankly, rudimentary; there are few beaches, fewer hotels and almost no tourist "attractions".

The experiences of La Palma are simple and are never thrust upon the visitor; they must be sought, and then re-lived in animated conversation in an ash-floored *bodegon*, around a wooden table heaped with uncomplicated plates of grilled fish and meat, salty potatoes (*papas arrugadas*) with *mojo palmero* sauce, and strong red wine made from grapes grown 200 metres away.

Preceding pages: salt pans at Fuencaliente; Santa Cruz de la Palma. Left, a harsh shoreline. Right, a Palmero.

The island map is a Rorschach inkblot test administered by a psychologist to test the mood of the viewer: it can look like a heart, or a stone axe. Seventeen miles (28 kms) from east to west, 29 miles (46 kms) from the rounded coast of the north to the pointed tip at the south, La Palma is the fifth of the Canary Islands in area (282 square miles, 730 square kms) and the third in population (80,000 inhabitants), a quarter of whom live in the capital city of Santa Cruz de la Palma. The island rises to a height of 7,874 ft (2,400 metres) at the Roque de los Muchachos, at the edge of a gigantic volcanic crater which dominates the island's northern half.

The coast is peppered with white houses, surrounded by gardens of green banana plants, scarlet poinsettia, pink and cream oleander, blue morning-glory and geraniums of every hue. Above the coast, the foothills of the mountains are cut with terraces, some abundant with crops of vegetables and fruit, some sad and neglected. Many Palmeros have fled to better paid jobs in

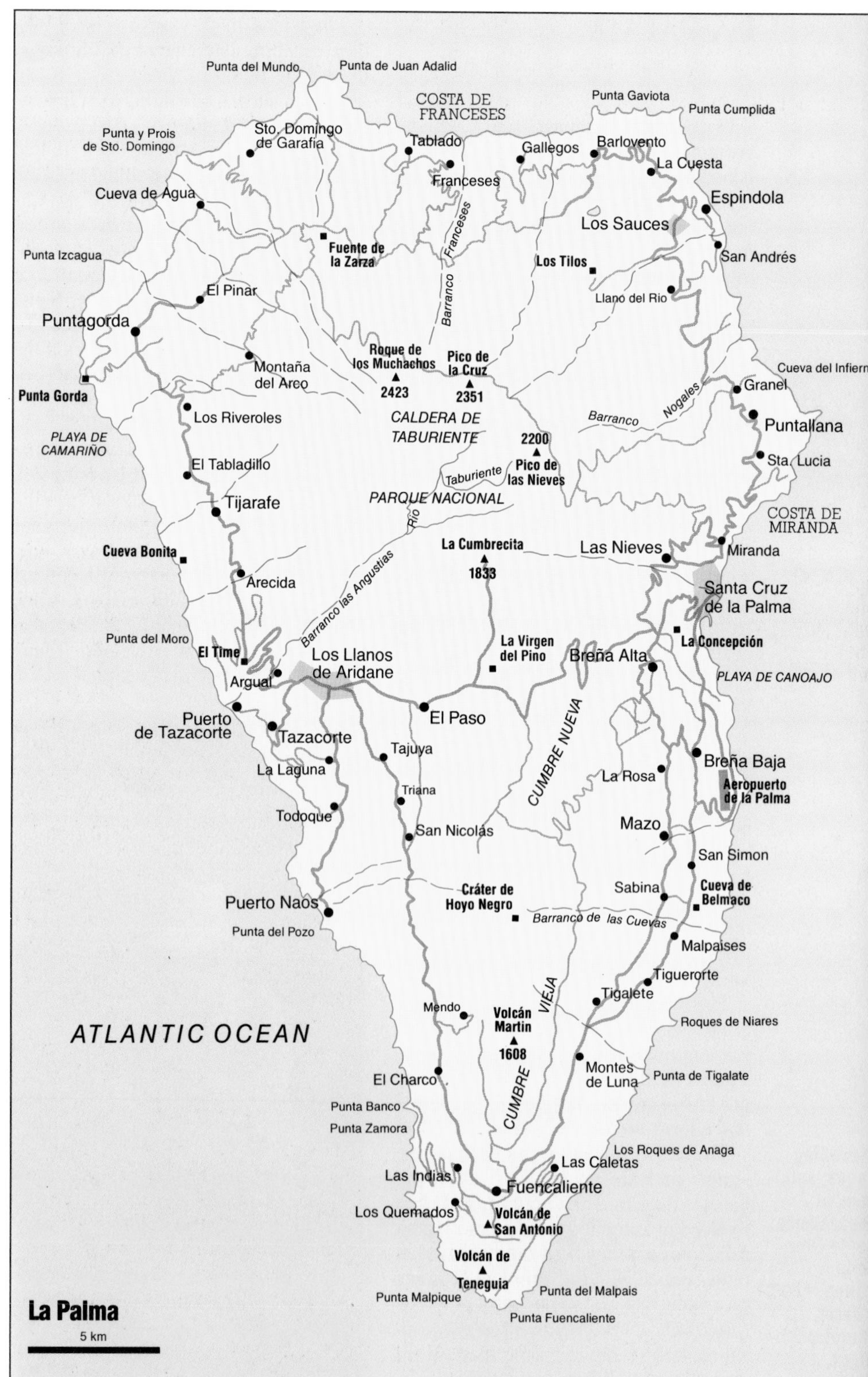
Punta del Mundo
Punta de Juan Adalid
COSTA DE FRANCESES
Punta Gaviota
Punta Cumplida
Punta y Prois de Sto. Domingo
Sto. Domingo de Garafia
Tablado
Gallegos
Barlovento
La Cuesta
Franceses
Cueva de Agua
Espindola
Los Sauces
Fuente de la Zarza
Barranco Franceses
Los Tilos
San Andrés
Punta Izcagua
El Pinar
Llano del Rio
Puntagorda
Roque de los Muchachos
2423
Pico de la Cruz
2351
Montaña del Arco
Cueva del Infierno
Punta Gorda
Granel
Barranco Nogales
Los Riveroles
CALDERA DE TABURIENTE
Puntallana
PLAYA DE CAMARIÑO
2200
Pico de las Nieves
Sta. Lucia
El Tabladillo
Taburiente
Tijarafe
PARQUE NACIONAL
Rio
COSTA DE MIRANDA
La Cumbrecita
1833
Las Nieves
Miranda
Cueva Bonita
Arecida
Barranco las Angustias
Santa Cruz de la Palma
Punta del Moro
La Concepción
El Time
La Virgen del Pino
Breña Alta
Los Llanos de Aridane
Argual
PLAYA DE CANOAJO
Puerto de Tazacorte
El Paso
Tazacorte
CUMBRE NUEVA
Tajuya
Breña Baja
La Laguna
La Rosa
Aeropuerto de la Palma
Triana
Todoque
Mazo
San Nicolás
San Simon
Sabina
Cueva de Belmaco
Cráter de Hoyo Negro
Puerto Naos
Barranco de las Cuevas
Punta del Pozo
Malpaises
Tiguerorte
Tigalete
Mendo
Volcán Martin
1608
VIEJA
Roques de Niares
ATLANTIC OCEAN
Montes de Luna
Punta de Tigalate
El Charco
CUMBRE
Punta Banco
Punta Zamora
Los Roques de Anaga
Las Caletas
Las Indias
Fuencaliente
Los Quemados
Volcán de San Antonio
Volcán de Teneguia
Punta Malpique
Punta del Malpais
Punta Fuencaliente
La Palma
5 km

the cities of peninsular Spain and of Venezuela.

The middle slopes of the mountains are wooded with the laurel forests, and above them, pines. In the distance, the peaks are rocky, with grey-green shrubs and, in winter, dazzling white snow.

City tour: The port is not only the point of entry into the city of **Santa Cruz de la Palma** but also its centre of business life. At *Carnaval* (held, like Mardi Gras, before the start of Lent) the harbour hosts the "Burial of the Sardine" a mock funeral satirising the established authorities of church and state, a fiesta with bacchanalian origins. (The official guides never even hint at the meaning of the tradition of throwing talcum powder at every one in the street).

Near the port a cobbled street surprisingly named Calle O'Daly (named after an Irish banana merchant—thanks to their religion and their American connections the Irish did well out of New World Trade from the Canaries) leads north to the centre of the city. This street, which at an ill-defined point becomes the Calle Real, is lined with the rich houses of the colonial merchants of the 17th and 18th centuries.

plica of lumbus' *nta Maria* Santa uz.

It is claimed that, in the 16th century, Santa Cruz de la Palma was the third-ranking port of the Spanish Empire after Seville and Antwerp. Whatever the truth of this boast, in 1553 the town was rich enough to be looted and razed to the ground by the French pirate François le Clerc, known as Pie de Palo ("Peg Leg"). With the aid of a royal grant, the town was rebuilt. Since the city centre was created at a single time, it has an architectural unity found nowhere else in the Canaries.

In the **Plaza de España**, the city echoes with past imperial splendour. Built in the shape of a triangle, the Plaza is bordered on its long side by the Calle Real and the **Casas Consistoriales** (1563), now the Town Hall (Ayuntamiento) of the city. Its arched colonnade supports an ornamented façade of stone carved with a bust of Phillip II, and the coats of arms of the Austrian Hapsburgs and of La Palma; within the portico is a spendid wooden ceiling, and inside the building an impressive staircase leads past murals to the Alcalde's (mayor's) office, with the conqueror de Lugo's flag in a glass case. The Three Kings annually visit the Ayuntamiento at the Epiphany fiesta (6 January), as part of the Christmas celebrations.

Facing the Town Hall is the **Iglesia de el Salvador**, the Parish Church of the Saviour, whose Renaissance portal dates originally from 1503, having survived Peg Leg's fire. The interior of the church is dominated by a Mujedar ceiling carved and painted by Moorish craftsmen with geometric designs originating from Portugal.

The church is regarded by the Palmeros as a cathedral, and the culmination of its year occurs on Good Friday. From here a procession sets out watched by a sombre crowd dressed in their best clothes. Men labour under the weight of heavy palls, bearing holy statues, but the most impressive and disturbing of the marchers are dressed in long black robes and pointed hoods with slit eyes (so that they may not be recognised and praised for their piety). Bare foot, with anchor chains attached to their ankles and dragging on the cobbles, they carry heavy crosses or contemplate the instruments of the crucifixion which they bear on black cushion. The ladies walk behind dressed entirely in black and wearing, for this important occasion, beautiful lace *mantillas*.

The Calle Real is crossed by the Avenida el Puente—the bridge supports the Calle Real itself, over a river now tamed and running, when it runs, through tunnels. Up the hill is the traditional **Mercado** where the produce of the island is sold—cigars, avocados, almonds, prickly pears, bananas, fish and smoked, pressed goats' cheese (*queso blanco*). On Saturday mornings the surrounding area is a blaze of colour with a flower market. At the head of the Avenida el Puente are the towers of the **Bellido** windmills, their sails long gone.

North of the Avenida el Puente, the Calle Real becomes the **Calle Perez de Brito**, winding through small squares with fountains and crosses which are decorated with flowers, coloured paper and satin during fiestas (particularly for the *Dia de la Santa Cruz* on 3 May, a proud day for the residents of the city).

At the end of the Calle de Brito is the **Barco de la Virgen**, housing a **Naval Museum** whose opening hours are a mystery to all tourists and residents alike. The museum is in the shape of a boat as its name implies—in fact it is a full sized concrete replica of the *Santa Maria*, the ship in which Christopher Columbus sailed to America. Palmeros like to believe that Columbus visited La Palma: he didn't. However, he did visit neighbouring Gomera where his ships were provisioned and he was entertained by the Countess Beatriz de Bobadilla, a woman notorious for the number of her lovers.

Across the valley on a promontory overlooking the mouth of the river are the ruins of the **Castillo de la Virgen**, and as you walk back towards the centre of the town along the sea front (Avenida Maritima) you will pass the star-shaped **Castillo Real**. Both castles were used to

One of man[y] town squares.

fight off the attacks of the pirates, raiders and corsairs of the 16th, 17th and 18th centuries. Another famous person who didn't visit La Palma was Francis Drake, whose piratical attack from the sea was repelled by the guns of these castles in 1585. South of the Castillo Real is the Canary Islands' finest façade of traditional wooden balconies, overlooking the sea.

The principal road system of La Palma is in the form of a rough figure of eight with a coastal road around the island's circumference and a road between Santa Cruz and Los Llanos de Aridane (the second city of La Palma) cutting across the diameter of the island. It is feasible to tour each loop in a day. There is also a new dorsal road which strikes across the highest point on La Palma, the Roque de los Muchachos, to the town of Garafia.

Southern loop: Numerous eruptions over the last thousands of years have filled the valleys with lava and ash and smoothed the steep volcanic contours with jumbled basalt rocks and deep drifts of ash; the southern part of La Palma is still volcanically active.

South of Santa Cruz, the road cuts in a tunnel through the wall of **La Caldereta**, an old volcanic crater which has been compacted by being overlaid by recent eruptions and then re-exposed by wind erosion and by the sea, which has sectioned the crater like a knife. It is worth stopping at the **Mirador de la Concepciòn** on the edge of La Caldereta to view Santa Cruz.

Las Nieves village contains the Real Sanctuario, the spiritual centre of La Palma as well as the **Chipi Chipi** restaurant, with its flower-covered wooden cabins for dining. Some distance along the route signed to **El Paso** (rather than Breña Alta) the road dives into a tunnel through the backbone of the island. It is a strange sensation to enter the high tunnel on the east in mist and cloud, and burst out of the other side in the bright sunlight: the central ridge of mountains (**Las Cumbres**) divides the climate on the island into two. Often, from the western side, you can look

**'açade of
alconies in
anta Cruz.**

back to the central ridge and see the cloud flowing over the ridge like a waterfall, a *cascada*, which provides the name for a bar from which this sight may be enjoyed.

If you are confident enough of your car to take it on unmade roads, drive over Las Cumbres to El Paso via **Breña Alta**, **San Pedro** (visit the embroidery workshop and sales centre for fine traditional designs), **San Isidro** and **El Pilar**, a clearing in the mountain forest which is quiet on weekdays and where, on Sundays and fiestas, Palmeros bring their picnics—a light meal of *sopa de garbanzos* (chick pea soup) and roast pigs, perhaps. Above El Pilar the road passes through a lunar landscape of ash ejected from the eruption of **Tacande**, when an enormous lava stream flowed westwards and now dominates the landscape towards El Paso.

The date of this eruption is usually given as 1585 but recently established carbon-14 dates of trees embedded in the ash and lava give a pre-conquest date for the Tacande eruption of some time between 1470 and 1492. The historical records of the 1585 eruption have been mis-identified and, in fact, refer to part of a twin lava stream at Jedey near Puerto Naos, most of which was from an eruption of 1712.

At the summit of this road there is a magnificent view westwards and northwards into the central caldera of La Palma. White spots atop the vertical far wall of the caldera mark the observatory domes at **Roque de los Muchachos**.

The road forks north and south at this point. The southern spur runs along the ridge to the **Volcan de San Juan**, the mouth of the lava flow of 1949, a jumble of sharp and dangerous black basalt, with a lava tunnel within which the hot lava flowed and eventually ebbed, leaving the cool walls of the tunnel still standing. The north spur drops down to join the paved road to **El Paso**.

A wide road, lined with golden California poppies, by-passes El Paso, but the narrow side roads of the village pass small houses built in traditional style, with ornamental chimneys like little

Inland transport, and one of the family.

Worshipping The Virgin Of The Snows

The Church of Nuestra Señora de Las Nieves is set in the plaza of Las Nieves with pavements figured in geometrical patterns of cobbled stones, dusted in April or May by the fallen blue flowers of the jacaranda trees. In a corner of the square is an open restaurant amidst flowers, and the square is bordered by the church buildings constructed in traditional style.

The church's name, (literally "Our Lady of the Snows"), refers to a miracle of the fourth century in Rome when the Virgin appeared during snow in August). It was founded during the time of the Conquest; its present building dates from the 17th century and has a polychrome wooden decorated ceiling of the Portuguese style.

The church contains several 16th-century Flemish statues (note especially the Calvary); these are typical of the church art of La Palma, brought from the northern limit of the Spanish Empire at the time La Palma flourished.

But the glory of the church and of the island is a small 14th-century terracotta image known as the Virgen de las Nieves. Venerated since 1534, the Virgen is the patroness of La Palma. She is credited with miracles; naive paintings on the church walls depict the many incidents in which she has saved ships from wreck.

The Virgen is housed over a Baroque silver altar, robed in clothes richly ornamented with pearls and rubies. Altar boys sometimes can be seen sitting on the church steps, surrounded by the silver altar pieces, brushing them, as if they were boots, to a gleam in which the reflections of the altar candles can sparkle.

The Virgen de las Nieves spends most of her year in the church, but once a year, in August, she is carried out of the side entrance of the church. As she appears the massed, gossiping crowd falls silent; then there is an explosive cacophony of sound as the church bell rings out, fanfares blare and fire crackers bang in the sky. She is carried around the church in a triumphal procession before returning to the altar.

Every five years (1990, 1995 and so on) there occurs the *Bajada de la Virgen*, the Descent of the Virgin, the greatest fiesta of La Palma when the small terracotta image is carried on a more extensive pilgrimage, around the island. At the start of the fiesta, pilgrims (*romeros*) carry the pieces of the silver altar down the Camino Real and past the Barco de la Virgen in Santa Cruz to the Iglesia de el Salvador; later they carry the Virgen herself.

The *romeros* are dressed in the traditional costumes of the island. The women wear long plain-coloured skirts and full-sleeved blouses with hems and cuffs decorated with hand-stitched patterns in black. The overskirts may be hitched up at the sides, the better to display this decorative work. The women wear flowing white head scarves topped by charming small straw hats in a variety of styles.

The men's costumes are in the same idiom: dark gilets and wide short trousers are worn over the top of white long-sleeved shirts and knee-breeches, cuffs and hems decorated with the same dark embroidery as the womenfolk. Broad, fringed cummerbunds and hats or caps with neck and earflaps are features of the men's dress.

The colours red, black and cream predominate and differences in style denote the places of La Palma from which the pilgrims have gathered. Bands of musicians pluck guitars and other stringed instruments, the *timple* (a sort of small guitar) being the most characteristic of the Canaries, and played like a mandolin. At their belts the men carry leather bottles of wine: there are frequent stops for refreshment during the course of the long pilgrimage.

Associated with the *Bajada* or descent is a long fiesta. Processions of giants (sometimes men on stilts, but always wearing large heads) and dwarfs (normal-sized men in costumes which disguise their height) parade and dance in the streets and plazas. Impromptu displays of arts, crafts, folk dancing and *lucha canaria* (Canary Island wrestling) are common.

Make early preparations for a visit to La Palma in the summer of the years of the *Bajada*: the month-long festivities attract many emigrants to Central America to return to their home, with friends and relations.

houses with pointed roofs, reminiscent of Thai spirit houses. The prickly pear cacti which infest the uncultivated gardens are left over from earlier times when the cactus was cultivated to host the cochineal insect, harvested as a red food colouring. The insects cling to the succulent leaves in grey mouldy-looking clusters. Other small working creatures in El Paso are the silk worms in the silk farm, where a silk tie costs £30-£40.

A detour off the main southern route route leads to **Puerto Naos** which has the biggest beach on La Palma, with fine black sand. But unsightly hotels are being slowly constructed, floor by floor as the money is found. The road south of Puerto Naos is still blocked by the lava flow of 1949.

Back on the main road at **Tamanca** a restaurant has been built in wine caves cut in the hill-side. The large barrels are still used to store the wine which you may drink with a *parilla mixta* (mixed grill) of several kinds of spicy sausages and chops.

Volcanic landscape: At the southern point of the island two packed-ash (*picòn*) roads lead, through vineyards which produce a rich, sweet wine, to the perfectly formed cinder cone of the **Volcan de San Antonio** (an eruption of 1677) and the striking jagged rocks, lava flows and coloured basalt of **Teneguia** (26 October 1971, the most recent eruption in the Canary Islands). The unsurfaced roads are easily passable but stay on the signposted ones—an imprudent driver can bog a car up to the rear axle in dust.

You can easily walk around the circumference of San Antonio (it commands wonderful but cold and windswept views of the coast and the Atlantic Ocean: southwards there is nothing between here and the ice of the Antartic). If you don't suffer from claustrophobia slither into the quiet centre of the cinder cone, and listen to the gentle touching of the needles of a few pine trees, the only sound.

The Teneguia eruption is, of course, still within memory. A tourist who had bogged his car in the dust around

The Volcan de San Antonio.

THE LA PALMA OBSERVATORY

Inaugurated in 1985 by kings, queens, princes, princesses, dukes and presidents from Spain, Denmark, Eire, Germany, the Netherlands, Sweden, and the United Kingdom, the Observatory on La Palma contains astronomical telescopes for studying the sun and the whole universe. It is the home of the William Herschel Telescope, the largest telescope in Europe and the third largest in the world.

The observatory was founded by the Instituto de Astrofisica de Canarias (La Laguna, Tenerife). It, and its sister observatory on Tenerife are here because the heights of the western Canary Islands are among the half-dozen best places in the world for astronomical viewing, with the darkest sky against which to pick out the faintest, most distant quasars and the clearest, steadiest atmosphere through which to see sharp detail.

The reason for the excellence of the astronomical conditions is the special geographical location of La Palma. It is under the influence of the oceanic climate of the northwest Canary Islands, with the cloud tops regularly (80 percent of the time) below the mountain top. The clouds trap dust and mist at the sea surface below. In the sea itself the cold Canary Current flows southwards from the latitudes of the British Isles, past Portugal. This cold sea current stabilises the air across the Roque de los Muchachos.

You can confirm for yourself the clarity of the air by looking horizontally with binoculars. El Teide is 80 miles (130 km) away, but it is possible to see the headlights of individual cars driving in Las Cañadas, as well as the brighter lights of Playa de las Américas on the near shore of Tenerife. At night it is also possible to see the lights of aircraft as they approach and land at Madeira, 250 miles (400 km) to the north. Stars rise and set without fading much at the horizon.

From the Roque de los Muchachos you can see the large dome of the William Herschel Telescope belonging to the UK and Netherlands. The dome opens as the sky darkens and the telescope's giant 13.8 ft (4.2 metre) mirror is able to be used to record light from exploding galaxies at the edge of the universe. In the foreground of the observatory is the small building containing the Carlsberg Automatic Meridian Circle, moved here from Denmark; if the computer inside senses that the weather is suitable, the shed will roll to one side, and the telescope will automatically seek out and measure the positions of the stars.

Near at hand, on a spur to the north of the Roque de los Muchachos, is the Nordic Optical Telescope, with an 8.2 ft (2.5 metre) mirror, competed in 1989. A tall tower to the right of the William Herschel Telescope contains the Swedish Solar Telescope. The telescope points vertically upwards within the tower and looks at the sun via a mirror called a coelostat—you can see it atop the tower. Beyond the solar telescope are the 24-inch (61-cm) Swedish Stellar Telescope, the 8.2 ft (2.5-metre) Isaac Newton Telescope (UK-Netherlands) and the 3.3-ft (one-metre) Jacobus Kapteyn Telescope (UK-Netherlands-Eire), all used to study stars, nebulae and galaxies.

Astronomers visit the observatory from all over the world. Those who study the sun keep relatively normal hours, but those who work through the night will be sleeping as you visit the Roque de los Muchachos; the dormitories are in the residencia near the observatory gate. Stern notices ask you to keep away in the night time so as not to disturb the delicate observations with car lights and in the daytime so as not to disturb the astronomers' sleep!

If you are at the Roque de los Muchachos as the sun sets, watch the fore-shortened triangular shadow of the mountain on which you stand point towards Tenerife on top of the clouds. The sunset will probably be undramatic, a golden glow, contracting to the west; the astronomers who are dashing in their cars to the telescopes will hope so, anyway, since spectacular red skies signify a murky, cloudy atmosphere.

At full darkness, if it is clear and there is no moon, you may well see the cone of the zodiacal light stretching upwards from the point on the horizon where the sun disappeared. This is sunlight scattered off a dusty nebula which surrounds the sun; it is seldom seen from Europe.

Teneguia was pulled free by a Palmero with his landrover. As the tourist bought him and his many friends drinks in a Fuencaliente bar (they all chose fine whisky, in the tourist's honour as an Englishman, they said), the Palmero described the eruption. He had stood 150 ft from the 650 ft fountain of lava. Was it dangerous? asked the tourist thoughtfully. No, the Palmero said confidently, the wind was blowing the red-hot lava away from him.

The throat of the Teneguia eruption is easily accessible, and you can experience geothermal energy in the flesh by sitting on a rock for a few minutes.

Fuencaliente ("Hot Spring") is a small town at the southern point of the island. A road, paved most of the way, zig-zags down below Teneguia, through dry steep slopes rich in succulent Canarian flowers, to a deserted lighthouse (El Faro) overlooking turbulent seas and a stony, steeply-shelving sea-shore. At El Faro sea-water evaporation tanks produce salt. There are few sea birds here; most of the European sea-shore is shallow, and near estuaries, the nutrient and warmth of which support small sea animals. Around La Palma the cliffs plunge almost direct into deep ocean waters. The Teneguia eruption has created nearby beaches of sterile new *picòn*, and, near a beach house which survived the eruption only by feet, is a thankful shrine where the lava flow stopped.

Northwards from Fuencaliente a pretty drive leads through pine forests with sea views and dramatic wayside flowers. Beyond, right beside the road, the cave of **Belmaco** was once occupied by Guanches. The oven now built into the cave is recent, but the carvings on the stone faces are original. Nobody knows what these carvings of meandering mazes and spirals represent, if anything. Other carvings elsewhere have the superficial appearance of a written language.

In the scree falling from the cave are small fragments of dark brown Guanche pottery. At **Mazo**, a couple of miles further north, at the **Ceramico Molino**,

The lighthouse at Fuencalient

Ramòn and his wife Vina produce highly sought-after replicas of the few score Guanche pots and scoops which have survived intact enough to copy. The black oil-rubbed surfaces of the ceramics are decorated with complex, rhythmic patterns of simple, impressed lines and Ramòn will show customers the photographs, measurements and rubbings of the very pot for every replica he sells.

Mazo celebrates the fiesta of Corpus Christi (the Thursday 60 days after Easter Day) by decorating the village with amazing arches and carpets of patterns made from flowers, seeds, leaves, lichens and fruits. On the feast day itself, a procession from the church, filled with the scent of a mass of lilies and carnations, is led by the priest who walks on the fragrant carpet.

Near the army barracks at the approach to Santa Cruz is the beach of **Los Cancajos**, crowded by the people of Santa Cruz on Sundays between the times of Mass and lunch, and protected somewhat from the surging sea which crashes over the rock pools. There is a fine view of the city across the harbour.

Northern loop: The northern loop of La Palma's road system passes around the geologically old part of La Palma, with deep cut, water-eroded valleys around which the road curves in hair-pin bends, with magnificent scenery. The road north from Santa Cruz leads through Puntallana to San Bartoleme. Two interesting options are open to you when the road forks. Follow the left fork and just before you reach **Los Sauces** turn off the main road to **Los Tilos**. This park has preserved some of the small amount of surviving original laurel forest in the Canaries. Never logged, the woods contain plant species not found anywhere else in the world, flourishing in the wet mist amongst the mossy tree trunks.

Alternatively the right fork at San Bartoleme takes you to the attractive small town of **San Andres** and the exposed headlands nearby. At Puerto Espindola a natural swimming pool, El Charco Azul, is breath-takingly blue,

raditional ottery at lazo.

calm in the encircling protection of the cliffs and constantly replenished by the waves from seaward side.

Just south of Los Tilos is the **Caldera de Marcos y Cordero**. Take waterproofs and torches and follow the water channels upstream as they run around the steep sides. The flowery, metre-wide path is scratched in the vertical cliff face and tunnelled darkly through rocky outcrops, dripping with water. At the source, water cascades into the channel from the heart of La Palma.

Beyond Los Sauces is **Barlovento** where an ever-empty and now disused reservoir, looking like a moon crater, testifies to the porosity of the volcanic soil. The road is unmetalled from here through Roque Faro to Garafia, passing through unlined, wet, dripping tunnels to one of Spain's most remote and poorest regions.

Until the completion of the road from Santa Cruz a generation ago, **Santo Domingo de Garafia** communicated weekly with the rest of the island by a messenger who walked with a mule across the mountains, and with the rest of the world through an unbelievable "port" below. Downhill from the cemetery, the road gradually deteriorates; take your car as far as you dare and walk on, to the edge of the cliffs, to view the islands offshore, the sea surging through natural archways. Ospreys nest on this coast. At the top of the cliffs a litter of steel cabling is the remains of a bosun's-chair which once hauled loads from boats bobbing in the white water below. Crumbling steps lead down the cliffs to the dock.

Garafia includes the land of the observatory on the Roque de los Muchachos above and it was its Mayor who welcomed the King of Spain at the observatory's inauguration in 1985, handing him the walking stick which signified the temporary transfer of authority over the town while the King was in Garafia. A small man, the Mayor swelled to the King's great height when embraced by him and the moment was photographed, the two men shoulder to shoulder, by an aide using the mayor's

Rough shor near Garafia.

own Kodak Instamatic. No doubt it is a picture that the Mayor has much cherished since.

Around onto the west side of the island the road runs first through almond trees, pink with blossom in January, and then through pines and bananas, through Punta Gorda and Tijarafe to **El Time**, on the edge of the rift valley which forms the outlet of the Caldera de Taburiente.

A restaurant balcony perches precariously over the sheer drop, with a view into the crater, over Los Llanos and Tazacorte, and south over the bananas of the western plains. The peninsula formed as the 1949 lava flow cooled in the sea is now covered with bananas, irrigated by water from the mountains and carried through pipes which drop almost vertically down the valley wall and feed the tanks which dot the landscape below. A reminder that La Palma is the most water-rich island in the whole archipelago.

The road zig-zags down the valley wall to the river. A spur leads west, through Las Angustias and its beautifully restored church to the port of **Tazacorte**. Here in 1492 Alonso Fernández de Lugo, the conqueror of Gran Canaria, landed and with unscrupulous and underhand tactics wrenched control of the island from the native Guanche kings to whom it was known as Benahoare ("Land of my forefathers"). Now, fishing boats and yachts tie up in the well protected harbour, and, at the sea-shore itself, restaurants offer whatever fish have been caught that day—*samas* and *viejas* may be untranslatable but are very palatable species available on local menus.

Tazacorte itself is a charming town with steep streets of traditional houses and balconies. In the central square old men and young play chess and gamble with Spanish packs of cards beneath a flowery arbour.

The road back towards Santa Cruz passes through **Los Llanos**, La Palma's somewhat anonymous-looking wine-rich second city, with a pleasant church and central square.

cal fish a eciality in zacorte.

THE CALDERA DE TABURIENTE

The Caldera de Taburiente forms the most spectacular scenery on La Palma. It is the central hollow of an extinct volcano, revealed when the peak of the volcano collapsed—the "roof material" now lies fractured and jumbled as a series of hills and rocks on the crater floor. The collapse, which was far larger than the similar 19th-century explosion of Krakatoa, occurred 400,000 years ago and stopped further volcanic activity in the northern half of La Palma: recent activity is confined to the southern half of the island.

The crater is 5.5 miles (nine kms) across—not, as claimed, the largest in the world, but perhaps the most impressive—and the inner wall of the *caldera* is an almost sheer drop of 2,300 ft (900 metres); the strata of the innumerable eruptions of the volcano before the collapse have been revealed in the inner walls.

At the time of the collapse, a rift valley opened up to the southwest of the crater. A river, Rio de las Angustias, now flows in the rift valley and has cut an erosion valley in its floor. It is fed by two tributaries, los Rios de Taburiente y de Almendro Amargo which meet at the junction of Dos Aguas ("two waters").

There are numerous walking trails into the Caldera de Taburiente, which has the status of a national park operated by ICONA, the forestry agency. It is forbidden to be in the park at night except at the authorised camping place.

There are two routes into the *caldera* for cars. The easier is from El Paso, where a paved side road leads to La Cumbrecita. This is a look-out point from which to view the opposite wall of the *caldera* below Roque de los Muchachos. An unpaved road leads to another, quieter look-out.

In addition, there is a road which starts well, in Los Llanos near the church, and goes on through plantations of avocado trees, but becomes adventurous and unpaved as it enters the rift valley. The road descends sharply to the river. Usually the rocky river bed of grey stones is fordable, except after storms or as the spring melt-water pours from the mountains. Then the river runs deep and fast with brown water which carries the very substance of La Palma out into the sea.

On the other side of Dos Aguas the road ascends through tobacco farms and their drying sheds to a look-out virtually in the centre of the crater, below Roque de los Muchachos. As the setting sun casts long dark shadows and the orange of the evening light intensifies the colours in the rocks, a chill strikes from the evening air and the sky darkens. In the distance, the spire of the Roque Idafe stands up from the crater floor. It is a monolith regarded as a sacred place by the original Guanche inhabitants of La Palma who made offerings there to their god Abora.

It was below the look-out that the conqueror of La Palma, Alonso Fernández de Lugo, tricked the Guanche chief Tanausu in 1492. On landing at Tazacorte, de Lugo received the immediate surrender of the tribes of Aridane, Tihuya, Tamanca and Ahenguareme; he fought and conquered the Tigalate tribe, thus subduing the southern half of the island. In the wooded hills of Acero (the Guanche province within the *caldera*) de Lugo met stiff resistance from Tanuasu and could not win by fair means: he ignobly descended to foul. He sent a messenger inviting Tanuasu to negotiate. Ignoring his adviser Ugranfir, who claimed that de Lugo did not want peace, Tanuasu agreed to talk. At the meeting place in the Barranco del Riachuelo, Tanuasu was ambushed and captured by de Lugo and his troops, after a battle in which there was considerable bloodshed, Tanuasu was sent into exile. Repeatedly crying out *"Vacaguare, vacaguare"* (I want to die), he refused to eat on the voyage to Spain, after he had lost sight of his island, and he died of hunger.

It is easiest to view the *caldera* from above by driving on the dorsal road to the mountains. At any time of the year the mountains can turn cold—and, in winter (January to April), it will certainly be icy with snow at the top of the mountain road: take warm clothes on this trip, no matter how fine it appears to be as you set out.

Northwards out of Santa Cruz, you turn left and drive up hill to Mirca, past a pretty church surrounded by eucalyptus, and ascend on the road signposted to El Observatorio Astrofisico.

The road climbs steeply and at some stage you are almost certain to enter the mist of the cloud layer, bursting out later into clear sunny skies. The ascent quickly reveals the stratification of the zones of vegetation, each extending over a suitable range of temperature and rainfall—an evergreen forest, with tree heath and faya trees, extending from 1,300 to 3,300 ft (400 to 1,000 metres). The pine forest extends from there to 6,200 ft (1,900 metres) and montane scrub takes over in the heights, with small rare flowers such as La Palma violets.

The road zig-zags up a deep cut valley with views to Santa Cruz. At one point it crosses a narrow-gauge railway line which is used in the cutting of a water mine into the mountain. The owner tunnelled horizontally until he found a descending stream of water within the mountain; he now bottles and sells the water at Mirca. You might pass a gang of peons cutting the coppiced faya trees—these stakes are a main stay of banana growing, holding the easily bruised bananas away from the main trunk of the plant, and a prop for the building industry where they are used as scaffolding.

If you are lucky you may see by the side of the road one of La Palma's unique pininana flowers, a 13-ft (four-metre) high spike of blue florets, a biennial plant which flowers in the spring. It is related to Tenerife's scarlet equivalent, which is known as the Pride of Tenerife.

The laurel forest gives way to Canary pines as you ascend, and at Fuerte de Olen (Olen's spring) the pines are beautiful, with what the English call Spanish moss hanging from the branches (in Spain it is known as Englishman's Beard).

From here there are different views through the pines to Tenerife. In the springtime there are pink and white cistus and for several weeks the almost ubiquitous small shrub, the cordeso, will be found flowering abundantly at successively higher levels on the mountain, covered with a mass of fragrant bright yellow blossoms. Fuente de Olen is a picnic area, within which are the ruins of a cylindrical stone-lined pit, which was used in the days before refrigerators to store winter ice for later use.

At about 6,500 ft (2,000 metres) the pines quickly become stunted and give out, leaving the ground bare except for isolated juniper trees. The road passes red and yellow drifts of ash, formed into fantastic shapes, some given fanciful names (look out for the formation known as the Yellow Submarine). The road circles 90 degrees of the *caldera* rim towards the north of the island.

The rim of the crater narrows down to the width of the road and as it enters the cutting known as Los Andenes (the railway platforms) there are views into the *caldera* to the south and, on the other side, down to the northern coast.

In the cuttings embedded walls of basalt have been formed by molten lava welling up through cracks in ash deposits. Walls which have been exposed as the ash has eroded away ("dykes") can be seen standing in the surrounding country, including the Pared de Roberto (Roberto's Wall), misclassified as archaeological remains in some guide books. The cuttings have also revealed "bombs" of volcanic lava which, spinning through the air, solidified as spheres and were buried in the wind-drifted ash. Yellow or orange ash which has been covered with hot flowing lava has been baked red from the top. The rocks are covered with flat, plate-sized, thick-leaved aeonium plants, some flowering with golden blooms.

At the observatory gate the road turns left and ascends to the Roque de los Muchachos, the highest point on the island at 9,900 ft (2,400 metres). The Muchachos (the boys) themselves are the columns of solidified mud on the peak. The horizon is wide as you look down on the sea and onto the tops of the white cloud, perhaps pierced to the south west by the island of Hierro, and to the south east by Gomera; almost certainly to the east the peak of El Teide on Tenerife will show through the cloud. This area of sea is equal to the area of the United Kingdom.

On the next peak east is the Observatorio del Roque de los Muchachos. The silence of the Roque is emphasised by the sound of the flight of the swifts overhead in the summer and by the distant neck bells of herds of goats. It is not unusual to see a mouflon (a wild sheep).

From the Roque de los Muchachos the road descends towards Garafia.

El Hierro

El Hierro has grown vain in recent years—it now has more *miradores* than policemen. The best is also the newest, the **Mirador de la Peña**, now graced by a restaurant designed by César Manrique in 1988 in a characteristic harmony of local wood and stone. Only when you stand at its edge, as the clouds form on your hand, as the precipitous cliffs of El Risco drop sheer below, do you sense the full drama of Hierro. For the sky falls not to shadow-bright sea but to El Golfo, pawed out of the mountains, reprieved by the waves, a green secret lying low in the upthrust crater of an extinct volcano.

Hierro gives no clues to such surprises. Whether arriving by ferry at the tiny **Puerto de la Estaca** or flying in at the new airstrip, built on reclaimed land in 1972, visitors only meet the steep mountains of the island's eastern coast climbing into cloud. A sprinkle of high white houses give a hint of its capital Valverde, caught in the hills like snow in a gully. Its highest peak, **Malpaso** (4,920 ft, 1500 metres), is lost in a line of close rivals guarding another secret: the high mountainous plateau, the **Nisdafe**, that runs the island's length.

Bleak landscape: Rolling back from the broad curve of El Golfo, the Nisdafe has determined life for the herreños (locals). A bleak tracery of dry stone walls and lava-slab tracks decorate the pastureland where many inhabitants still own patches of land, a legacy of not-so-distant days when many migrated up here in summer to grow cereals and graze livestock, later returning to the coast to harvest figs and vines. **San Andrés**, a gaggle of homes in its centre, still bears the raw stamp of farm life high up on a windy *meseta*, where ancient prickly pear and figs are hallowed by stone circles and thick capes and hats shroud their owners.

'receding ages: the ell-tower t Frontera. eft, erreño. ight, plash of olour in a leak andscape.

Agriculture still dominates the island, from the old men forever cropping *tagasaste* (albuminosa) for fodder to the new lorries now taking *queso herreño* (cheese) to the ferry. Every day milk churns line the roadside, destined for the new Co-operativa Ganadera (by the road junction to Isora) that cannot produce enough of this cheese to meet demands. Once made in every herreñian home, three types of *queso*—blended from cow, goat and sheep milk—are now available: *ahumada* (smoked), *curada* (mature) and *blanco* (white). The *curada* is the most popular.

Never abundant, water has proved crucial to the island's survival—epitomised perhaps by its emblem the **Garoë Tree**, growing in a valley to the north of San Andrés. Surrounded by small pools of water, the present tree (a lime) planted in 1957 marks the site of an earlier Garoë destroyed by a hurricane in 1610. Cartographers of the time frequently depicted Hierro as the mysterious island of "Pluvialia", with its rainy *Arbol Santo*, the sacred tree whose leaves could distil water and bring life to a waterless land. In fact the phenomenon is not so rare; water condenses on many trees and plants as the clouds

swirl across Hierro—enough to provide an annual 40 gallons a square ft (2,000 litres per sq metre), more than eight times the island's rainfall.

In the north the Nisdafe spreads six miles (9.6 km) wide, its hills clustered with pines apparently electrocuted by the wind. The villages of **Guarazoca**, **Erese** and **Mocanal** (the highest on the island) are quiet, the corner-stones of their simple churches typically left unpainted. The deserted village of **Las Montañetas** is even quieter, its tight-bunched houses and lava walls well-preserved by the climate, its fruit trees still blossoming.

Down on the coast another deserted village, **Pozo de las Calcosas**, offers more reveries and a swim in its man-made seawater pool, a common solution for an island without beaches. Such places are busy in summer, especially **Tamaduste**, where on Sundays a bus brings trippers down from Valverde to enjoy its sheltered beach and bars. **La Caleta** on the other side of the airport offers a similar lava-scaped pool, some breezeblock houses and a bar playing Leonard Cohen songs. Many herreñian families have summerhouses on the coast, and it's quite usual to own two houses—a legacy of emigration and an arduous terrain. Many are now being restored thanks to new prosperity.

In town: Modernisation is also quietly turning the capital **Valverde** inside out. Visitors still say "Is that it?" as they suddenly find themselves out among the goats after a walk down the high street, but when the Victorian adventuress Olivia Stone arrived in 1884 there wasn't even an inn. "All is poverty", she noted, deducing from her reception that she was probably the first Englishwoman to set foot on the island. She would have seen the newly-built windmills (now the football pitch) used to make *gofio* (maize flour), but was two years too early to see the new clock, brought all the way from Paris in 1886, and installed in the church tower.

Today Valverde has a youthful atmosphere generated by the island's high school students, who board in the

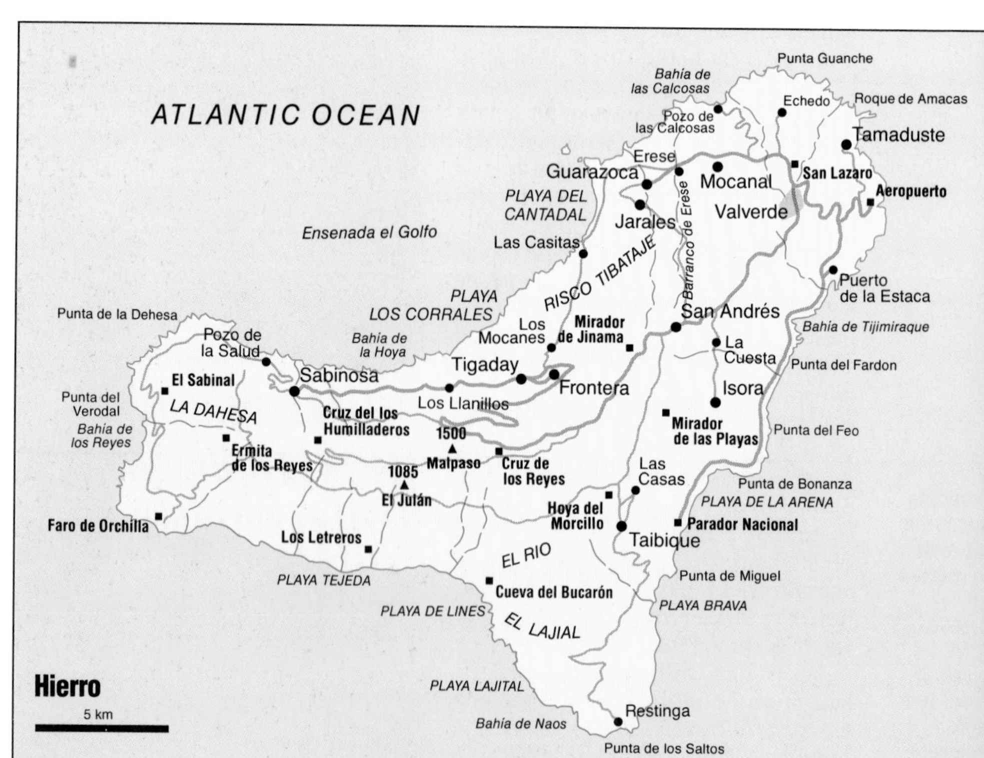

capital during the week. A new bus station on the edge of town threatens to kill off the heart of island life, the taxi-rank opposite the Bar Los Reyes.

The tower of **Nuestra Señora de la Concepciòn** (1767) was reputedly built to keep watch for the pirates that forced Hierro to keep its capital inland. Civic virility is also responsible for the 18th-century Juzgado and Plaza de Quintero Nuñez (1913) above the church, the latter named after an herreño who rose to become Mayor of Manila. Two small museums offer idiosyncratic diversions. The private **Casa-Museo** (walk down from the *Cepsa* garage) contains an intense collection of things herreñian, Canarian and antiquarian, including an altar built by its courteous owner Juan Padron (bang on the door) that plays choral music. The second, next door to the **Tourist Office** (open 9.00 a.m.-2.30 p.m.) in the high street, houses ethnographic and archaeological finds (nominally open 10.00 a.m.-2.00 p.m.) assembled by its energetic curator Angeles Fernández Quintero.

Hierro's cuisine is simple but good. The **Bazar El Placer** (Dr Quintero 23) sells its famous *quesadilla*, a cheese-cake flavoured with vanilla, aniseed and lemon. Try the **Noche y Dia** restaurant for a quintessentially herreñian meal: *vino herreño*, *solomillo* (sirloin) and *piña* (pineapple). As for nightlife, you're on the wrong island. The star attractions here are in the sky.

On the road: In 1914 work began on the island's first proper road, leading down to the small harbour at **Puerto de la Estaca**. Little has changed there since the 1930s when steamers regularly called at its cobbled quay to collect figs, wine, almonds and goat-skins.

A new road continues south now, opening up the island's eastern shore to development. So far, two bars and a *pension* attend the small black sandy beach at **Timijiraque**: most of the narrow cliff-lined shore remains a rocky sea-blown wilderness only crossed by a black crochet of lava walls. Fierce weather and rockfalls make the road so hazardous that a section approaching

heltered arbour at amaduste.

the photogenic Roque Bonanza is patrolled daily. At its end the **Parador Nacional**, built in 1976, shelters behind a tall curtain of cliffs, serving isolation and luxury to its guests.

Known as **Las Playas**, the *parador*'s spectacular setting is actually a semi-submerged crater similar to El Golfo, best viewed from the **Mirador de Isora** above. The **Mirador de las Playas** opposite offers another angle, with long-range views to Gomera and Teide. Its giant pine trees are impressive examples of the ancient pinewoods that cover much of the central Nisdafe, their floors inches deep in long needles. Many walks lead through these sweet-smelling woods—a good starting point is the picnic site at **Hoya del Morcillo**.

Pinewoods also give their name to the southern town of **El Pinar**, its steep streets now closely entwined with its neighbours Taibique and Las Casas. Most of the thatched roofs here have disappeared but the 500 residents still live a rural life—the Communist Party HQ (near the Bar Chachi) a sign of their traditionally left-wing sympathies. At the top of town (turn hard right uphill by the Calle El Lagar) the **Museo Panchillo** (No 53) has a display of local curios and sells honey and figs. Behind it the **Artesania Ceramica** (follow the sign of the snail) sells pottery. An old lady at No 45 sells rag rugs and *talegas*, the durable wool bags that are a must for any herdsman's back.

South of El Pinar the land gradually falls toward the sea, pines give way to figs, grassy fields become a scorched no man's land of volcanic clinker. Unbelievably there's life at the end of the road, just. **La Restinga** is a small fishing port slowly waking to the fact that every summer the Teutonic desire to get to the end of things draws hundreds of Germans to its austere finality. A sense of their priorities is clear from the lone German who set up the first bar (now the Kai Marino Hotel) in the 1960s, even though running water didn't arrive until 1974.

Pool tables and "Lohengrin" cocktails now grace a resort-in-progress

In the bar a Taibique.

with good underwater swimming but a poor beach (most head west to Tecoron or Lajial). Its restaurants have good fish—try the *peto* (similar to tuna) or the small white *viejas* or *cabrillas*, and don't be put off *lapas a la plancha* (limpets), sometimes translated as "grilled slime".

Hard lessons: It was at the nearby **Bahia de Naos** that the Norman adventurer de Béthencourt first landed in 1403, as deserted then as it is now. His main problem in conquering the island's aboriginal inhabitants, the Bimbaches, was finding them: partly because they hid in the mountainous Nisdafe, but also because they were so few—their numbers having been decimated by Moorish slave-traders.

In the end he used a captured Bimbache as an intermediary to invite their leader Armiche to peace talks. Armiche agreed terms and he and over a hundred men surrendered their arms, whereupon de Béthencourt promptly imprisoned them. Hopefully the herreños will not be quite so naive now tourism begins to invade their isle, for de Béthencourt subsequently sold most of the Bimbaches into slavery and installed his own Norman families as rulers.

Hierro learnt some more ways of the world when English sailors landed here in April 1762, four months after England declared war on Spain in the Seven Years War. An early alarm, signalled across the mountain-tops to Valverde, resulted in their capture, along with nine rifles that became the focus of a preposterous dispute. Requisitioned by the Tenerife government, the arms were only returned to the islanders after the intervention of Carlos III, a king almost as popular in the Canaries as the brandy named after him.

A mile (1.6 km) north of La Restinga lies the **Cueva de Don Justo**, a labyrinthine system of volcanic tunnels said to total over 20,000 feet (6,100 metres) and be the sixth largest in the world. A concealed entrance lies below the red cone of the aptly named Montaña de Prim, though one should not enter without a guide, which can be arranged by

…epherd …d his …ck.

TRANQUILIDAD

There's a gentle riddle going round Hierro. Something active yet passive, something you can feel but not translate, something that hits but doesn't hurt. Something born on an isolated island at the end of the world, where steep mountains set the pace of life, where for centuries mule-paths and lava-paved tracks formed the only link between twelve hamlets and a capital still called simply "La Villa". Something grown on an island where nature seems to provide everything but whose people had nothing, an island that had no roads till 1926, where telephones didn't ring until 1945, where many still talk in a pure Castilian, unelided by the rush of modern life.

"*Tranquilo, tranquilo!*" they joke, your first clue. "See how the dogs sleep in the road?"

There's a different clock on Hierro. Ask when's the next *lucha canaria* match and your reply comes in phases of the next moon. "Stop, *amigo*. Stand in a doorway. Sit in the sun."

Suppose you're looking for the Garoë Tree. "Why do we need a sign?" the barman laughs, "Everybody knows where it is". Then he closes his bar and takes you there.

Tranquilidad. An age-old conspiracy to live peacefully, a plot with 7,000 characters. Born of necessity, grown from trust, now relished by islanders still attentive to friendship, still absorbed in a rural life neither quaint nor sad.

Until recently a hard agricultural life was all that faced most herreños, many families sought brighter futures elsewhere. The first emigrants went to Cuba—you'll still see *arroz cubana* on the island's menus—but the majority found work in Venezuela. One of Hierro's most famous sons, Juan Fransisco de Leon, even led a revolution for independence from the Spanish in 1794.

Most islanders still have brothers and sisters in South America. It's likely that that wizened old man collecting figs, who looks like he's never left the slopes of his *finca*, has just flown back from a behatted and gift-laden visit. On the walls of his *casa* will be varnished crocodiles and brilliantly-coloured butterflies brought home as souvenirs.

Many emigrants found work running small shops or working in hotels, sending money back and sometimes returning to the island themselves, newly prosperous. Often they have come back to the same house they were born in, where they build a grand new front, install aluminium doors and windows crowned with a marble plaque proclaiming "Gracias Venezuela". Ties still run deep—many households continue to make *hallacas* at Christmas, a favourite Venezuelan speciality of meat and spices steamed in a wrapping of banana leaves.

"They still eat the leaves over there," laugh the locals, bettering the hand that fed them.

Some of the young still leave, for everywhere the disco voice of Playa de las Américas calls from the radio.

Others are content to stay, better off as living standards rise. There's even a slight immigration, as other Canarios and foreigners join the conspiracy of *tranquilidad,* but sooner or later most herreños try a spell abroad, if only on military service. Few seem tempted by the outside world. Instead they return to their tiny island, happily forsaking big money for a quiet life.

Tourism may now offer the chance to have both. Holiday bungalows are being built, *miradores* multiply. The airport runway is to be extended 500 ft (152 metres) to allow bigger planes to land. Some look forward to the prosperity and security the tourists will bring, others are more dubious. *Tranquilidad* is more important. Local politicians say they will restrict development, but the pace of change has quickened. Perhaps the welcoming grins of the herreños are the smiles of seals greeting their cullers?

Walking amongst the bees and wild flowers of the Nisdafe, along the azure shore of El Golfo, amid the timeless pines of El Julan—it seems impossible that *tranquilidad* could not survive.

History would seem to be on its side. That first road on the island took 12 years to build. Another to El Golfo, planned in 1914, didn't arrive till 1962. There was even an attempt to introduce telephones in 1914, but that failed after three years because no one used them.

"*Tranquilo señor, tranquilo.*"

Maximo Morales in the Bar Avenida.

Rough shores: The southern coast of Hierro is known as **El Julan**, a line of barren, windswept slopes falling sharply to steep cliffs. Curiously the remotest part of the island is also home to **Los Letreros**, a bizarre set of primitive inscriptions made in the flat surface of lava-streams. As yet undeciphered, their alphabet-like doodles have also been found at La Caleta and other parts of the island. Some think their authors belonged to an early Berber civilization, others link them to similar inscriptions in La Palma and the Cape Verde Islands. Vandals have had their say too and Los Letreros are now guarded—you'll need written permission from the Tourist Office before making the difficult journey to their site.

A high forest track runs the length of El Julan, a bumpy but invigorating drive that circles round the coast and back to El Golfo. Allow a full day, but avoid the route (clockwise is safest) if there's been heavy rain. Towards its end lies the remote Ermita that's home for **Nuestra Señora de los Reyes**, the island's spiritual patroness.

A popular place for newly-weds on their *luna de miel* or honeymoon (a key is available from the Ayuntamiento in Valverde) Our Lady of the Kings sits diminutively in the silver sedan chair used for the Bajada in which she "descends" to Valverde for a month-long fiesta held in her honour every four years (the last was in June 1989). It takes a day for the colourful procession to wind across the Nisdafe, stopping beneath Malpaso for lunch at the Cruz de los Reyes.

The legend itself tells of how a French ship was mysteriously becalmed off El Julan for weeks on end, its crew only kept alive by the generosity of the herreñians who took food to the stranded sailors. Having no money to pay for this the captain gave the islanders the statue of the Virgin Mary from his ship. That same day, 6 January 1577 (The Day of the Kings), a breeze suddenly blew up...

Stunted forest: A track north from the Ermita leads to another of Hierro's sur-

he Ermita uestra eñora de s Reyes.

prises: **El Sabinal**, a forest of *sabinosas* (juniper) bent double by persistent winds. Bowed but not defeated, every tree is a stunted compromise, its twisted trunk worn silver-smooth, its branches hairy with green lichen. Further ahead lies the **Mirador de Bascos**, bright with wild flowers and giving fine views over El Golfo to the islands of La Palma, Gomera and Tenerife.

Today a switchback road eases the steep descent to **El Golfo**, for so long only accessible by tracks creeping down its crater walls. **Frontera** below offers comfort to travellers in the shape of **Nuestra Señora de la Candelaria** (1818), remarkable for its bell-tower placed on the volcanic cone behind, and a bar opposite serving good *tapas*. The grey amphitheatre beside the church is the **lucha canaria** stadium with the best view in the world.

A ribbon of houses line the road at **Tigaday**, where vines and wine presses show it is the centre for herreñian wine. One of the few things known about the Bimbaches was that they were the only early Canarians to distil alcoholic liquour (using laurel berries)—a tradition fiercely continued in the local *mistela*, more palatably in *vino herreño*, a growing export. Another surviving sign of Bimbache intelligence is a scarified skull which was found in the Cueva de los Jables (now in the Museo Arqueologico in Santa Cruz de Tenerife), showing they practiced a rudimentary sort of brain surgery.

Largest lizards, smallest hotel: Some Bimbache food still lives up in the cliffs of **El Risco**, the giant lizards (*lacerta simonyi*) long thought extinct on Hierro. The Roques de Salmor on the eastern corner of El Golfo were reputedly the last refuge of a primeval lizard once as long as 30 ft (nine metres), though only five ft (1.5 metres) fossils have been found. Their survival was dramatically discovered in 1975 when an Englishman was caught leaving the island with a bag full of their descendants, now down to two ft (60 cm) in length. It is thought that about 1,000 lizards still live a tenacious existence up

Looking down onto El Golfo.

among the basalt crater walls, the oldest part of the island.

Also near the base of El Risco is the deserted village of **Guinea:** like Las Montañetas it was one of the original settlements made by the Norman colonists brought over by de Béthencourt in the 1450s. El Golfo must have appeared as idyllic then as it does now to the guests settling into the four rooms of the Club Puntagrande at Las Puntas. Recognised by the *Guinness Book of Records* as the smallest hotel in the world, the Club stands on the old *embarcadero* where up until the 1930s many of the island's supplies where shipped in.

A new road cuts across the gulf to **Pozo de la Salud** through fields growing bananas and pineapples on land once dead with lava. Here a *Finca de Experimentacion* researches into new crops that could help the island's vulnerable economy. Bananas were only tried in Hierro in 1960, their cultivation later stimulated by a drought in 1968 when the Nisdafe's pastures failed and many families were forced to leave the island. Ten years later a world glut forced a switch to pineapples. Today the *finca* is offering farmers strawberry plants at five pesetas each as an incentive to diversify.

Spa waters: One early export from the *embarcadero* was mineral water from **Pozo de la Salud**. In the 1890s this Well of Health developed a reputation as a therapeutic spa where patients benefitted from the radium content of its waters. An analysis of 1915 suggested it could treat everything from indigestion to venereal disease, recommending hot baths and daily draughts washed down with chicken soup. A new *balneario* is under construction, but treatment is still available from the cat-mad owner of the Casa Rosa. More substantial sustenance can be found in **Sabinosa** above, where the **Casa de Huespedes** does a fine example of a local cake made from cheese, figs, nuts and orange juice.

A track leads out from Pozo de la Salud to Hierro's desolate western coast, past a popular lizard-shaped rock (more obvious as you return). Gradually the land turns violent, scene of the island's most recent eruption in 1793. Towering cliffs are striped with rockfalls, mountains streaked with dark cinders. The island's best beach is out here, **Playa del Verodal**, the fortunate result of a more recent landfall—its red gravel was pushed down to the sea during a project to build a coastal road.

Another track leads to the island's south west corner and the **Punta Orchilla**, its name derived from the orchil (a moss-like lichen found on rocks and used for dyes) that brought traders to the Canaries, and was Hierro's first export product (after slaves). Here the waves attack a coast of lava badlands mouldy with euphorbia, fittingly sinister for a point so long thought the end of the world. In A.D. 150. Ptolemy placed his zero meridian through Hierro, a line universally accepted up until the 19th century and finally transferred to Greenwich in 1884. Nearby a lighthouse stands with a sign commemorating this lonely corner of the world, the "*tristeza y alegria de los herreños emigrantes*".

A twisted Sabinosa tree.

Gran Canaria and the Eastern Isles

The eastern province of the autonomous region of the Canary Islands, comprising the islands of Gran Canaria, Fuerteventura and Lanzarote, is surprisingly different in character to the Western province as described elsewhere in this book.

A reader has only to flip through these pages to ascertain that the western province is surprisingly lush and green on high ground. In general the eastern province is drier and harsher as a human environment than the islands to the west, with less resultant vegetation. Fuerteventura, closest to the African mainland (60 miles, 96 km), is little more than a chip off the block of the Sahara, hot, sandy, and waterless. And yet by contrast the highest points in the mid-north of Gran Canaria occasionally receive snow in the winter, to the exhilaration of the locals.

Inter-island rivalry in the Canaries is intense, but nowhere is it more intense than between the two leader-islands, Gran Canaria and Tenerife. These two have fought over the captaincy of the archipelago for centuries, with Tenerife having the better of the past couple of centuries, but Gran Canaria currently in the ascendancy as the seat of the autonomous government.

Such is the rivalry that natives of one island will often go out of their way to avoid having to go to the other, and agencies that function in one province often do not in the other. Government offices are in Gran Canaria; shipping business is in Gran Canaria, and regional television is in Gran Canaria, but the university is in Tenerife; the latter became such a subject of debate (Las Palmas wants its own university) that it caused the collapse of the government late in 1988.

The islanders know instinctively whether a newcomer is a pure outsider or from a rival island. One resident tells the story of the tinerfeño (Tenerife islander) barber who travelled over to Gran Canaria only once, a decade ago, and went into a barber's shop for a haircut to see how it was done there. Just as he was preparing to sit down he overheard the barber mutter something about the smell of sardines (Tenerife has a festival featuring the mock burial of a sardine). The tinerfeño stormed out without his haircut, and hasn't been back to Gran Canaria since.

Foreign residents are just as widespread in this province as they are in Tenerife, with extensive numbers of English, Germans, Indians, Koreans, Japanese and Scandinavians in Gran Canaria and limited numbers of English and Germans on Lanzarote and Fuerteventura. Although tourism really started on Tenerife, the islands of Lanzarote and Gran Canaria in particular have more than made up for lost time.

Gran Canaria: The third largest of the Canary Islands (592 sq miles, 1,532 sq km), Gran Canaria, which has a population of approximately 600,000, is often described as a miniature continent because it has everything; its capital, Las Palmas, the seat of Canarian govern-

'receding ages: the 'laya :anteras ·each in Las 'almas; :esar Aanrique, anzarote's elebrated ırtist and ırchitect; ;ran ;anaria's entral nountains. .eft, ıgriculture lominates ;ountry ives. Right, .as Palmas.

ment, is a major city on any terms, with a major port, major airport, major traffic problem, extensive areas of slums, of elegance, of shopping, of tourism and an active red light area. The city (population 355,000) has a sea frontage of over six miles (9.6 km) in length, and a reputation for being one of the worst cities in Spain for drug addiction and drug-pushing.

The port and the airport were once major stepping-stones between the continents of Europe, Africa and South America, but now that aircraft have longer ranges and that the steamship days are over, the levels of transit traffic have decreased, to be replaced by charter holidaymaking traffic.

Notable in Las Palmas are Las Canteras, the sea-front promenade of the capital city's own resort, one of the oldest on the island and the most popular with Spaniards themselves, and Vegueta, the old quarter of the city where the aristocrats once lived and where they built in Spanish colonial style. The cathedral, Columbus' house and museum are also located here, although some local historians (from Tenerife province) maintain that Columbus never set foot in Las Palmas.

Surrounding the capital are various semi-industrial areas for warehousing, assembly and manufacturing, and visitors will have to travel some miles down the southeast coast before getting clear of the sprawl. This coast, with major towns like Agüimes and Telde inland, away from the arid heat of sea-level and the danger from pirates, is not appealing to the eye. Half-way down and slightly inland is the Barranco Guayadeque, a long ravine honeycombed with caves which have proved a treasure trove of Guanche remains.

In the south the developments around Playa del Inglés (which alone has 350 restaurants and 50 discos) and Maspalomas make a continuous belt of urbanisation, with some apartments a considerable distance from the sea. As recently as 1963 a guide book author noted that Maspalomas was about to get itself a "new town of hotels which will take away some of the wildness from this

KASBAH

comparatively remote spot." It most certainly has.

Tourism has taken root in the south because of the sun and sand (notably the famous dunes at Maspalomas, now isolated in front of a belt of development), but there's little on the neighbouring hinterland of real interest, which is why the southern shore was never inhabited in the first place. Further round the coast the smaller resorts of Puerto Rico and Mógan, however, are more attractive and consequently more upmarket.

Beyond Mógan the west coast becomes a wild and difficult place to live, with most inhabitants pursuing their original livelihoods of fishing or agriculture. In the northwest the two attractive towns of Agaete and Galdar are very active in the island's cultural life, with festivals and guanche remains.

Inland Gran Canaria has a landscape to rival the best of Tenerife, with patches of ancient forest and a cluster of peaks rising to 6,496 ft (1,980 metres) at Pico de las Nieves. There is an excellent view of the central summits from Cruz de Tejeda, where the island's *parador* (now a restaurant) is situated. Gran Canaria's most distinctive peaks are the Roques Bentaiga and Nublo, which appear on most of the mountainscape postcards.

In these inland areas many of the islanders live in caves, as their Guanche forefathers did, particularly in Artenara and Atalaya, although most have been so altered from the exterior that it is difficult to distinguish cave houses from more conventional ones. The precipitous roads around these areas are not for the driver with vertigo, although they are now made more reliably than they were 25 years ago, when a guidebook author advised motorists not to "drive too near the edge of the road, which may be left soft."

The elegant, the aristocratic, and the foreigners on Gran Canaria tend to live either in the Garden City in Las Palmas, which divides the old Vegueta district from the port and resort area in the north, or up in the hills behind Las Palmas around the villages of Tafira

Preceding pages: Playa del Inglés. Below, fishing boat in Mogán.

and Santa Brigida. Some of the best restaurants and most atmospheric hotels are found here, and many are a legacy from an era when the British dominated trade and industry.

Lanzarote: The fourth largest of the seven islands (307 sq miles, 795 sq km), Lanzarote has a population of 50,000 and a landscape which is something of an acquired taste. It has, however, attracted a surprising number of artists of various sorts who now live on the island.

At the wrong times of year, when the light is sluggish and the ground dead (the little planted greenery is often partly shielded from the intense sun), the island looks like what it is, the scab of an old volcanic wound, still bubbling hot, red and raw underneath. At other times there are moments of rare beauty in this landscape, where the earthly colours and sparse, minimal features come together in a memorable way. They say that the islanders paint their windows and doors green to compensate for the lack of it in the landscape.

You have to admire the ingenuity with which the islanders have made use of their volcanic landscape; they pile up lava and paint it white for houses, flatten it for roads, make walls of it for fields, powder it for sand for beaches, and use volcanic ash instead of earth, growing a surprising quantity of vegetables, farming in lava is not an easy task, but it is achieved on Lanzarote.

The prickly pear cactus is widespread on the island, either growing wild or hosting colonies of cochineal beetle (in a kind of white dust on the side of the plant) which is used as a food dye; once a major industry, cochineal export died almost completely with the introduction of synthetic colourings, and now staggers on only for the benefit of a few consumers all over the world who for one reason or another prefer their food colourings to be natural.

Lanzarote is a major success story of the new tourism on the Canaries, attracting a more peace-loving, higher-spending visitor who appreciates the finer things in resorts. They say that the

eavy ing: rmers till nzarote's va.

idea for the very successful British TV series *Eastenders* was dreamed up here by a couple of BBC men who were taking a winter break.

Part of the influence in the appeal of an island that has no real immediate beauty is the work of resident artist and Lanzarote native César Manrique, who has been personally responsible for some of the more memorable features such as cave conversions (Jameos del Agua and Cuevas de los Verdes), museums and viewpoint restaurants (Castillo de San Gabriel and Mirador del Rio), and who has always maintained a high profile on the low profile of tourist urbanisation: as a result, nearly all developments are no more than two storeys in height, and many conform to some sort of local style. The exception is the capital city of Arrecife itself, which Manrique condemns as an urban disaster, and which has no appeal for the temporary visitor.

Spain has nine national parks, no fewer than four of which are in the Canaries. One of these, and perhaps the most unusual, is that of Timanfaya, the massive wasteland on Lanzarote created by volcanic eruptions between 1730 and 1736. In Timanfaya the *mal-pais* or badlands are so bad that barely a patch of moss or film of lichen manages to grow, and the park area is littered with the twisted, solidified rock that spewed out of the Montañas del Fuego, the fire mountains. The park rangers give dramatic and much photographed demonstrations of the continuing power of the earth, and the park's restaurant (El Diablo) cooks with volcanic heat. Camels are the best form of transport over the sharp, rugged terrain, and extensive camel trains of tourists trail over the sides of the mountains.

Fuerteventura: If Lanzarote is not everyone's cup of tea, there is even less to look at in Fuerteventura, the second largest island (668 sq miles, 1,731 sq km) with a tiny population of 25,000. If you are something of a desert connoisseur then this is the island for you. Like neighbouring Lanzarote, Fuerteventura does not have the height to be able to

Fuerteventura's barren landscape

prod the passing clouds into disposing of some of their water, and years pass with little more than a single miserable shower of rain.

The island used to be more prosperous and its higher land was once wooded with palms, but over the last few centuries the climate has become increasingly unkind. The economy (a fragile one) is based on goats, tourists from Germany and the military. The capital city of Puerto del Rosario, which surrounds the port, is straggling and unattractive. Inland, the ancient city of Betancuria is little more than a hamlet.

Most of the resort areas (Fuerteventura has the best and most extensive beaches of all the Canaries) are either on the northern tip at Corralejo, where there are two large hotels, or on the southern Jandia peninsula. The Jandia peninsula was at one time separated from the rest of the island by a wall, La Pared, erected by the original Guanche kings. This southern part of the island was isolated again during and after World War II, when it was given by General Franco to a German, who built an airstrip and excluded all *majoreros* (Fuerteventura islanders). Rumours about what actually went on behind that wall are still circulating.

Fuerteventura is the home of the Spanish Sahara Armed Forces, the Spanish Foreign Legion, who are on the island both because it affords good training space and because Fuerteventura is closest to that area of Africa that used to be known as the Spanish Sahara, and which is now the discontented property of Morocco. The soldiers, who can be unruly at times, are not much liked by the *majoreros*.

There are plans afoot to build what is said to be the biggest resort in the world on Fuerteventura, and if the island had had its own water supply that resort would probably already be under way. As it is, Fuerteventura remains an austere isle, and the *majoreros*' diet is still based on *gofio* (ground maize) and his main preoccupations are his goats, his dogs, and the occasional bit of wrestling and stick-fighting as entertainment.

oatherd in a Oliva, uerte- entura's ncient wn.

Going To Africa

Although politically part of Spain since the early 16th century, the Canary Islands are geographically part of north-west Africa. This is particularly true of Fuerteventura, the second island of the archipelago in size and the closest to the African coast—just 60 miles (100 km) away. It and, to a lesser extent, the other islands are geologically similar to the desert regions and Atlas mountains of the north and west of Africa.

Unsurprisingly, therefore, many of the customs and even the physique of the islands' first inhabitants, the Guanches, are closely related to the indigenous inhabitants of what is nowadays Morocco, Algeria and Mauritania. Theories abound concerning the original settlers, but it is believed that a Berber tribe, possibly one known as the Canarii, came to the islands from North Africa 6,000 years ago following the decay of local regions of forest and vegetation.

This belief is supported by the appearance of the Guanches and the Canarii, (tall and with a fair complexion), the similarity of language and symbols, worship and burial habits, animal and crop husbandry, tools and weapons.

However, the Canarian Stone Age ended in 1496, with the conquest of Guanche Tenerife by the Spanish under Alonso Fernández de Lugo (the latter's first attempt to subdue the natives of Tenerife failed at the village of La Matanza, "the massacre", but succeeded three years later at what is now appropriately called La Victoria).

With the Canaries firmly under Spanish control—the vanquished Guanches were even baptised and given Christian names—contact with Africa largely disappeared as the axis shifted 700 miles (1,100 km) northwards to Cadiz and Seville in southern Spain. It was not long, however, before the conquistadores were annexing parts of Africa for the Spanish Empire; Ceuta and Melilla, enclaves on the north coast of Morocco still governed today from Madrid as well as Spanish Sahara, a vast area of desert over 100,000 sq miles (280,000 km), ceded by Spain to Morocco in the mid-1970s.

Since then Morocco, Mauritania and the Polisario Front have been arguing about—among other things—who should have the right to mine the rich phosphate deposits near El Aiún, the former capital of the Spanish Sahara.

Hopefully gone are the days when Moroccan gunboats machine-gunned Spanish (especially Canarian) fishing boats which strayed too close to the Moroccan coastline. Only recently have relations improved sufficiently between Spain and Morocco for official regular sea and air communications to be re-established.

Getting there: Royal Air Maroc and Iberia are the main air carriers. From Las Palmas de Gran Canaria (airport Gando) RAM has flights to Agadir (Wednesdays), Casablanca (Mondays, Wednesdays and Fridays), Marrakesh (Wednesdays), Oujda (Wednesdays) and Tan Tan (Fridays).

The Spanish state airline, Iberia, operates to Abidjan on the Ivory Coast on Sundays, to Dakar in Senegal every Monday and Friday and to Melilla each Monday, Friday, Saturday and Sunday. All these flights operate from Tenerife South airport (Reina Sofía).

From Las Palmas de Gran Canaria Iberia has departures to Dakar on Mondays, Wednesdays and Fridays; to Abidjan on Sundays; to Melilla every day of the week except Tuesdays and Wednesdays; to Nouakchott in Mauritania each Tuesday, Thursday and Saturday; and to Noudhibou in Mauritania, on Tuesdays and Saturdays. Royal Air Maroc also operates flights to Abidjan, to Libreville in Gabon and Malabo in Equatorial Guinea, all on a Sunday and all departing from Gando airport in Gran Canaria.

So much for flying there. The only regular passenger boat service (some cargo boats have limited passenger accommodation but are infrequent) is by Compañía Marroquí de Navegación with its car ferry *Rif* sailing weekly Las

receding ages: a wn in the ades alley, orocco; in mosque in orocco. eft, the eckoning harms of frica. ollowing age, late fternoon vents on e Djemma Fna begin.

Palmas-Agadir-Las Palmas, the one-way journey taking 18 hours. The company hopes that it will be able to extend this service to other ports on the Moroccan coast soon.

Further information on this can be obtained in Las Palmas from Guillermo Sintes Reyes SA Calle Artemi Semidan N. 11, 3rd floor (Tel. 277153/277208/274114); in Agadir—Comanav, Boulevard Mohamed V, BP 201 (Tel. (8) 20446/20452/20646); in Casablanca—Comanav Casablanca, 7 Boulevard de la Résistance (Tel. 302412/301825); in Paris—SNCM Paris, 12 rue Godot de Mauroy 75009 (Tel. (1) 4266-6019); or through Viajes Martin Travel Las Palmas Tel. 222500/04/08; Puerto de la Cruz, Tenerife Tel. 387209/387112/387197; Puerto del Carmen, Lanzarote Tel. 825925/826527; and finally in Fuerteventura Tel. 876326/876349.

Travel wisdom: Briefly, the places mentioned have something to recommend to those wanting a holiday with a difference, but take care with money and valuables (as always) especially in potentially dangerous places such as the densely crowded alleys and the markets or *souks*.

Geographically the nearest to the Canaries, Morocco is probably the likeliest destination with Marrakesh, Casablanca, Agadir and El Aiún on travel agents' lists for short package holidays. But further afield, Dakar in Senegal, Libreville in Gabon, Abidjan on the Ivory Coast and Malabo in Equatorial Guinea are worth visiting and can easily be reached by air either from Tenerife or Las Palmas.

Coming from northwest Africa to the Canaries are three unwelcome visitors. Locusts, fortunately, are infrequent and short-lived, although recent years have seen an increase in their numbers; the *Scirocco* (fine wind-borne sand and dust) which covers everything, even indoors, and which visits the islands four or five times a year, and lasts between a day and a week; the *Calina*, sand in suspension, is also an African export and hangs heavily over the islands for periods of up to several days, seriously limiting visibility.

HEADLINES AND BAR GOSSIP

The late 1980s have been untypical in so far as items in the news are concerned. Politics are not the islander's favourite topic in the press or in conversation, but in the late 80s political issues surfaced more often in the newspapers than usual because of a resurgence of inter-province rivalry. The debate was prompted by Gran Canaria's intention to have its own University rather than share the only regional Universidad de la Laguna, established in Tenerife in 1774.

Tinerfeños believe that a second university in such a small region is not only unnecessary but detrimental, as the cost of two universities in the Canary Islands will impoverish both. The issue caused a change of presidents in the Canary Islands Autonomous Government and a major political crisis. This issue might yet cause a split of the present single Canary Islands Government into two separate Autonomous Governments—a really ridiculous situation.

Media: The average islander does not read the newspapers at all. Literacy is not all that high and perhaps only 38 percent of the population reads a newspaper, and even less a book.

How many of the population watch television and listen to the radio is difficult to assess, but almost certainly the vast majority gather news from those media alone. The island newspapers do not attempt to compete for international news with the mainland press. Those interested enough in the latter subject buy *El Pais*, a bulky daily flown in from Madrid and even so costing less than the local papers.

Major international events are reported in the local press, but in succinct form usually on an inner page. All papers devote more space to local sports—wrestling, basketball and especially soccer. Bull-fighting is not included for the simple reason that it no longer takes place on these islands, having given way to soccer, and being too expensive to arrange.

Festivals of every sort and kind, be they village or town affairs or the hugely important *Carnaval* are a favourite topic of conversation, covered extensively by the press. *Carnaval* exceeds all else in terms of column-inches, in daily reports and special supplements, before, during and after the annual event. The time, effort and money spent on *Carnaval* in these islands is enormous. If the same effort was expended on business or industrial activity the Canaries would probably be top of the EEC's economic league.

Preceding pages: shepherdess; chewing over the latest. Left, swapping views in Puerto de la Cruz. Right, potato prices are much discussed.

Bar talk: The topics of conversations in bars depend on the type of bar and its location. In the wine shops or *ventas* in the country districts it is probable that the potato crop will be the most frequent topic. Potatoes of many excellent varieties are grown here and harvested up to four times a year, and the subject comes up in conversations in unexpected places, such as ladies' hairdressing salons, elegant dinner tables and cocktail parties. *Papas* and their prices are discussed in the latter places as ardently as stock prices in the City of London.

In more sophisticated places such as *tapas* bars in Santa Cruz or Las Palmas you might hear the latest jokes about Gomerans, the undeserved butt of jokes, rather as are the Irish in the UK and the Belgians in Europe. "Why does a Gomeran keep an empty bottle in his fridge? To cater for visitors who do not drink." Or "Why is cold milk not available on Gomera? Because the Gomeran cannot fit his cow into his refrigerator".

The name of a recent cabinet minister gave rise to a constant string of Moronic/Moranic jokes told amongst the more educated society. One concerned his reply to a journalist's question about the Israeli position at an international conference in Madrid; the minister said it gave his wife hiccups.

One might expect tourism to be a frequent subject of conversation or press comment amongst the inhabitants of these tourist-supported islands. Travel agents, hotel managers or car hire operators may discuss the matter, but the general public seldom bothers with the topic unless it is to comment upon the latest barbarity committed by the lager louts in Playa de las Américas or Playa del Inglés. The newspapers carry occasional statistics on visitors to the islands—a continual breaking of records. Timeshare, which seems to be considered to have negative effects on the tourist trade because all payments are made outside the islands, is a fairly frequent topic.

The break-down of nationalities visiting the islands is often reported in the press. It may surprise many British visitors who feel themselves heavily outnumbered by Germans, (the latter somehow manage to get into the hotel lifts and swimming pool sunbeds first) that they, the Brits, outnumber the Germans and other nationalities by a considerable margin in all the islands except Fuerteventura, where the Germans win.

Crime: Drugs, robberies and traffic accidents are frequent, if not daily issues in the newspapers. These islands, because of their Free Port status and their strategic position are naturally attractive to the drug dealers. The large number of foreign visitors and Spain's very lenient anti-drug laws are other attractions for the dealers—almost amounting to an invitation. In one court case in Tenerife a young English heroin addict called the islands "Heroin Paradise" which, thank God, it is not.

Theft is commonplace here, especially in those urbanisations with numerous temporarily absent foreign residents. The police tend to get bored with so many reports and with catching the same delinquents at regular intervals.

There has been a very steep rise in the number of fatal traffic accidents over the last two or three years as also in the number of vehicles on the road (7,000 new cars every month). The roads themselves are quite good; it is speed, inexperience, drink or drugs that causes most of these fatal accidents, occurring usually during the early hours of weekend mornings. In Tenerife alone, 140 people, most of them under 25, died in car and motorcycle accidents in 1988, a frightful figure for a small population.

Environment: The poorly-understood subject of ecology comes up when new urbanisations or hotel buildings begin—a pretty frequent occurrence in the south of Tenerife and Gran Canaria these days. It is also a topic when, with unwelcome regularity each summer, forest fires break out in the lovely forests of Gomera, La Palma, Tenerife or Gran Canaria. Many hundreds of hectares of pine forest have been ravaged by fires in the last few years, and a big one in Gomera in 1984 claimed the lives of 21 people, including the newly appointed Civil Governor of Tenerife Province who, tragically, put politics before safety.

The only satisfactory outcome of these disastrous fires is that they increase membership in the ecological groups.

While the development of a barren, arid wasteland in the south of an island might cause an uproar of protest, nothing is said, and far less is done to stop the uncontrolled, unplanned and unlicensed construction of cement-block houses on the fringes of towns and villages on all the islands. Politics is the reason why a blind eye is turned to these real eyesores on the landscape, as more residents mean more votes for the councillor who looks the other way.

Left, auctioning stall space for *Carnaval*. Above, the roads are good, but the drivers may not be.

Separatism: Independence is a word appearing often in the newspapers and in graffiti messages sprayed on walls. Its meaning is often misunderstood by visitors who see it as a desire on the part of the islanders to separate from Mother Spain. There does exist a small group of radicals who desire complete independence from Spain on ethnic grounds. This group was originally represented by MPAIC established in 1963, today calling itself AWANAK, whose initials translate roughly as "The Canary Islands Popular Front" written in the ancient Guanche language.

The symbol or logo-type displayed by this party is the spiral labyrinth, and this can sometimes be seen accompanying a written invitation to *godos* (the nickname for the Peninsular Spaniard) to go back to the mainland. The uninitiated visitor who thinks he's in Spain is completely bewildered when he sees an occasional message written in English which says "Spanish Go Home".

The other meaning of independence, used in the title of some local political parties, is independence from any of the main peninsula-based parties such as the Spanish Labour Party (PSOE), the alliance of Conservative parties (AP), the Liberal Party, or the left-of-centre Social Democrat party (CDS).

The Association of Independents of Tenerife (ATI), of Canary Independents (ACI), and of the independents from Hierro, are not separatists. They want to establish their own identities in the same way as the Catalans, Basques, and Andalucians.

A final warning to innocent visitors to these islands (and to mainland Spain for that matter): beware of the newspapers and stories you may read or hear on 28 December, the day of the Holy Innocents. This is Spain's April Fool's Day, when the newspapers publish elaborate or dramatic reports on their front pages which need to be taken with a pinch or two of salt.

WATER

"These islands enjoy a fortunate climate in consequence of the barely perceptible change of the seasons. "

Plutarch, *Life of Sertontus*

The western group of the Canary Islands are more fortunate than their eastern neighbours in that they receive triple the amount of natural water. Supplies come from three sources: rain, snow—which covers the slopes of El Teide on Tenerife for about five months per year—and moisture from the clouds collected by the vegetation on the upper regions of all four islands in the western province.

Water from these three sources soaks through into underground natural deposits, although about 80 percent is lost by run-offs to the sea or by evaporation. And in contrast to the eastern group there are no water desalination plants, as yet, in the western islands.

Water is extracted by two methods. Firstly, by blasting *galerias* or tunnels horizontally into the mountainsides, aimed at the underground deposits. This method began in 1860 and today there are about 940 *galerias* on Tenerife alone, measuring a total of 1,300 miles (2,000 kms). Visible evidence of these tunnels are the mounds of excavated rock at the mouths of the *galerias*, which are usually about five feet (1.5 metres) in diameter and are commonly accompanied by a small square building housing a simple water distribution device.

The second method, begun in 1925, is the drilling of vertical wells aimed at the same underground deposits.

In addition to these man-made taps, nature has provided a few springs, which are found at various levels on the islands where water encounters an impermeable layer of rock. The volume of water from these springs decreases in the summer and they are seldom visible from the roads.

At present all water on the Canary Islands is produced and owned by private enterprise. Municipalities contract to buy their requirements from owners and distribute to individual consumers who are charged on a metered basis. Irrigation water is also sold by water companies or individual owners and is distributed via standard-sized pipes or open channels, for an agreed number of hours per day, week or month, according to contract. It is measured in *pipas*, each *pipa* being equal to 480 litres or 105 gallons. Each hour of water down one of these channels equals 100 *pipas* or 10,500 gallons (48,000 litres).

Water for irrigation is stored in open tanks, visible all over the islands, and filled from *galerias* or wells. The agreed amounts must be released from the holding tank on the given time and day, in order to avoid overflow, even if it is raining.

Water and political power: The private ownership and production of water recently became a hot political issue when in 1985 the Spanish Parliament in Madrid promulgated a new Water Law, replacing that of 1879. In spite of general local opposition to this law in the Canaries, where very many owners of water are small humble farmers, the Canary Islands Autonomous Government, dominated at that time by the Socialist Party,

Preceding pages: water is central to fruitful fields. Left, underground water in an old well. Right, most properties have their own supply.

approved the new law.

In June 1987, after a statutory four year term, a General Election was held throughout Spain. In the Canary Islands, as a direct consequence of the unpopular Water Law, the Socialist Party was voted out of office. The newly elected, centre-right government promptly suspended the new law, proposing new water legislation which has still not appeared at the time of writing.

But besides the affairs of politicians and costs of the water supply, the more immediate problem concerns quality rather than quantity. In the Orotava Valley of Tenerife, one of the areas of heaviest usage, a few wells have been closed due to pollution. On

this side of the island an excess of natural fluor in the water has caused problems to teeth, especially in young children, and in the south certain areas suffer from brackish water of disagreeable taste. Visitors and residents can take comfort from the fact that the authorities apply strict health controls on domestic water, but even so it remains a wise precaution to drink only from bottled water.

On the smaller islands: La Palma has the greatest rainfall in the Canaries with an average of 25 inches (64 cms) per year, earning it the title "Isla Verde"—Green Island. Water on La Palma comes mostly from ga*lerias* with a few supplementary wells. An exceptional feature are the various streams in the great Caldera de Taburiente.

Gomera, from whence water was taken by Columbus to bless America, still obtains its water from wells—there are only three *galerias*. An important contribution comes from the exuberant forests from the upper regions of the island where wild laurel trees and giant briar shrubs condense astonishing amounts of water from the clouds all year.

Hierro, the most westerly and least developed of the islands has the most complicated and the quaintest sources of water. Because of the extreme porosity of the terrain, water can only be recovered from wells at sea level, from where it is pumped up to towns and villages high up on the island. Accordingly water cisterns, some quite ancient, are to be found all over the island. Most have wooden lids provided with a hole just large enough to admit a bottle on a string, and custom allows passers-by to fill one bottle—a relic of the kindly consideration of former times.

Hierro also has an ancient medicinal spring Pozo de la Salud—the "Well of Health" at Sabinosa, whose waters are believed to produce cures for a variety of ailments. The "Holy" or "Fountain" tree of Hierro, called the Garoë by pre-Hispanic inhabitants, was once famous for its water-producing qualities. George Glas, writing in 1764, tells how "its leaves constantly distil such a quantity of water as is sufficient to furnish drink to every living creature in Hierro, nature having provided this remedy for the drought of the island". And nature today, assisted by the Spanish Conservation of Nature Institute (ICONA) continues to provide this "remedy for the living creatures of Hierro". Basins of stone have been placed by ICONA near the roadside at Los Aljibes de Binto, where trees in the cloud belt distil quantities of fresh, clear water—as many as 220 gallons (1,000 litres) in just one night. In the future the fast development of tourism in the south of Tenerife will require sea water desalination plants, if only to distil brackish water and keep the golf courses green.

Because of drip-feed methods and shrinking areas of cultivation agriculture will survive on natural water for years to come.

Left, Tenerife's rivers are rarely more than trickles, but (right) the woods of Gomera are water-rich.

RECOLLECTIONS OF A HAPPY MONTH

Marianne North, artist, spinster and traveller, spent much of her life roaming the wilder parts of the world, recording its natural history in a remarkable series of paintings now housed in the Marianne North gallery in Kew Gardens in London. In 1875 she visited Tenerife. She recalled her impressions of the month she spent on the island in her two-volume autobiography, "Recollections of a Happy Life", published in 1892. Here we reprint part of that autobiography, and some of her paintings.

On the morning of the 13th we landed at Santa Cruz. We drove on the same day to Villa de Orotava, creeping slowly up the long zigzags leading to Laguna, where everyone (who is anybody) goes to spend the hot summer months; in the New Year's time it was quite deserted, and looked as if every other house was a defunct convent. All had a most magnificent yellow stone-crop on their roofs, just then in full beauty; ferns too were on all the walls, with euphorbias and other prickly things.

After passing Laguna, we came on a richer country, and soon to the famous view of the Peak, described so exquisitely by Humboldt; but, alas, the palms and other trees had been cleared away to make room for the ugly terraces of cacti, grown for the cochineal insect to feed on, and which did not like the shade of other trees.

Some of the terraces were apparently yielding crops of white paper bun-bags. On investigating I found they were white rags, which had been first spread over the trays of cochineal eggs, when the newly-hatched insect had crawled out and adhered to them; they are pinned over the cactus leaves by means of the spines of another sort of cactus grown for the purpose. After a few days of sunshine the little insect gets hungry and fixes itself on the fleshy leaf; then the rags are pulled off, washed, and put over another set of trays.

The real cochineal cactus had had its spines so constantly pulled off by angry natives who object to having their clothes torn, that it sees no use in growing them any longer, and has hardly any. When I was in Tenerife people were beginning to say that the gas-colours had taken all their trade away, and had begun to root the cactus up and plant tobacco instead, but they could not re-grow the fine trees.

These cactus crops did other damage to the island. The lazy cultivators when replanting it, left the old plants to rot on the walls

Preceding pages: Teide and the north coast. Left and right, Marianne North's lifelong enthusiasm was for painting natural history.

instead of burning them, thereby causing fever to rage in places where fever had never been before.

The roads were very bare, and the much-talked-of Peak with its snow cap was spoiled for beauty by the ugly straight line of the Hog's Back on this southern side. Nevertheless the long slant down to the deep blue sea was exceedingly beautiful, and a certain number of date-palms and dragon-trees, as well as the euphoria and other fleshy plants, gave a peculiar character to the scene I have not seen elsewhere.

We found there was a hotel (and not a very bad one either, in its own Spanish fashion), and we got possession of its huge ball-room, which was full of crockery and looking-glasses, and some hundred chairs all piled up on the top of one another. This room had glass doors, besides other rooms opening into it, but served to sleep in well enough; and I determined to stay and make the best of it, for the climate and views were quite perfect. I did stay more than a month.

The people at Orotava were most friendly, the gardens lovely. The nobles who owned them were of the very bluest blood of old Spain; but not rich—they seldom went out of the island, and had kept all their old habits and fashions. The ladies walked about in mantillas, flirting their fans, and wore no

other costume even at their evening receptions, merely adding some jewels, and flowers stuck most becomingly behind their ears. They had no education beyond what they got in some convent, but were thorough ladies. One old lady seemed to reign supreme amongst them—the Marchesa della Florida. She was good enough to take me under her protection, and even asked me to come and stop in her house; but I valued my time too much to try such an experiment.

Dr Hooker had given me a letter to the Swiss manager of the Botanic Gardens, who also kept a grocer's shop. He was very kind in taking me to see all the most lovely gardens. The famous Dragon Tree, which Humboldt said was 4,000 years old, had tumbled into a mere dust-heap, nothing but a few bits of bark remaining; but it had some very fine successors about the island, and some of them had curious air roots hanging from the upper branches near the trunk, which spread themselves gradually round the surface, till they recoated the poor tree, which had been continually bled to procure the dye called Dragon's Blood. When the good people found my hobby for painting strange plants, they sent me all kinds of beautiful specimens.

The landlady gave me a smaller room opening into the big room with a good view into the street, where I could live in peace and quiet, without fear of interruption and they fed me there very kindly too. Any one who likes bread and chocolate can live well all over Spain; I did not care if I got nothing else. My friend the gardener arranged with the farmer at the Barenca da Castro to take me in for three day; so I took some bread and a pillow, mounted my donkey, and rode thither through lovely lanes, mounting over the high cliffs till I came to my destination—an old manor-house on the edge of one of those curious lava cracks which run down to the edge of the sea, filled with large oaks, sweet bay-trees, and heath-trees thirty feet high. Half-way down was a stratum of limestone, from which a most delicious spring burst out.

The ground was covered with sweet violets. There were green beds of water-cresses all about the sweet clear pools on the little theatre of green at the mouth of the cave, and then some pretty falls to the lava rocks on the beach some thousand feet below. People and animals were always coming and going, and were very picturesque. The men wore high top-boots, blankets gathered in round their necks, and huge Rubens hats. The women had bright-coloured shawls draped gracefully over their heads and shoulders, with red and black petticoats; sometimes hats on the top of their shawl-covered heads. They were all most friendly.

My quarters at the old house above were very primitive. A great barn-like room was given up to me, with heaps of potatoes and

Left, Dragon trees in the garden of Mr Smith. Right, still life, flowers and cochineal cactus.

corn swept up into the corners of it. I had a stretcher-bed at one end, on which I got a very large allowance of good sleep. The cocks and hens roosted on the beams overhead and I heard my donkey and other beasts munching their food and snoring below. From the unglazed window I had a magnificent view of the Peak, which I could paint at my leisure at sunrise without disturbing any one. The family much enjoyed seeing me cook my supper and breakfast—coffee, eggs, and soup; soup; eggs, and coffee, alternately. I returned by a lower road, close to the edge of the sea, under cliffs covered with sedums, cinerarias, and other plants peculiar to the Canary Islands.

I stopped a while at the Rambla de Castra, on the sea-shore, standing almost in the sea, surrounded by palms, bamboos, and great *Caladium esculentum*. It was a lovely spot, but too glaring. After this little excursion I remained quietly working in or about Orotava till the 17th of February, when I moved down to Mr Smith's comfortable home at Puerto de Orotava. Mr Smith when I stayed with him had a second wife, a most lovable Scotchwoman. He was 70 years old, and talked quite calmly of taking me up the Peak, not minding 15 hours on horseback; but the weather fortunately remained too cool for such an attempt. I believe he knew every stone on the way, and had shown it to Piazzi Smyth and all the travellers one after the other. The latter gave me a letter to him.

I had a room on the roof with a separate staircase down to the lovely garden, and learned to know every plant in that exquisite collection. There were myrtle-trees 10 or 12 feet high, bougainvilleas running up cypress-trees (Mrs S used to complain of their untidiness), great white lancifolium lilies (or something like them), growing high as myself. The ground was white with fallen orange and lemon petals; and the huge white cherokee roses covered a great arbour and tool-house with their magnificent flowers. I never smelt roses so sweet as those in that garden. Over all peeped the snowy point of the Peak, at sunrise and sunset most gorgeous, but even more dazzling in the moonlight. From the garden I could stroll up some wild hills of lava, where Mr S had allowed the natural vegetation of the island to have all its own way.

Magnificent aloes, cactus, euphorbias, arums, cinerarias, sedums, heaths, and other peculiar plants were to be seen in their fullest beauty. Eucalyptus-trees had been planted on the top, and were doing well, with their bark hanging in rags and tatters about them. I scarcely ever went out without finding some new wonder to paint, lived a life of the most perfect peace and happiness, and got strength every day with my kind friends.

The town of Puerto was just below the house, and had once been a thriving place, some English merchants having settled there. Now only a few half-bred children remained, entirely Spanish in education and ways, though they talked their fathers' tongue after their fashion. I went off with a donkey-boy and a couple of donkeys for a week to Echod (Icod), all along the coast, sometimes high, sometimes low, with fresh views of the Peak up every crack. At Echod there is the best view of all; and a few miles above that place are forests of the Canary pine, which is something like the Weymouth, with very fine needles, but drawn up into slender trees of 100 or more feet high.

Echod is a lovely old place, full of fine big houses, with exquisite views up and down; but it rained most of the time. The Marchesa de la Florida had written to her cousin the Count of Sta Lucia, who took me to see some fine coast-views, and insisted on walking arm-in-arm over ploughed fields and slippery pavements at an angle of 45 degrees, much to my embarrassment.

Some other grandees, with terribly long strings of names, were most hospitable, showed me their beautiful villas and gardens at Corronel and Gorachico, (Garachico), and even pressed me to stay. The latter place is built on glacier of black lava, and the next eruption will probably send the whole town into the sea. It was one of the most frightful bits of volcanic scenery I ever saw. The day I was there was wintry and dark with storm-clouds; the white waves ran in between the dark rocks, and sent up great jets of foam with an awful crashing and roaring.

Santa Cruz, to which I at first took a dislike, I found full of beauty. Its gardens were lovely, and its merchants most hospitable. I stayed there till the *Ethiopia* picked me up, on the 29th of April.

Right, the peak, with bananas and date palms in the foreground.

THE CANARIAN DOG

About 2,000 years ago a galley loaded with explorers from Roman Mauritania reached Gran Canaria. The explorers found a fertile land with soaring mountains and exotic flowers and trees.... and dogs such as they had never seen before.

Dogs everywhere—slender, sinuous, tiger-striped. Dogs that were wild but not savage, intelligent, beautiful to look at, easy to train and quick to obey.

The explorers chose a pair of pups and took them back to King Juba II of Mauritania. The boy-king Juba had been educated in Rome and had returned home with a thirst for discovery which brought him fame, and it was he and his people who put the Canary Islands onto the map of the world with a name that has never changed—the island of *canes*, of dogs.

This theory of the naming of the islands is the most widely accepted by historians and scholars through the ages, starting with the Roman naturalist Pliny. There are other, less attractive theories. Thomas Nichols, the first Englishman to describe the islands, suggests that the islanders actually lived on dog flesh. Historian Francisco Gomara says there were no dogs at all when the conquistadores came from Spain, and that the island was named after a red grape *uva canina*.

The 19th-century Spanish writer and naturalist Viera y Clavijo had two theories; first, that the vassals of the Italian kings, Cranus and Crana, settled in one of the islands and named it Cranaria. His second was that Canarias derived its name from the Latin verbs *canere* or *cantare*, to sing, and that canary birds are thus responsible for the islands' naming. In addition many archaeologists now believe the name of the island group comes from a North African tribe, the Canarii, from whom the islanders are descended.

An awesome creature: The Canary mastiff, known as the Verdino (also called the Bardino, the letters V and B being almost interchangeable in Spanish) because of its green shading (*Verde* = green), has probably been on the islands for 2,000 years. It is presently an unregistered breed, although the Spanish Kennel Club has recognised it and is setting standards by which to judge a true specimen.

The Verdino is a rustic, smooth-haired, heavy guard-type dog with a broad jaw, usually brindle coloured in stripes, or sometimes golden with white flashes on the chest. It weighs in at between 90 and 110 lbs (40 and 50 kilos). At its best it is an awesome creature of obvious strength and it has all the characteristics of a dog which has for centuries been assisting man in all manner of agricultural work; it is affectionate to known friends, highly faithful, but also highly territorial.

Left and right, man and his dog, ancient and modern.

Whether or not the dogs so admired by King Juba were true Verdinos is open to discussion. Certainly there were other dogs on the islands, and that of Fuerteventura has its own tradition, being commonly longer and leaner in the body and faster across the ground. Every major incoming influence since has brought with it more dogs; the conquistadores imported their own favourites, and the preponderance of small lap-dogs and variations on a Pekinese theme in the streets of Puerto de la Cruz on Tenerife are descendents of the sofa dogs brought out to Puerto by holidaying ladies of gentility earlier this century.

Despite all these influences and cross-breeds the Verdino is championed as the true Canarian dog unique to the islands, possibly because it is yet another symbol of the independence of the islands from the mainland.

Dr Luis Felipe Jurado, professor of the La Laguna (Tenerife) veterinary faculty of the university, has studied the Verdino for many years. He accepts the Juba theory of the naming of the islands, and is convinced that the dogs preceeded men on the Canaries. How did they get here? On rafts from Africa, he theorises; not man-made ones but great storm-knarled platforms of fallen trees and bushes that drifted here after floods in the rivers of the mainland.

Dogs of prey: However they came, whenever they came, history accepts the Verdino as an integral part of the islands' past and a sad one at times. The conquistadores so feared these animals that in Tenerife they condemned most of them to death, allowing each shepherd only one to guard his flock.

This law, issued in May 1499, must have been glaringly ignored by the islanders, judging by the number of times it was made public and the fines that were imposed. Offenders faced being scourged, but they continued to keep and protect their precious dogs. However, with many of the original islanders dead as a result of conquest, some of the Verdinos turned savage and attacked herds of goats. A price was put on their heads and they were termed "worse than wolves".

At one stage a gold coin was paid to anyone producing the head of a Verdino, but eight years later the Spanish ruler Castellano, who was in love with a Guanche princess, annulled the order, saying that the Verdino was "an honourable dog and that he (Castellano) didn't wish to judge it".

But life was difficult and death almost inevitable for the dogs during those bad years. In Fuerteventura where for centuries they had guarded goats and sheep, a general "licence to kill" was issued against dogs of prey, as they were termed. One was allowed for each flock, with the proviso that a young boy should stand guard over it.

Somehow the Verdino managed to survive, only to face a new threat in the last century when British and German dog-fighting enthusiasts settled in the islands, bringing with them the bull terrier. Cross-breeding to produce stronger, fiercer animals in this cruel sport threatened the purity of the breed.

The dog-fighting is officially outlawed now, and staged fights are rare. Lovers of the Verdino are also fighting, to preserve the purity of the breed. Most are strongly opposed to selective breeding, but choose—with care and difficulty—mates that are not closely related, because of the dangers of interbreeding. Verdino owners and organizations such as Solidaridad Canario are generally stimulating public awareness and interest in the Canarian breed.

Lack of money is a continual problem, and Verdino enthusiasts, professional or otherwise, often disagree on all but the most basic issues. Efforts to breed the dog, to "follow through" on pups and to arouse government interest have all been hampered by so many difficulties that today it seems the Verdino banner is flown by individuals, not groups.

However public awareness and interest in the dogs is flourishing and the price of a pure-bred Verdino pup (about £250) has increased accordingly—even if the owner would part with it. Shepherds and goatherds in Fuerteventura, where the Verdino is still a working dog, have replaced the basic *gofio* and water diet with a higher-protein one, and are careful to remove ticks and other parasites which have always sapped the dogs' strength.

Left, faithful, strong, and unique to the islands. Above, an early representation of the Fuerteventuran dog.

Rescued breed: A brighter day is dawning for the Verdinos. These days they are guarded as zealously and lovingly as they once guarded their masters.

In Tenerife the Club Español del Presa Canario ("presa" literally means bulldog) arranges regular meetings and competitions of Verdinos, which take place in the main square of La Laguna, in Geneto, Tegueste and other venues.

It isn't easy to find a Verdino, at least not in Gran Canaria, where they are now pets-cum-guard dogs. Veterinary surgeon Enrique Rodriguez Grau Bassas has acquired one from Fuerteventura (where he carried out in-depth genetic research on the dog for the University of Cordoba some years ago); Ico—named after a legendary Lanzarote princess, daughter of a Guanche queen and a Spanish nobleman—is six years old and hopefully will be a mother of many Verdino pups. She is quite small—the average height of a bitch is 22 ins (57 cms) from neck to ground, but over the past ten years Verdinos have grown and with a good diet will further increase in size.

Like all her breed, Ico likes to sleep by day and is active at night. She growls but doesn't bite. She has lovely gold-flecked eyes and is friendly but not fawning, demonstrative only with her owner. But beware that friendliness—she would attack anyone approaching her owner's house or car. She is as agile as the mountain goats her ancestors guarded, and resistant to disease. She has, says Dr Rodriguez, a certain daintiness—on her first visit to a restaurant she sat quietly behind him and delicately accepted the food he passed to her.

The writer and historian Viera y Clavijo describes this dog better than any other: "...apart from its svelte figure, vivacity, courage and speed, it possesses that delicate and exquisite sentiment that allows it to enter society with man. The Verdino understands man's desires, fights for his security, obeys and helps him, defends and loves him, and .... knows exactly how to gain the love of his owner."

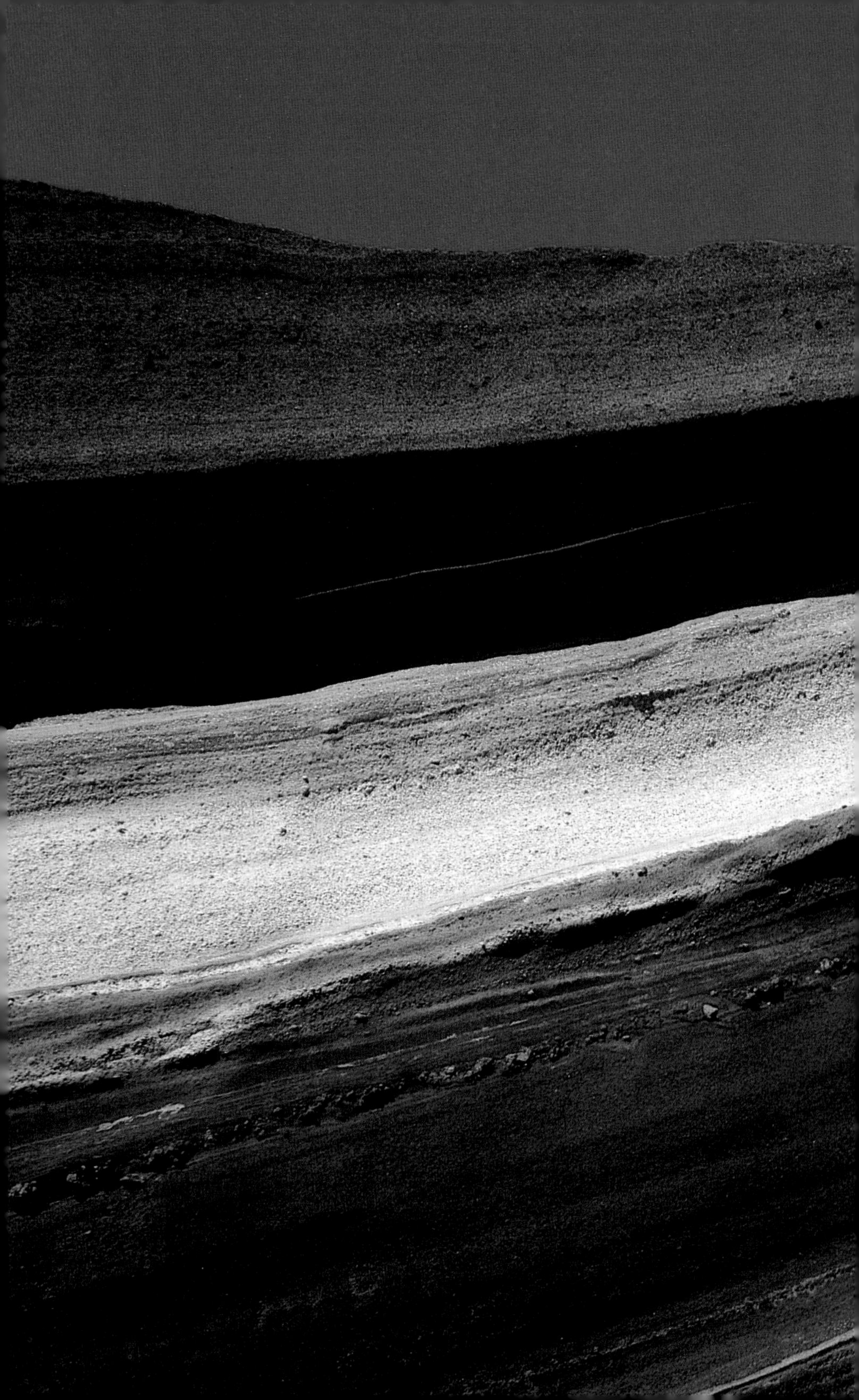

"The human mind simply cannot imagine the power of soulless nature. Out of the mountain came a slow, oh so slow river of fire, growing by the minute, till it stood over ten feet high and two hundred yards across. Its edges turned black as it cooled; the top too was black—scaley and scarred like the hide of some antediluvian monster. On it came. No-one could hold it back. No-one could turn it aside. Everything in its path was obliterated. Everything. Houses, farms, orchards..."

La Palma: The awesome power of a volcanic eruption on the island of La Palma was brought home to the rest of Spain by Radio Tenerife in 1949. It was by no means the first eruption on the island to be described by eyewitnesses—nor was it to be the last.

La Palma suffered two explosions that year and the southern quarter of the island was completely cut off by lava.

The volcanic activity of the islands has no less impressed other, more sanguine observers. The level-headed Italian engineer, Torriani, was almost lost for words when he witnessed the eruption of Tegueso in 1585—"I believe, indeed, that not even the most ingenious spirit is capable of describing such horror, fear and calamity." He soon regained enough composure to devote a full chapter to the event. "Tegueso... burned each day and more fiercely with resplendent flames and many coloured plumes of smoke. This smoke changed from golden black, to golden white, yellow, sky-blue and red..."

Captain Andrés de Valcáred, a military man, who saw his aunt's La Palma farm buried by lava in 1646, was more impressed by the noise than the colour. "There was such a noise and terrible rumble as if there was a great number of artillery pieces being fired off, and with such loudness that it was heard in all the islands. And there were thrown out stones in such numbers that they seemed like flocks of birds and so many that they were seen everywhere on the island. By night they were seen the more clearly for it seemed each stone was a living streak of fire."

Preceding pages: volcanic crater near El Teide; lava strata. Left, a blanket of lava. Right, the La Palma eruption of 1971.

But in all the descriptions there is a common pattern of events. Before the eruption proper comes a series of earthquakes which steadily increase in frequency and violence. The quakes eventually rip open the earth and molten rock emerges to form a series of small cones which are built up by more molten rock and ash.

The most recent eruption in the Canaries—Teneguia, La Palma, in 1971—is estimated to have produced the equivalent of

two million lorry loads of lava. And the eruption was a relatively small one, lasting from 26 October to 18 November. The lava flow made the island a few yards longer.

In both the 1646 and 1971 eruptions volcanic bombs were thrown out of the volcano's mouth. Once living streaks of fire, they litter the surface of the lava flows and look like petrified Cornish pasties. These bombs are formed as solid chunks of rock that are hurled through liquid lava in the throat of the volcano. Their crusts are usually crazed, revealing an inner core of solidified frothy lava.

The recent lava of Teneguia, south of the

town of Fuerteventura on La Palma, is solid but still warm under foot, and the cracks in its surface still emit scorching gases. The whole of La Palma's southern tip is a wasteland of black cinders, rubble and what appear to be streams of hardened tarmac. The area looks like the scene of an immense industrial disaster of which the visitors are the sole survivors.

Volcanoes and lava flows are to be found throughout La Palma and the word *caldera*, which is now used by geologists to describe large basin-shaped hollows in a volcano, comes from La Palma's Caldera de Taburiente, now a National Park. A *caldera* is Spanish for a boiling-pan or kettle and when you stand beside the Roque de los Muchachos Observatory and look down into it, you can understand its appropriateness. The enormous basin below is full of cloud which bubbles and heaves like boiling porridge.

The German geologist, Leopold von Buch, first applied the term *caldera* to volcanic features. But, despite its sheer walls and their rainbow coloured lavas and ashes, the Caldera de Taburiente is not a vast volcanic crater. For what nature can build up, nature can tear down again. The Taburiente *caldera* is the product of the inexorable process of erosion. As La Palma has gradually risen from the Atlantic, streams have cut into the soft ashes of the island mass. Large chunks of the *caldera's* walls have simply slumped into the five mile (eight km) basin to be broken down by and carried seaward by the constant flow of water. So great has been the power of erosion that at the very base of the Caldera, rocks of the pre-island Basalt Complex have been exposed.

Below the clouds, the Caldera de Taburiente is a wooded Shangri-la, accessible only on foot. At its centre is a knife-sharp slab of rock, Idafe, which was sacred to the native islanders before the conquest, which saw its last act played out in the natural fortress of the Caldera.

Tenerife: From La Palma the view eastward is dominated by Tenerife, still a substantial snow-capped pyramid even at a distance of nearly 60 miles (90 km).

Tenerife has been built up by the two most violent types of volcanic eruptions known—Plinian and Peléan. A Plinian eruption is a stupendous uprush of boiling gas several miles high. Peléan eruptions are equally explosive, but in this type of eruption the boiling lava and gases roll out from the volcano in a glowing incendiary avalanche. A normal avalanche is propelled by gravity alone, but these *nuées ardentes* (burning clouds) have internal sources of energy which make them move faster, further and more devastatingly than any simple landslip or normal lava flow.

It was the work of such eruptions which constructed a huge volcano much higher than the present Mount Teide, which dominates Tenerife, and is in fact the highest mountain in Spain at 12,199 ft (3,718 metres). These cataclysmic eruptions emptied the magma chamber under the volcano

and the upper part collapsed under its own weight. The base of the walls of this original vast volcano are all that remain, defining a sheer walled *caldera*.

The flat white expanse between these walls and the peak of Teide itself are known as *cañadas*. They are formed of fine sands and gravels eroded from the *caldera* walls. In a wetter era many centuries ago the Cañadas was covered with lakes.

The area of the Las Cañadas National Park, which includes the peak of Teide within its limits, is not one but two *calderas*. The separating wall is Los Roques de García, a distinctive barrier of dark mauve and pink rocks protruding from the white *cañadas*.

Volcanic activity on Tenerife is today centred around El Teide and its several parasitic cones which have sprouted on the northern edge of the *caldera*. The most recent eruptions have been explosive, forming a small *caldera* at the very summit of Teide in which a new cone is growing.

The most recent eruption of Teide was in 1909, and there were three eruptions in the 18th century. Christopher Columbus saw smoke and ash emanating from Pico Viejo as he sailed for the New World in 1492. Las Narices de Teide (Teide's Nostrils) on the south flank of the mountain blew in 1798. The road to Chio now cuts through its dark grey lava flows and clinker. Little or no vegetation grows there among the scattered volcanic bombs, and its jagged surface is a malevolent landscape for walkers. The drab, fresh lava flows here contrast with the older lava flows in the park, which are altogether smoother and surprisingly colourful.

Teide is classed as a strato-volcano; it is made up of different lavas and ashes which have spilled out in a series of eruptions from several craters at different times, which explains why the rocks around it are so varied in texture and colour.

Lava types: The Hawaiian islanders may have given geologists the names for the different types of lavas but the Canaries can boast as wide a range as Hawaii. Around Teide there are flows of pahoehoe lava, literally lava fields that you can walk on barefoot. This is smooth, satiny lava, sometimes formed into coiled strands like rope. Pahoehoe lava cooled slowly and remained viscous for some time, allowing the gases to ooze out through the steadily solidifying "plastic" skin.

Ahah lava is a complete contrast. This type of lava cooled quickly, the gases were spat out ripping the surface into jagged blocks. Walking across it even in hiking boots is not to be done for pleasure—at best it means wrecking a good pair of boots.

Left, the broken lava of the Cañadas is harsh on the feet. Above, quiet product of massive underground energy.

But if the textures are varied, it is the colours of Teide that impress the most. Solid rivers of chocolate and russet browns run alongside frozen oranges and burgundies. Here and there streaks of jet-black obsidian (a natural glass) glint in the sunlight, and huge spheres of lava that broke away from the main lava flows lie stranded on the buff-white back-drop of the Cañadas. And above, the sky is the clearest blue.

The Cañadas and the peak of Teide are

easy to get to. In the Visitor Centre the National Park authorities screen a film about all the parks on the islands, and there is a display of rock specimens and a model showing the geological development of Teide. Information on the natural and archaeological interest of the area is also available in the centre; plants like the tiny Teide violet or the bizarre Tajinaste are found only here.

The Tajinaste grow around the *Parador*—the only place to stay (unless you fancy overnighting at the refuge as you hike up to the peak itself), and a good stop for coffee. From here there are sweeping views up to the top of Teide and nearby is the picnic site at Roques de García, the ancient remnants of the wall which divides the *caldera* into two. Erosion has carved the Roques into weird and wonderful shapes.

Between the Visitor Centre and the *Parador* is Teide's main attraction—the cable car which runs up to near the summit. The thin air, laden with sulphur, and the cold make the trip to the very top unsuitable for people with heart complaints, and even fitness freaks will find the scramble from the cable car to the summit exhausting. Nevertheless, hundreds of visitors make the trip daily—if the cables are not iced up or the wind blowing too hard.

Teide's very popularity and its accessibility are threatening the mountain top's special character. On some days the summit seems as busy as the resort of Puerto de la Cruz, and thousands of pairs of feet have worn tracks across the summit. And such is the desire of visitors to take home a souvenir rock that the park authorities are seriously worried about the survival of the peak itself—tons of rock are removed by souvenir hunters each year.

Tenerife's recent volcanic history is not confined to the National Park of Las Cañadas. The coastal town of Garachico was destroyed by lava flows in the spring of 1706. The peninsula of black lava which can be seen today jutting out to sea covers the former harbour, once of major importance in the Spanish route to the Indies. The town was rebuilt on this lava and some of the older houses are made of the black pumice produced in the eruption.

Gomera: Many parts of Tenerife have underground water with temperatures over 70°F (20°C) and even 85°F (30°C). In places brine and other hot liquids rise close to the surface and have deposited their salts in the volcanic ashes, staining them unusual shades of bright green and blue.

By way of contrast Gomera has no signs of recent volcanic activity. Yet it does possess spectacular volcanic scenery. The most impressive example is Los Organos (the Organ Pipes), which are best seen from the sea just west of Vallehermoso's beach. This cliff of basalt columns looks just like a giant church organ. When the lava cooled, it shrank and cracked into six-sided columns which have weathered to different heights to produce this remarkable feature—60 ft (20 metres) wide and 240 ft (80 metres) high.

Volcanic domes of thick viscous lava and dykes of resistant rock which stand out as natural walls in the deeply cut ravines may also be seen in the centre of the island in the Garajonay National Park.

Hierro: The smallest island of the Canaries, Hierro has seen no eruptions in historic times, though it has suffered volcanic activity more recently than Gomera. El Golfo on the west of the island is the semi-circular remnant of a former crater dissected by the sea to reveal several hundred metres of lava flows lying one above the other. Most of the island's surviving basalt core is pockmarked by hundreds of small craters.

Origins: How did the islands come about in the first place? Certainly not through the drowning of Atlantis. Quite the reverse, although geologists argue over the details.

The general view relies on the theory of plate tectonics. Essentially the world's surface is made up of a number of thick slabs, or plates, of rock which are constantly moving—slowly—relative to one another. These movements are caused by currents of heat generated within the molten core of the Earth.

Over hundreds of millions of years the plates on which Africa and South America sit drifted apart, forming the Atlantic Ocean. As Africa rubbed along the southern edge of Europe the enormous pressure built up here folded up the Atlas Mountains in North Africa. As the Atlas chain was folded, huge blocks of rock in the Atlantic were shoved upwards. Local releases of pressure around these blocks let liquid rock flow upwards through cracks. Volcanoes formed where the cracks reached the surface.

Outcrops of these original basement rocks have been exposed at the bottom of La Palma's Caldera de Taburiente and in the cliffs of northern Gomera. On these western isles these rocks are relatively recent, going back a mere 20 million years or so, but on the eastern island of Fuerteventura they date back 37 million years.

Tenerife, the three smaller islands in the western province, and Gran Canaria are purely volcanic. They are separated from each other by deep-water trenches and almost certainly were never linked to Africa.

And the chances of seeing an eruption? Fairly remote. The last was on the island of La Palma in 1971. Teide still oozes sulphurous trails of smoke and Timanfaya on Lanzarote burns away just beneath your feet. It is just a matter of time—next week, next month, next year, next century, or maybe not for another million years or so.

Varied textures...the gravel of Teide, left, and ropey lava on Hierro (above).

But whether you will be warned of an impending eruption will be a matter of luck. Despite the large resident and tourist populations the Canaries have a scanty network of seismographs to record geological movements. Contingency planning is almost non-existent, though estimations have been made of the ash falls that Teide might produce.

So far the historic eruptions have occurred in sparsely inhabited areas and have not been too calamitously sudden. But historic time on the Canaries is a mere five centuries, and the next eruption could be above Puerto de la Cruz or Los Cristianos. Who knows.

CANARIAN COMBAT

Judging by match attendance Canary wrestling or *lucha canaria* is the third most popular sport of the islands. But among the native-born islanders it is a clear favourite. Wrestling clubs and rings are on all the islands—there are, for example, 15 clubs on Fuerteventura alone, one club for every 1,200 *majoreros*.

The sport's governing body has tried to get the wrestling recognised for the 1992 Olympics to be held in Barcelona, arguing that *lucha canaria* is international because Canarian emigrants introduced it throughout South and Central America as well as mainland Spain. The rejection of the proposal by the Olympic Committee is seen as yet another slight by Madrid on *lo nuestro*, "our own", though cutting the televised final bouts of the 1986 inter-island championship match caused more obvious indignation at the time.

How Canarian *lucha canaria* is may be an open question, but it certainly has pre-Spanish origins. Nevertheless similar styles of wrestling can be seen in northern Spain, the Swiss Alps, western Britain and even in parts of Africa.

Ancient and modern: The 17th-century poet, Viana, described a wrestling match held in Tenerife just before the conquest in such detail that it is possible to identify all three throws that the winner used. The prose chroniclers recorded notable bouts too, like that held in Tenoya, Gran Canaria, between Adargoma of Gáldar and Gariragua representing Telde. The two champions fought over the two kingdoms' grazing rights. In the best traditions of *lucha*, both wrestlers claimed the other had won. This must be one of the most gentlemanly and chivalrous contact sports.

These pre-conquest matches generally took the form of personal duels or trials of combat, like the Tenoya fight. Wrestling was also a form of training for war and an entertainment at festivities—the bouts described by Viana formed part of the official merry-making at a royal wedding.

According to the early European writers, special places were set aside for native wrestling bouts. "They had public places outside the villages where they had their duels, which was a circle enclosed by a stone wall and a place made high where they might be seen," wrote one visitor.

In its modern form, *lucha canaria* is no longer an individual contest but a team sport. There are 12 wrestlers in each team, only one man from each team fighting at any one time.

Left, stick-fighting, vicious and skilful. Right, *lucha canaria* is part of the islands' heritage.

The individual bouts or *bregas* are fought within a sand-covered ring between 30 and 33 ft (nine to 10 metres) in diameter.

The rings—often built and owned by the local town council—are known as *terreros*, a word of Portuguese origin and probably acquired during the various temporary alliances of native islanders and Portuguese against the Spanish.

At the start of a *brega* the wrestler takes his opponent's right hand in his and grasps the rolled hem of his opponent's shorts with his left. As the two wrestlers come together their right hands brush the sand-covered floor of the *terrero* and the *brega* is under way.

Using a combination of trips, lifts and sheer weight each man tries to unbalance his opponent, gripping onto shorts or shirt. The *brega* is lost if any part of the wrestler's body—except, of course, his feet—touches the ground. If both wrestlers are toppled the man who hits the ground first is the loser. Each team member must grapple to win the best of three *bregas* or bouts to gain a point for his side.

Until the Spanish Civil War *lucha canaria* retained much of its original character. A style of wrestling similar to Cumbrian wrestling from the north-west of England was to be found in Tenerife and other stylistic differences occurred on other islands. The presence of a *comisionado*, or wrestler's second, harked back to the duels of pre-conquest days. In Gran Canaria the two opposing teams used to be known as North and South—preserving the former ancient division of the island into two separate Guanche kingdoms.

In the 1920's *lucha* was the sport of the country people practised on the grain-threshing circles. These days threshing floors are few and far between, but even the modern city-dwelling Canario will occasionally wrestle with a friend or cousin during a Sunday barbecue in the country. And *lucha* has even been taken up by some foreign residents—two German brothers, brought up in the islands, are members of the Hierro team.

Sport or art?: Less common as a tradition on the islands is *juego del palo* or stick-fighting (known as *banot* in Tenerife), though it is currently undergoing a revival. A controlling body for the sport—or perhaps art form—has been set up, and classes are now being given in branches of the *Universidad Laboral* throughout the islands.

In pre-conquest days stick-fighting formed part of a more dangerous game. When two Canarios challenged each other to a duel, they went to the place agreed upon, which was a raised arena with a flat stone, big enough for a man to stand upright on at each end. Both competitors stood on their stones, with three stones each for throwing and with three more which served for wounding, and with the stave called a *magodo* or *amodeghe*.

First they threw the stones, which they dodged with skill, weaving their bodies without moving their feet. After that they stepped down to the ground and faced each other with the *magodos*, trying to smash each others' forearms and using the thin stones between their fingers as a kind of vicious knuckle-duster.

The stone throwing preliminaries and the stone knuckle-dusters went out of fashion years ago, but the stick-fight has survived—just—in areas like Fuerteventura, where goat-herding still plays an important role in the economy.

The staff is about six ft (1.8 meters) long and about an inch (2.5 cm) thick. Almost any wood can be used as long as it will provide a straight staff and will not shatter easily. The Canary Island bush, *membrillo*, or the introduced cherry are preferred.

A pole of appropriate length is cut green, stripped of its bark and left to season. The seasoned pole is then cured with pig fat to make it more resilient—linseed oil is sometimes used, though few practitioners of the sport would readily admit to using a manufactured product.

As with wrestling there are differences between the islands. The Fuerteventuran "school" prefers a defensive style, sacrificing speed for power, whilst adherents of the Tenerife style go for speed. Even the name of the staff varies from island to island—in Gran Canaria it is called a *garrote*, on Tenerife a *banot* and in Fuerteventura it is known as a *lata*. Throughout the islands herdsmen still carry these staves.

Juego del palo (stick-fighting) was a rural sport, like wrestling, though the practitioners were mainly goat-herders. In living memory herdsmen in Fuerteventura met occasionally in a "Corral Council" to resolve disputes between individual herders. If agreement could not be reached by negotiation the matter was eventually determined by a stick-fight between the two men or their representatives.

Left, he who hits the ground first, loses. Above, a form of combat with a long history.

Banned and forgotten: A variant on the theme was developed in the last century when camels were first introduced to Fuerteventura as beasts of burden or for ploughing. In this type of stick-fight a camel-driver's crop, a stick of about three feet long (one metre) is used.

In 1860 Pedro Pestano introduced the *palo camellero* to Tenerife and by the 1920s there was a thriving group of stick-fighters on the island who used the short stick. This style, however, has all but died out.

And the same almost occurred with *garrote* on Gran Canaria. This was banned after the conquest by a Spanish law which forbade native islanders from carrying weapons, although goat-herders were exempt on the grounds that they needed a suitable stick to protect their flocks.

Lucha was more difficult to control. Indeed in 1527 wrestling bouts were held in Tenerife as part of the festivities to mark the birth of Felipe II of Spain.

By the 19th century, however, the *cultos* (cultured) of society were of the opinion that "spectacles of this kind should figure only in the memory". With the Franco era *lucha* generally met with malign neglect but, since the democracy was re-established in 1976 much more public interest—and money—has been invested in the sport. Nowadays most of the main *luchaderos* (rings) are modern buildings.

Demonstrations of both *lucha* and *juego del palo* are given during most festivals, and Fuerteventura offers the best chance of coming across a wrestling match in a local *luchadero*. Otherwise look for posters in bars off the tourist run—or on the wall of the Lopez Socas stadium in Las Palmas, Gran Canaria, near which is a bronze statue of two wrestlers set in a bleak park off the Avenida Escaleritas.

Matches are televised surprisingly regularly on the local TV channel; check the local papers for details.

Festivals Of Queens And Sardines

There is nothing tinerfeños (Tenerife Islanders) love quite so much as a fiesta, and the locals think nothing of travelling from one end of their island to the other to immerse themselves enthusiastically in some of the best.

It's said that on just about every day of the year, there's a fiesta in full swing somewhere in the archipelago, though the majority tend to fall in the summer months.

Mostly they are small local affairs and unless the visitor happens to be in the village concerned on the appointed day, they are likely to go unnoticed, intruding on the outside world only when the strains of music and laughter float down the valley followed—much later—by the staccato report of fire-crackers and the sudden blossoming of fireworks in the clear night sky.

There are exceptions of course, and the most important and widely-celebrated religious fiesta (after Christmas and Easter) is the **Octavo** (Eight Days) **de Corpus Christi**, revered in all Catholic countries. In Tenerife it is held principally in La Laguna and La Orotava, two ancient towns whose deep-rooted rivalry is reflected in the extravagantly-designed and painstakingly fashioned carpets of flower petals and coloured sands with which the streets and squares are strewn, as town attempts to outdo town in its acts of devotion.

Works of art comparable to superb religious paintings and tapestries, these carpets of flower and sand are months in the intricate preparation and planning stages—destroyed in a few short moments by the feet of the devout taking part in the solemn procession.

Traditionally, the religious festival of **Corpus Christi** was followed closely by the **Romería**, a colourful fiesta where food, wine, music and dancing are the order of the day. So popular have these rustic celebrations become—with flower-decked oxen pulling carts laden with Canarios in national costume, tempting the crowds with choice morsels washed down with local wine—that in recent years, towns and villages have co-operated with each other so that instead of clashing, *Romerías* are held at intervals over a period of several bacchanalian weeks.

King of fiestas: For tinerfeños, **Carnaval** is an all-consuming way of life. A kind of incipient madness that slowly infiltrates and takes over their lives, bringing (as it moves into top gear) the commercial and business sectors of the islands to a near standstill.

The word *Carnaval* is believed to derive from the Latin *carne valle*, meaning "Goodbye to meat", devout Catholics by tradition being expected to exclude meat from their diet during the 40-day period of Lent.

According to Juan María Canals of the National Liturgy Secretariat, prior to Christianity, carnival was celebrated in Italy and Greece as a festival heralding Spring, while in mainland Spain, it was to become a fiesta protected by Felipe IV and Carlos III, who introduced the masked balls reminiscent of the Italian celebrations.

Much later, during Franco's dictatorship, carnivals were banned throughout Spain as it was feared that fancy dress parades would create the ideal climate in which crime could

Preceding pages: band at local fiesta; the extravagant colours of *Carnaval*. Left, queen for one day. Right, after a hard day's celebrating.

flourish undetected. Never ones to give in easily (as the conquistadores had already discovered), the tinerfeños were quick off the mark at re-naming their *carnavals Las Fiestas De Invierno* (The Winter Festivals), thus cleverly side-stepping the unwelcome prohibition.

Being familiar with Tenerife and knowing there was little organised crime in the islands, Franco turned a largely blind eye on the continuing revelries, but he did draw the line at individuals masquerading as either religious or military figures. Since his death (in 1975), anything goes, with Ayatollah Khomeini and Fidel Castro clones often seen at *Carnaval* time.

only surpassed by those of Rio de Janeiro and New Orleans, although organisers in Las Palmas, Gran Canaria, make similar claims for their fiesta.

In 1988 some 20,000 people took part in the Santa Cruz *Carnaval*, with more than 200,000 spectators on the day of the *Coso* (Grand Parade), while figures for Puerto de la Cruz four days later were only slightly less, at 150,000 for the main parade.

In 1987, more than 240,000 people crammed themselves into Santa Cruz's Plaza de España and its surroundings for the open-air dance marking the end of *Carnaval*, and earning a place in the *Guinness Book of Records* as the largest carnival ball ever.

Almost 190 years ago, in 1802, Puerto de la Cruz (or Puerto de La Orotava as it was then known) was already fully dedicated to enjoying itself at the *Carnaval*, a fact supported by the diaries of the Viscount of Buen Paso, Juan Primo de Guerra, whose entry for 12 February of that year states: "My sister says...that she would be happy, if I am in agreement, to take a house in Puerto de la Orotava for a few days to enjoy the diversions of the *Carnaval*..."

Carnaval today: Declared officially as being of "international interest touristically", Tenerife's *carnavales* are widely accepted as the best in Europe and probably

Events on such a huge scale naturally call for careful forward planning, with extra police drafted into the area and the recent introduction of *pipís moviles* (mobile lavatories), to try to prevent the city's gutters from flowing. Many of the older houses still have very discreet urinals behind the open doors in their entrance ways, the result of an ancient law requiring house-owners to provide such facilities to the general (male) public.

Carnaval is thirsty (and hungry) work. *Una cubata* (Pampero rum with cola) is the traditional drink to order, and in Santa Cruz well over 100 refreshment kiosks pack into the Plaza de la Candelaria and Plaza de

España area alone. The sites are auctioned off in advance by the town hall, and a site for a *churrería* (*churros* are a type of deep-fried doughnut) goes under the hammer at 2,000,000 pesetas (approx £10,000).

In September or October the scores of *agrupaciones* (*Carnaval* groups) start their nightly rehearsals, the majority of them sponsored by their local town halls and/or Caja Canarias (a leading bank). At this time newspaper articles on the preparations begin to appear on a daily basis.

Queens amongst queens: *Carnaval* always kicks off with the election of its Queens, adult and juvenile. Costumes are lavish beyond belief, costing millions of pesetas and taking many months to complete. So jealous of their costumes are top designers that they refuse even to tell organisers the dimensions of their creations, many of which necessarily are fitted with hinges to enable their wearers to pass through stage doors without mishap.

Traditionally, *Carnaval* has always had a strong gay element, repressed during the Franco years but now enjoying a new-found freedom and respectability. In 1988, *murga* "Los Rebeldones" chose for their *Carnaval* repertoire a topical song controversially entitled *Avoid AIDS*, and donated the entire proceeds from their show to local victims of the disease.

Lasting some nine or 10 days, high spots of *Carnaval* include the Grand Procession (on Shrove Tuesday in Santa Cruz, the following Saturday in Puerto); the Burial of the Sardine (on Ash Wednesday), when a "sardine" of monstrous proportions is accompanied by its entourage of wailing "widows" before being burnt ritually. Fireworks and an open-air ball follow; and *Carnaval* comes to a climactic close with *Piñata Sabado y Domingo* the following weekend.

Ear-splitting, vibrant, brash, shameless, frenetic, sensual, smelly, crowded, aggressive, gaudy, magnificent...*Carnaval* is all things to all people. At the end of the 1988 celebrations, town hall workers in Santa Cruz had swept up 786,133 lbs (356,590 kilos) of rubbish and had hosed down the streets with 297,184 gallons (1,351,000 litres) of water and disinfectant.

But when the party has ended in Santa Cruz and Puerto de la Cruz, it's only just beginning in Los Realejos, Icod, Candelaria, Tacoronte, La Orotava, Los Cristianos and the lesser islands, as the ripples of *Carnaval* spread ever outwards from the twin epicentres and spill over into Lent itself.

***Carnaval* scenes...a record-holding event for the participants, and (right) for rubbish left behind.**

TRAVEL TIPS

Getting There

The Canarian archipelago, variously called "The Land of Eternal Spring", "The Garden of the Hesperides", or "The Fortunate Isles", stretches out in a chain of seven main islands and three smaller ones, some 300 miles (480 km) long. The nearest point to the African coast—only 60 miles (96 km) away—is the island of Fuerteventura, sometimes described as a piece of the Sahara that drifted away.

BY AIR

All but one of the seven largest islands has an airport; Gomera, the exception, can be reached by ferry only at the moment. All others are linked by frequent inter-island flights, and by far the busiest airports are Reina Sofia (South Tenerife) and Gando in Gran Canaria, into which principal scheduled international air traffic comes. Spain's national airline Iberia has regular services to Tenerife and Gran Canaria from most major European cities, with daily flights to and from Amsterdam, Brussels, Düsseldorf, Frankfurt, Geneva, London, Paris, Rome, Vienna and Zurich. Iberia's HQ in the UK is at 130, Regent Street, London W1 (tel. (1)-437 9822). From the UK the principal charter—and limited scheduled—flights are operated by Air Europe, Britannia Airways, Monarch and Dan-Air.

BY SEA

The ferry company Trasmediterranea runs between Cadiz and Santa Cruz (Tenerife) or Las Palmas (Gran Canaria) three times a week, with a journey time of 36 hours. Sailings go on to Lanzarote once a week. Ferries link all seven islands with frequent sailings between Tenerife and Las Palmas, Gran Canaria.

A regular jet-foil service runs (except when the sea is too rough) between Santa Cruz and Las Palmas, and, three times weekly, to Morro Jable in the south of Fuerteventura. This is also operated by Trasmediterranea and is much quicker than travelling by conventional ferry, the hydrofoil "flight" between Santa Cruz and Las Palmas taking just 80 minutes.

The island of La Gomera is linked to Tenerife by Ferry Gomera (a subsidiary of the Fred Olsen Scandinavian ferry company) which piles between Los Cristianos (Tenerife) and San Sebastian de la Gomera.

RMS ST Helena sails from Avonmouth to Cape Town every 60 days, with stops in Tenerife, Ascension Island and St Helena. The trip from England to Tenerife takes five days.

Cruise ships such as *QE2*, *Canberra* and those of the Fred Olsen line also call occasionally at the two main ports. Compania Trasmediterranea: Marina 59, Santa Cruz de Tenerife – tel. 277300; Muelle Ribera Este, Las Palmas de Gran Canaria – tel. 267766; St Helena Shipping Co. Ltd., Helston, Cornwall, UK. – tel. (326) 563434.

BY RAIL

Being rugged and mountainous, the Canaries have no rail network, but the Spanish national rail system (RENFE) will deliver passengers to the station at Cádiz. From there to the islands, see the above section "By Sea".

BY ROAD

Road users travel through mainland Spain to Cádiz and thence by ferry to Tenerife or Gran Canaria, and the other islands.

Any size of vehicle can be brought across and most standards of accommodation are available on board. Pets are charged extra. Imported vehicles used on the islands for more than six months will need Spanish licence plates. The importation of foreign vehicles involves much red tape, such as an International Driving Licence, car registration papers, a Green Card and a Spanish bail bond.

The principal French **tour operators** are: FRAM, Nouvel Horizon and Jet Tours, each with offices in the provincial capitals and holiday resorts. For detailed information regarding scheduled flights to Tenerife and Gran Canaria, contact Air France agents: there are daily flights between various French airports and the Canaries.

German tour operators such as Touristik Union International, Neckermann Reisen and Tjaereborg are also well represented in the archipelago, while the German airline Lufthansa runs a regular scheduled service to and from the major airports.

Apart from the Cadiz ferry, there are no fixed sailings between mainland Europe and the islands, other than cruise ships which, as already mentioned, call at irregular intervals at the ports of Las Palmas and Santa Cruz.

TRAVEL ESSENTIALS

VISAS AND PASSPORTS

Spain joined the European Economic Community on 1 January 1986 and will become a full member state on 31 December 1992, so citizens of EEC countries, the USA and Canada need only valid passports, while visitors from Australia, New Zealand and South Africa must have a **visa**. Make sure your passport is stamped on entry, especially if you intend to stay for more than three months. If this is the case you must obtain a visa from a Spanish Consulate at home, and later, a *permanencia* from the offices of the Civil Governor of the province and the police station of your local town.

The Canary Islands have different **customs regulations** to mainland Spain, and passengers' personal baggage from Europe is not normally subjected to Customs inspection. Prohibited goods, however, include narcotics and pornographic material—both incidentally readily available in the cities and tourist areas.

PORTER SERVICE

Do not expect **porter service**, except at the best hotels. One can usually ferret out a luggage trolley at the main airports, although there is an inexplicable lack of them at Tenerife's Reina Sofia airport.

HEALTH

Tips for a **healthy stay** are: drink bottled water and beware the origin of ice-cubes, don't overdo the sun-worshipping, it's only too easy to become badly burned in the Canaries' unusually clear atmosphere; take care over eating and drinking (measures of spirits are much larger than in other countries and generally far cheaper, too).

Visitors with severe respiratory complaints should avoid the major cities of Las Palmas and Santa Cruz because of the high level of petrol and diesel fumes and dust, some of it from the Sahara, and anyone with heart trouble on Tenerife would be well advised to give the trip to Teide (Spain's highest mountain) a miss.

Citizens of EEC countries enjoy reciprocal **medical benefits** (in your home country, the local social security office will provide you with a form E111 for temporary visitors, or E121 for pensioners). State facilities generally mean adequate treatment and medical skills, but lengthy waits for outpatients, with few nurses and doctors speaking anything other than Spanish. However, names of doctors with some knowledge of a foreign language are available at local tourist bureaux and in English and German newspapers and magazines.

Private medical care is preferred by foreign visitors and usually implies prompt attention, good standards, staff who speak foreign languages, but relatively high costs. Foreign visitors should arrange sickness and accident insurance before departure and cover of £10,000 is not excessive.

Recently a few foreign doctors (mostly British or German) have begun to practice in the Canaries, though this is by no means the norm. Bear in mind, that in both state and private hospitals, a patient's family is expected to help out with basic nursing duties, which could prove problematical if on one's own.

ANIMAL QUARANTINE

There are no quarantine regulations as such for those bringing their **pets**, but you will need the usual vaccination certificates issued by your veterinary surgeon back home, and preferably translated by a Spanish consular official in the country of origin.

Dogs need a current certificate to prove that they have been inoculated against rabies—though no case of the disease has been reported in the Islands since 1927. Dogs are not allowed on beaches, in taxis, buses or restaurants. Pets arriving at airports in the Canaries are treated as baggage (meaning they are simply collected from the luggage carousels) assuming they have travelled on the same flight as their owner. If they have flown out unaccompanied, they are treated as freight and cannot be released from the airport until passed as fit by the airport veterinary officer.

Getting Acquainted

GOVERNMENT AND ECONOMY

The Canaries form two of Spain's 50 provinces. The province of Santa Cruz de Tenerife, consists of the islands of Tenerife, La Palma, Gomera and Hierro; and the province of Las Palmas de Gran Canaria, comprises the islands of Gran Canaria, Lanzarote and Fuerteventura.

Although an integral part of the Spanish state which reverted to being a monarchy after the death of General Franco in 1975, the Canaries became an autonomous region on 16 August 1982. Governed by the Gobierno de Canarias, which is responsible for strictly Canarian decisions, it has various councils in the role of local ministries called *consejerías* and the members of the parliament are of several different political colours and persuasions.

A *cabildo*, or local council, deals with matters related to each island. Each municipality has a mayor (*alcalde*) whose well-paid job it is to take an active and positive interest in his town's life and development. The town hall deals with purely urban matters, such as the town's police force (mainly concerned with traffic control nowadays), rates, fines, permits (foreign residents can now obtain a 30 percent discount when travelling by Trasmediterranea or Iberia, between the Canaries and mainland Spain, or 10 percent in the case of inter-island travel) and various taxes and charges levied on businesses. Further, each province has both a civil governor and a military governor, appointed from Madrid.

The **economy** relies on tourism, commerce and agriculture—bananas, tomatoes and avocado pears being the principal products exported to mainland Spain and Europe besides being grown for home consumption. Tourism is by far the biggest growth industry with an annual increase approaching 20 percent, each province receiving around 1-1/2 million visitors every year. Both Las Palmas (Gran Canaria) and Santa Cruz (Tenerife) have large ports, each handling more than 50 million tonnes of shipping annually.

GEOGRAPHY AND POPULATION

Totalling 870,000 inhabitants, the province of Las Palmas (Gran Canario, Lanzarote and Fuerteventura) is the more populous, while that of Santa Cruz (Tenerife and the other islands) has some 700,000 residents. The islands of Tenerife and Gran Canaria are the most densely populated of the seven.

The total area of the archipelago is just under 3,000 square miles (7,770 sq. km) and the geography, while based on volcanic activity, is infinitely varied; the lunar **landscape** of the crater of Teide in Tenerife, which was the location for the film *One Million BC*, starring Raquel Welch in 1966; Lanzarote, which the first American Apollo astronauts visited as the place in the world most closely resembling the moon; the fertile valleys of La Palma and Hierro; the sandy desert of Fuerteventura; the grass-covered mountains of Gran Canaria; the pine forests of Gomera and Tenerife—the list is endless.

Some 700 miles (1,100 km) southwest of the Peninsula, as the Canarios refer to mainland Spain, the islands lie between 27 and 29 degrees north latitude and 13 and 18 degrees west longitude.

CLIMATE

The **climate** has made the islands very popular in recent years. At the turn of the century, the Grand Hotel Orotava and the Hotel Taoro Park in Puerto de la Cruz (Tenerife) and the Santa Catalina in Las

Palmas (Gran Canaria) received the wealthy and the invalids from northern Europe. Nowadays the islands boast hundreds of hotels and apartment blocks of every level. Once a winter sunshine destination, the Canaries have become popular the year round.

There is little variation in temperatures between the four seasons (which do not have noticeable changes as happens in more northerly climes), ranging from 17 degrees centigrade in February, to 24.8 degrees centigrade in August.

However, between November and March, the temperature can fall quite sharply. Generally, the southern part of each island tends to be a few degrees warmer than the northern part, while at high altitudes the days and nights can be very cold in winter. Temporary visitors need not bring heavy clothing, and winter wear such as overcoats, gloves and boots is unnecessary, certainly in the tourist resorts.

TIME ZONES

The archipelago follows GMT. At noon in London and the Canaries, it is 1.00 p.m. in Madrid, 4.00 a.m. in Los Angeles and 7.00 a.m. in New York.

WEIGHTS AND MEASURES

Weights and measures are decimal (grams, kilos, centimetres, metres, kilometres, litres). Electrical current is 220 volts in modern buildings, and 110 volts in older properties, and it is unreliable, an *apagón* (power-cut) being quite frequent, especially in windy or rainy conditions. The better hotels and apartments, however, normally have their own generators.

HOLIDAYS

Fiestas, usually religious and sometimes merely historical, are celebrated in every hamlet, village, town and city in Spain, the Canaries being no exception, with each island having public holidays peculiar to itself. The bank holidays, when everything stops, are religious with just two exceptions and all apply to mainland Spain as well. January has two, the 1st (New Year's day) and the 6th (Epiphany or 12th Night or *Reyes*) when children receive their Christmas presents.

19 March is St Joseph's (Father's Day), while 7 May is Labour Day; 25 July celebrates St James' Day (he is the patron saint of Spain), and Santa Cruz fêtes its victory over Lord Nelson's attack on that day; 15 August, besides being the Feast of Our Lady of Candelaria (Candelaria is the patron saint of the Canaries), is the religious fiesta of the Holy Assumption.

Two months later, on 12 October, the *Día de la Hispanidad* celebrates Columbus' discovery of America on the same day in 1492: this date is commemorated in Latin America, too. 1 November is All Saints' Day (or "Day of the Defunct", when graves and tombs are garlanded with flowers). 6 December, day of the Constitution, is followed closely by the Immaculate Conception on 8 December. Christmas Day (25 December) closes the annual calendar of national holidays.

More parochially, the islands have a full timetable of **fiestas**, probably the most outstanding being carnival: the *Carnaval* (literally "goodbye to meat") processions and festivities of February in Puerto de la Cruz, Santa Cruz (both Tenerife) and Las Palmas (Gran Canaria)—the latter the most spectacular—are renowned and rival those of Río de Janeiro.

Noteworthy also is Corpus Christi in May or June, with the intricate sand- and flower-carpets of La Orotava and La Laguna in Tenerife.

In mid-September, *Las Fiestas del Santísimo Cristo* (the festival of the Most Holy Christ in La Laguna and Tacoronte in Tenerife), include firework displays, cattle shows, Canarian folklore and South American musical groups, *lucha canaria* (Canarian wrestling), a veteran car rally round the island and photographic exhibitions.

In June every fifth year in Santa Cruz de La Palma (La Palma), and every fourth year in Valverde, capital of Hierro, the "Descent of the Virgin" honours a 14th-century terracotta statue, when a religious procession accompanies this oldest of Canarian relics from the Sanctuary of the Holy Virgin of the Snows down to the capital, Santa Cruz de La Palma.

The calendar of fiestas and festivals is too full to be detailed, but local tourist offices (*Oficinas de Turismo*) can provide a breakdown. In brief, Tenerife can boast some 30; La Palma, eight; Gomera, five; Hierro, three; while in the province of Las Palmas, Gran Canaria can reckon on 24, Fuerteventura, six and Lanzarote, nine.

This count does not include every village feast day (it has been said there's one every day of the year somewhere), while some of those listed above last a week or more. The principal tourist offices are at: Santa Cruz, Plaza de España, tel. 242227; Puerto de la Cruz, Plaza de la Iglesia, tel. 384328; Las Palmas, Parque Santa Catalina, tel. 264623; Lanzarote, Parque Municipal, Arrecife, tel. 811860.

RELIGIOUS SERVICES

Spain, including the Canary Islands, is predominantly a Roman Catholic country and every town has its Catholic church. There are cathedrals in Las Palmas and La Laguna (previously the capital city of Tenerife and whose grid system of streets was used as the model for many Latin American cities on their foundation).

Today, the Roman Catholic authorities are much more tolerant and ecumenical vis-á-vis other religious denominations and sects. Long gone are the bad old days when Protestants who died on the islands were buried in the beaches, head down.

For 80 years there have been Anglican churches in Puerto de la Cruz (All Saints' Church, Taoro Park. Tel. 384038); Santa Cruz (St George's, Plaza 25 de Julio, behind the Civil Governor's residence); and in Las Palmas (Holy Trinity Church, *Ciudad Jardín* or Garden City); each having a resident chaplain. An Anglican Service is held every Sunday at 5.00 p.m. at the San Eugenio Church, Pueblo Canario, Playa de las Américas, Tenerife, tel. 387039, and Evangelical Services are held at 10.00 a.m. on Sundays in the TV Room of the Hotel Princesa Dacil in Los Cristianos and at the Tenerife Christian Centre, Apartamentos Teide, Calle Iriarte 6, Puerto de la Cruz, tel. 383179.

Tenerife and Gran Canaria both have Protestant cemeteries. The long-established and prosperous Indian community was allowed to build its own crematorium in Santa Cruz in 1988 to enable its dead to be burnt according to custom, although the practice had already existed for many years, during which time funeral pyres had been used for cremation purposes. The practice of burning the dead was of course long frowned upon by the Roman Catholic church. Other sects (for example the Jehovah's Witnesses) have increased in numbers in recent years.

LANGUAGE

While the language of the islands is Spanish, there are some variations on classical Castilian Spanish. The purest Castilian is reckoned to be still used in tiny Hierro, a heritage of westwardbound *conquistadores*.

Visitors familiar with the Spanish of the mainland, especially Castile, Leon and La Mancha, may notice the shorthand Spanish of the islanders: the endings of words are frequently dropped and the "th" quality of "proper" Spanish becomes an "s" sound. But that's how it's pronounced in South and Central America and even southern Spain itself.

Vocabulary peculiar to the Canaries includes *guagua* (bus), *malpaís* (lava-covered badlands), *papas* (potatoes), *bubango* (marrow), *luz* (for electricity generally) and *chicharerro* (an inhabitant of Santa Cruz).

COMMUNICATIONS

MEDIA

The islands, Tenerife in particular, are well served by English language and German language **newspapers** and **magazines**. For German-speaking readers the two magazines, the weekly *Teneriffa Woche* and the monthly *Teneriffa Monat*, are complemented by *Wochenspiegel*, a fortnightly newspaper printed, as is its English language counterpart *Here and Now*, by one of Tenerife's daily papers *Diario de Avisos*.

Magazines for English-speaking readers are the monthly *Tenerife Today* and *Island Gazette*, both of general interest with useful tips, telephone numbers, addresses and what-to-see sections, while *Tenerife Property Scene*, as its name suggests, is the island's only comprehensive property guide: all three are published and printed in Tenerife and widely distributed there and abroad. Other Tenerife-based Spanish-language newspapers are *El Día*, a daily, while *Jornada* appears on Mondays and concentrates on the weekend's sports results.

Gran Canaria has three newspapers—*Canarias 7*, *La Provincia* and *Diario de Las Palmas*. All major European daily newspapers are on the news-stands the day following publication.

Radio reception of European and American short-wave programmes is generally good, while *Radio Cadena* broadcasts in English, German and Swedish on weekdays from Las Palmas at 8.50 a.m. (Saturdays at 8.20 a.m.), giving local events, regional information, tourist tips, world news, weather, sports and exchange rates: tune in to 747 KHz, medium wave.

Spanish television offers two commercial channels, most of the programmes being relayed by satellite from mainland Spain and picked up by relay stations on Tenerife, La Palma and Gran Canaria. Some news bulletins and programmes of local interest originate from studios in Santa Cruz or Las Palmas. All are in Spanish, even the vast majority of non-Spanish programmes being dubbed.

POSTAL SERVICES

The **postal service** (*correos*) is normally quite efficient, although long delays can occur within the same island and between the islands. The price of a standard letter is seven pesetas (to a destination in the same town), 19 pesetas (within Spanish territory) and 45 pesetas inside Europe. A week is an average time for mail to and from other parts of Europe.

TELEPHONE AND TELEX

The **telephone service** Telefónica or Compañia Telefónica de España, has not been able to keep up with the demand for installation of new telephone lines. It is not unusual for private subscribers to wait more than two years for a telephone to be connected, and it is often easier (and clearer) to make a call to Europe than to ring another part of the same island.

Telefónica receive 2,000 complaints a week from dissatisfied customers in the Canaries. However, a welcome innovation has been the mushrooming of manned multi-cabin telephone centres, open from 9.00 a.m. to 9.00 p.m., though some stay open later. They are cheaper than kiosks, do away with the need to have precise change, are usually comfortable and the assistant does normally assist.

Telefónica also run a fax service in the major cities in case you do not have access to a private system. In Las Palmas (Gran Canaria) this is at Avenida 1º de Mayo 62, tel. (928) 371551, and in Santa Cruz (Tenerife), in the Plaza de España, tel. (922) 231202.

Also starting to appear on the islands, notably on Tenerife, Lanzarote and Gran Canaria, are satellite dishes able to pick up European and, soon, American television stations.

Dialling codes are 922- for Tenerife province numbers and 928- for Gran Canaria province when dialled from elsewhere within Spain. International callers should ignore the 9.

EMERGENCIES

SECURITY AND CRIME

There was a time when it was usual to be able to leave houses and cars unlocked without risk, there being little or no robbery on the islands. Not so now. Crime is on the increase, especially petty theft, as the writer discovered to his cost when four wheels of a mini-car were removed one night. To finance drug-addiction, burglaries and *tirón* (handbag snatching from pedestrians in the street) are rife.

Police and consular advice is emphatic. Never carry large sums of money, passports or important documents—use the hotel's safe or security box—and never leave anything in a car, especially a rented one, as even the boot can easily be broken into.

Las Palmas (Gran Canaria) has the worst record for crime at the time of writing, to the extent that some British, German and Scandinavian tour operators have threatened to find alternative holiday destinations if something is not done.

Popular resorts in Tenerife, such as Playa de las Américas, Los Cristianos and Puerto de la Cruz, are not far behind, it must be added. This, interestingly, is in spite of newspaper reports that Canarian police are almost top of the league in Spain for solving crimes.

If a visitor or resident is the victim of a theft or other criminal activity, there are several options available. If you are on a package holiday, contact your representative or guide who should take control of the situation. Others who are residing or travelling under their own steam should contact the nearest consulate (between 9.00 a.m. and 1.00 p.m.) by telephone: in Tenerife province the British Consulate is at Plaza Weyler

8, First Floor, Santa Cruz—tel. 286863, while Gran Canaria province is covered from Luis Morote 6, Third Floor, Puerto de la Luz, Las Palmas—tel. 262508, 262512 and 262516.

Outside of these hours, find an interpreter with a good working knowledge of Spanish and your own language (your hotel reception should be able to help) and report your loss to the nearest Policía Nacional or Guardia Civil police station. These can be found in the telephone directory or in daily newspapers. Full insurance cover for property lost or stolen is indispensable, especially as only a tiny percentage is ever recovered.

If you are involved in an accident, the police must be informed immediately—the nearest telephone kiosk will list local telephone numbers to contact the fire brigade, ambulance services and police (both Guardia Civil and Policía Nacional). Try to ensure that injured people are not moved until either an ambulance or police-van arrives on the scene. If there are no personal injuries, still make sure that insurance details are exchanged. Do not have your car repaired until given the go-ahead after a mechanic's assessment of damage.

MEDICAL SERVICES

Where there are no facilities for dealing with serious illnesses or accidents, such as in Lanzarote and the smaller islands, helicopters are used to airlift patients to the larger and medically better-equipped islands. Private clinics in Tenerife include the Tamaragua, whose 24-hour emergency service can be contacted by telephoning 383551 or 380512 in Puerto de la Cruz; the Bellevue (permanent medical service, telephone 383551—5 lines) also in Puerto de la Cruz; the San Miguel (330550, 333712 or 333798 for 24-hour service) in La Orotava; and the International Health Centre in Playa de las Américas (791600).

In Gran Canaria the British American Clinic is in Las Palmas (telephone 264538, 262059 and 270751); the Queen Victoria Hospital (telephone 254243); and the International Clinic (telephone 245643) also in Las Palmas. There are no clinics in Lanzarote or in Fuerteventura.

The alternative to paying the very high costs of private medical treatment, unless you have a very comprehensive insurance cover, is the Social Security sector (see *Health* section above).

Another option is the *Centros Médicos* (Medical Centres) which are often open 24 hours a day and which can cope with first aid, injections, X-rays and even basic dental treatment (a very expensive consideration in the Canaries, being entirely private). If, however, you are in urgent need of more skilled dentistry than a simple extraction, you should go to an *odontólogo/estomatólogo* (dental surgeon).

Getting Around

MAPS

In recent years, a profusion of maps and guides of varying quality and to suit various tastes has appeared on the bookstalls and in the *librerías* (bookshops/stationers). The first, and still the most accurate, is Spain's equivalent to Britain Ordnance Survey series. Previously available only from the military headquarters of the provincial capitals, these *mapas militares* can now be bought in leading bookshops.

Editorial Everest produce annotated maps in different languages and the Firestone set of three road-maps (the whole archipelago, T32; Santa Cruz province, E50; and Las Palmas province, E49) are more than adequate for the holidaymaker.

For the botanist, Hubert Moeller's *What's Blooming Where on Tenerife?* or Editorial Everest's *Exotic Flora of the Canary Islands* and David and Zoe Bramwell's *Wild Flowers of the Canary Islands* should prove satisfying; for the more energetic, the island governments (*Cabildos*) in conjunction with ICONA (the Nature Conservation Institute) have produced maps of forest and mountain trails for walkers. The *Landscape* series covers Gran Canaria, Tenerife and La Gomera, giving car tours, walks and picnic suggestions and is produced by Sunflower Books of 12, Kendrick Mews, London SW7 3HG. The historically-minded should obtain Salvador Lopez Herrera's *The Canary Islands Through History*, published by Gráficas Tenerife, or *All the Canary Islands*, the Escudo de Oro edition.

PRIVATE TRANSPORT

Car hire: international rental companies such as Avis (with offices on all seven islands) and Hertz (on all save Gomera) are probably the best bet. Every major town will have at least one and, as is the case in tourist areas, many, car hire firms.

Beware back-street concerns, with just one or two cars and incredibly cheap terms. Take care even with reputable companies as "only 2,550 pesetas per day" can mean 3,350 pesetas not counting additional insurance cover, taxes and petrol, so read the small print very carefully. Fully comprehensive insurance is a necessity.

Taxis are not strictly "private transport" as they must all carry the "SP" plate—"Servicio Público". In provincial capitals, taxis are metered but elsewhere, for longer journeys, demand to see the *tarifa* (rates between different destinations).

You can import your own car for six months in any one calendar year. British European and Japanese car manufacturers are well represented on the islands and cars are generally cheaper than in Britain. Insurance is higher, the road fund licence still very low, petrol relatively cheap, but anybody resident for more than six months must exchange their national driving licence for a Spanish one.

SHOPPING

Since the Canaries became a duty-free area in 1852, by Royal Decree, commerce has flourished. Even if the visitor of the late 1980s finds the cost of living to be generally higher than at home, some items are still a *ganga* (bargain). Imported cigarettes, wines and spirits are much cheaper (oddly, local wine is dear) and some electrical goods, cameras and watches are also cheap, due to a lower luxury tax.

Property and land prices are highest near to large urban areas such as Puerto de la Cruz, Santa Cruz and the southern Tenerife development zones, as are those close to Las Palmas and Playa del Inglés in Gran Canaria.

Shopping areas worthy of a visit in Tenerife are the Calle Castillo district in Santa Cruz, the Paseo San Telmo, and other streets near the sea in Puerto de la Cruz. In Gran Canaria the port area of Las Palmas and the Mesa y Lopez and Triana streets are the best, (the latter having the excellent department stores El Corte Inglés and Galerías Preciados). Shops and offices in the Canaries generally open between 9.00 a.m. and 1.00 p.m. and 4.00 p.m. to 8.00 p.m., although some shops stay open later than this, especially over the Christmas/New Year/ Twelfth Night period, while in the summer months, many businesses operate from 8.00 a.m. to 2.00 p.m.

Post Offices (*Correos*) dispense stamps, parcels and other business between 9.00 a.m. and 2.00 p.m. on weekdays, but larger branches stay open for telegram and giro services until 7.00 p.m. Garages (*gasolineras*) provide petrol, oil, water and air between 8.00 a.m. and midnight—all the islands have at least one 24-hour petrol station, the larger ones having more. Mechanical repairs are carried out in a *taller* (workshop) and bodywork in a *chapista*.

Banking hours, for many years between 8.30 a.m. or 9.00 a.m. and 2.00 p.m. (9.00 a.m. to 1.00 p.m. on Saturday) are now undergoing a change. Some 25 percent of High Street Banks will now be opening from 8.00 a.m. to 5.00 p.m. from Monday to Thursday, but with reduced staff.

COMPLAINTS

The visitor (or resident) wishing to lodge a **complaint** now has recourse to several organisations concerned with citizens' welfare. The Consumer Advice bureaux in the islands comprise the office in Las Palmas (Gran Canaria), situated in the Santa Catalina hotel (the autonomous government's department of Economy and Commerce), telephone 231422; in Santa Cruz (Tenerife) it is on the Avenida Anaga no. 39 (or alternatively at the Spanish Tourist Board in the Calle Marina no. 57); in Adeje (South Tenerife) call 793165 at Pueblo Canario in Playa de las Américas; and in Puerto de la Cruz, the number is 387060.

By law, all establishments used by the general public (hotels, bars, restaurants, apartment blocks, etc.) must have a complaints book (*Libro de Reclamaciones*) which is checked periodically by the Ministry of Tourism and Information. To register a complaint, write (in English if necessary) in the *Libro de Reclamaciones*, detailing your objections.

Special Information

DOING BUSINESS

A special visa is not necessary to start a business in the islands. It is important to secure one's residency and get a self-employed work permit (*la residencia con permiso de trabajo cuenta propia*) which does not define the business involved.

To obtain this card—which in theory should be easier after 31 December 1992 with Spain's full membership of the EEC—one should employ a *gestor* (a semi-official commercial agent). The nearest consulate's commercial attaché will advise about who to see, as *gestores* tend to specialise in different spheres of commercial activity: ring 262508, 262512 or 262516 for the British Consulate in Las Palmas and 286863 in Santa Cruz. In Las Palmas the German consulate can be contacted on 275700, in Santa Cruz telephone 284812. The French Consulate in Las Palmas can be contacted on 242371, and in Santa Cruz the number to ring is 232710.

Further information about setting up a business is contained in consular leaflets such as *Procedure and Documentation for Establishing Business in Spain* issued by the British Consul.

The consulates will also be able to provide up-to-the-minute information regarding **import and export** laws. Basically, personal and household effects (radios and TVs, fridges, electric or gas ovens, washing machines, floor polishers, bicycles and pianos, etc.) which are imported on establishing residence can be brought into the Canaries by presenting to the Customs a duplicate inventory, in Spanish and visaed by the Spanish Consul in the country of origin.

STUDENTS

Due to the number of foreign immigrants, **schools** based on British, German and American educational systems have developed since the late Sixties. The private Spanish schools in the Canaries have longer hours, Spanish-medium tuition and curricula and teaching methods very different from British, French and German systems. Parents settling in the islands may be looking for a more familiar scene than this for their children's formative years.

The British School of Gran Canaria is at El Sabinal, Carretera de Marzapan, telephone 351167; there is also the Canterbury School at Juan XXIII, 44, in Las Palmas. Lanzarote has the British School of Lanzarote in the capital, Arrecife, at José Antonio 7.

In Tenerife the British Yeoward School is at Parque Taoro, Puerto de la Cruz, telephone 384685. It was established in 1969 and, like the British School of Gran Canaria, takes children from three or four years of age through to GCE/GCSE level at age 16. In the south of Tenerife, the Wingate School, Calle Mirador de las Cumbritas, El Llano, Cabo Blanco, telephone 791002, some seven miles (12 km) from Los Cristianos and Playa de las Américas, offers a British education for children from four to 14 years of age.

The Colegio Alemán in Tenerife is in Santa Cruz at Calle Enrique Wolfson 16, telephone 273937, or in Puerto de la Cruz at San Antonio 1, telephone 384062. Both establishments provide a curriculum based on German and Spanish, as will the newer Colegio Alemán on the outskirts of Playa de las Américas.

The American School at Los Hoyos, Tafira Alta in Gran Canaria, telephone 350400, takes pupils up to the age of 18.

Tenerife has a full **university** at La Laguna, formerly the island's capital, where students from the whole of Spain and from other countries follow higher education courses. In Gran Canaria, the Polytechnic has some university faculties, such as Law.

These two higher education institutes, instead of being complementary, have too often suffered from the ingrained inter-island rivalry which also manifests itself in other walks of life.

PILGRIMAGES

Ever a traditional people, the Canarios—with their distinctive music and dancing varying slightly from island to island; their *lucha canaria* (Canarian wrestling) and regional cuisine–naturally have a long-standing religious tradition.

The section above covered fiestas in the main: however, two pilgrimages are peculiar to the principal islands of the archipelago. The whole of Gran Canaria venerates 8 September each year with the celebration of the Fiesta de la Virgen del Pino (Festival of the Virgin of the Pine-tree) when pilgrims progress, many on their knees, to the sanctuary at Teror, some 17 miles (27 km) from Las Palmas. Tradition has it that the Virgin Mary appeared to the islanders at this spot; a basilica now marks the exact place where the patron saint of Gran Canaria materialised.

The patron saint of Tenerife is Candelaria (therefore a popular name for girls and often shortened to "Candi"). Pilgrims set off on 14 August—some camping in the desolate mountains—in order to arrive at the basilica of Candelaria on the following day. The town square of Candelaria, just off the motorway to the south, is noted for its statues of the Guanche kings (or *menceys*) as well as for its basilica to the Black Virgin, and the most devout of Canarians will cross the square on their knees, taking two steps forward and one step back.

THE DISABLED

The Spanish have a very uncomplicated attitude towards the physically and mentally incapacitated. While not making a conscious effort, people accept them readily. The poorly-sighted are particularly well cared for: men and women with poor eyesight find sociable employment selling lottery tickets and the blind are cared for by Spain's most organised and effective charity—ONCE (Organización Nacional de Cieqos Españoles, or National Organisation of Spanish Blind).

GAYS

Following the advent of "democracy" since Franco's régime, many hitherto clandestine groups have emerged. Apart from the politically extreme left, who were obliged to live abroad until 1975/1976, socially and sexually different groups have also appeared. It is common now to find gay and transvestite clubs in the larger cities and tourist resorts. Live sex shows are obviously successful, and transvestites have long been accepted in the Canaries, especially at Carnival time.

FURTHER READING

Banks, F R. *Your Guide to the Canary Islands*. Redman, London 1963.

Brown, A Samler. *Madeira and the Canary Islands*. Sampson Low, London 1889.

Brown, Alfred. *Madeira and the Canary Islands*. Robert Hale, London 1963.

Cioranescu, Alejandro. *Le Canarien* (texts by Gadifer de la Salle and Jean de Béthencourt). Tenerife, 1980.

Dicks, Brian. *Lanzarote, Fire Island*. Dryad, London 1988.

Du Cane, Florence. *The Canary Islands by Du Cane*. Charles Black, London, 1911

Fernandez-Armesto, Felipe. *The Canary Islands after the Conquest*. Clarendon, Oxford 1982.

Glas, George. *History of the Canary Islands* (translation from Spanish). 1764.

Léon. *Gran Canaria, Lanzarote, Fuerteventura*. Editorial Everest, Madrid 1974.

Hayter, Judith. *Canary Island Hopping*. Sphere, London 1982.

Mercer, John. *The Canary Islanders*. Collings, London 1980.

Mason, John and Anne. *The Canary Islands*. Batsford, London 1976.

Piazzi Smyth, Charles. *Tenerife or the advantàges of a residence amongst the clouds*. 1852

Stone, Olivia. *Tenerife and its six satellites*. Marcus Ward, London 1887.

Wolfel, Dominik. *Estudios Canarios*. Burgfried-Verlag, Austria 1980.

Yeoward, Eileen. *Canary Islands*. Stockwell, Ilfracombe 1975.

GETTING AROUND

ORIENTATION

The four islands in the province of Tenerife consist of Tenerife, with an area of 790 sq miles (2,046 sq km) and a population of about 600,000 people. La Palma (not to be confused with Las Palmas, the capital of Gran Canaria) which lies northeast of Tenerife with an area of 280 sq miles (725 sq km) and a population of 80,000: Gomera, to the west of Tenerife which is much smaller at only 146 sq miles (378 sq km) and a population of 25,000: and finally the tiny island of Hierro, southwest of Tenerife and Gomera, which covers 107 sq miles (277 sq km) and has a population of a mere 7,000.

RECOMMENDED MAPS

All Tourist Information Centres and most hotels provide free maps of all the islands. These are detailed enough for most tourists, although they can be unreliable in more remote areas. For those people planning walking holidays however, it is possible to buy more detailed maps published by the Spanish Government and military in book shops.

AIRPORT/CITY

Note: All airports are provided with duty free shops although the prices are approximately double the ordinary shop prices.

Tenerife: there is a regular bus service running from the airport to Santa Cruz which is linked to scheduled flights from mainland Spain. The service does not necessarily operate all through the night. There is also a regular service to Playa de Las Américas, Los Cristianos and Puerto de la Cruz. Car hire facilities are available during the day. Taxis are also ever present but these can be expensive, particularly for a journey to the north of the island.

La Palma: regular bus services are available from La Palma airport, as well as taxis and car hire facilities. Hierro: airline buses, car hire and a fairly irregular taxi service is available.

WATER TRANSPORT

Ferry services operate between the islands on a daily basis. The timetable can vary; check at Tourist Information Centres, Travel Agencies, or in the local paper *El Dia*. Additionally specialist trips are available. On Gomera the *Alcatraz* motorvessel operates between San Sebastian and Valle Gran Rey, and twice a week it runs special trips to Los Organos, a spectacular rock formation in the shape of organ pipes and which is best photographed from the sea.

In Tenerife it is possible to hire a boat to go from Los Gigantes harbour to Masca and from San Andrés to Punta de Antequera but this service is not regular, usually requiring twelve persons or more.

PUBLIC TRANSPORT

There is no train service on the islands. The bus service is extensive on Tenerife and La Palma but more limited on the other islands. The buses are cheap and do, generally, run on time. Obviously the regularity of the service is in direct proportion to the areas of population—for example the service from Santa Cruz to Playa de Las Américas is hourly between 06.30 and 21.15. In general, there is a minimum service between towns of at least one bus each morning and afternoon. Express buses are also available on motorway routes.

It is worth noting that buses will pull off the motorway to pick up passengers provided they stand at a motorway turn-off.

Taxis around main towns are cheap and metered although an extra 50 pesetas can be charged at night. The traffic and parking problems in large towns are considerable and many local residents park their cars on the outskirts and use taxis. Try to avoid rush hours which are between 08.00 and 09.00, 13.00 and 14.30, 16.00 and 17.00 and the end of the working day between 19.00 and 20.00. At these times it would be quicker to walk.

Outside the towns taxis are not metered and it is advisable to check the price before hiring them. All taxi drivers should carry a tariff card.

PRIVATE TRANSPORT

Small motor bikes and scooters can be hired in the south of Tenerife but car hire is the normal system of private transport. In general the prices are cheaper than mainland Spain owing to competition and lack of V.A.T. A small car will cost 3,500 pesetas to 4,500 pesetas a day plus petrol, with discounts for long-term hire. It is worth shopping around for the cheapest deal. Some firms operate age restrictions on hire facilities because car insurance for under 25s is expensive. In Santa Cruz some firms are reluctant to hire to British tourists owing to problems in recent years. It is also possible with larger firms to leave the car in locations other than the original point of hire.

B.C. Rent a Car has offices on all the islands. Check availability of cars with their head office situated in Puerto de La Cruz, Edificio Masaru, Urbanisation La Paz, Tel. 385813 or 385849.

ON FOOT

Walking should be restricted to planned routes in the country and is certainly not recommended along major roads, where drivers are fast and accidents frequent. Also remember that the terrain is extremely rugged on all the islands and the distances between locations is often deceptive. One must also take account of the heat.

HITCHIKING

This is possible but difficult in major population areas. Lifts are easier to get in the smaller islands where people tend to have a natural inquisitiveness.

COMPLAINTS

For taxis take the registration number of the cab and lodge all complaints to the Policia Municipal who keep a register of all taxi owners and drivers. A "denunciation" could take a long time to process.

Lost property can be claimed from bus stations or the Policia Municipal.

Where to Stay

Pensions and hotels vary as everywhere, in quality and price. Whilst it is impossible to compete with package deal prices, a cheap pension should cost about 1,000 pesetas a night per person and an exclusive hotel 10,000 pesetas to 12,000 pesetas a night. Hotel prices include breakfast.

If you intend to stay a long time the smaller villages will often have rooms to let.

HOTELS

TENERIFE

Hotels in the tourist areas in the south (Playa de las Américas and Los Cristianos) and in Puerto de la Cruz are expensive for the itinerant tourist. If you wish to stay in this type of accommodation then it is best to obtain a cheap package holiday before travelling to the Canaries.

If you know where to look, there are alternatives There are a number of pensions in Santa Cruz in the area around Plaza Candelaria. Cheap accommodation in small hotels is also possible in Puerto de la Cruz but is more difficult to find. Details of room availability can be obtained from the Tourist Information Centre in Plaza de España, in Santa Cruz. The only time of the year when room availability is difficult is during *Carnaval*.

Rooms are also available in El Médano, Garachico, Adeje and San Juan. The government-run Parador at Las Cañadas is also worth staying in overnight, but must be booked well in advance.

Nautilus, (****) Av. de las Piscines 2, Bajamar. Tel. 540500. 268 rooms.

Neptuno, (***) Carretera Punta Hidalgo. Tel. 540404. 97 rooms.

Tinguaro, (***) Urbanizacíon Montaman. Tel. 541154. 115 rooms.

El Médano, (***) La Playa 2, El Médano Tel. 704000. 65 rooms.

Playa Sur Tenerife, (***)Los Valos. Tel. 704150. 70 rooms.

Aguere, (*) Obispo Rey Redonodo 57, La Laguna. Tel. 259490, 32 rooms.

Tenerife Tour, (***) Av. del Generalísimo 170, Las Caletillas. Tel. 500200.

Parador Nacional Las Cañadas del Teide, (**)Las Cañadas. Tel. 332304. 17 rooms.

Princesa Dacil, (***) Camino Penetracíon, Los Cristianos. Tel. 790800. 330 rooms.

Reverón, (**) Av. General Franco 26, Los Cristianos. Tel. 790600. 40 rooms.

Andrea's, (**) Av. Valle Menéndez, Los Cristianos. Tel. 790012. 42 rooms.

Bougainville Playa, (****) Urbanización San Eugenio, Playa de las Américas. Tel. 790200. 481 rooms.

Conquistador, (****) Av. Litoral, Playa de las Américas. Tel. 792399. 485 rooms.

Europe, (****) Av. Litoral, Playa de las Américas. Tel. 791308. 244 rooms.

Gran Tinerfe, (****), Playa de las Américas. Tel. 791200. 358 rooms.

Las Palmeras, (****), Av. Litoral, Playa de las Américas. Tel. 790991. 519 rooms.

Park Hotel Troya, (****), Playa de las Américas. Tel. 790100. 318 rooms.

Tenerife Sol, (****), Playa de las Américas. Tel. 791062. 523 rooms.

Flamingo, (***), Urbanización San Eugenio, Playa de las Américas. Tel. 791220.

Botánico, (*****), Calle Richard J. Yeoward, Puerto de la Cruz. Tel. 381400. 282 rooms.

San Felipe, (*****), Av. de Colón 13, Puerto de la Cruz. Tel. 383311. 260 rooms.

Semiramis, (*****) Calle Leopoldo Cologán 12, Puerto de la Cruz. Tel. 385551. 275 rooms.

Atalaya Gran Hotel, (****), Parque Taoro, Puerto de la Cruz. Tel. 384600. 183 rooms.

El Tope, (****), Calzada de Martiánez 2, Puerto de la Cruz. Tel. 385052. 216 rooms.

Florida, (****), Av. Blas Pérez González, Puerto de la Cruz. Tel. 385052. 216 rooms.

Meliá Puerto de la Cruz, (****), Av. Marqués Villanueva de Prado, Puerto de la Cruz. Tel. 384011. 300 rooms.

Orotava Garden, (****), Av. Aguilar y Quesada, Puerto de la Cruz. Tel. 385211. 241 rooms.

Valle-Mar, (****), Av. de Colón 2, Puerto de la Cruz. Tel. 384800. 171 rooms.

Casa del Sol, (***), Urbanización San Fernando, Puerto de la Cruz. Tel. 380762. 45 rooms.

Don Manolito, (***), Lomo de los Guirres 6, Puerto de la Cruz. Tel. 385012. 49 rooms.

Internacional, (***), Carretera de las Arenas 91, Puerto de la Cruz. Tel. 385111. 111 rooms.

Marquesa, (***), Calle Quintana 11, Puerto de la Cruz. Tel. 383151. 88 rooms.

Monopol, (***), Calle Quintana 15, Puerto de la Cruz. Tel. 384611. 92 rooms.

San Telmo, (***), Calle San Telmo 18, Puerto de la Cruz. Tel. 385853. 91 rooms.

Maja, (*), Calle Iriarte 9, Puerto de la Cruz. Tel. 383853. 24 rooms.

Los Gigantes-Sol, (****), Acantilado de Los Gigantes, Puerto de Santiago. Tel. 867125. 225 rooms.

Maritim, (****), Calle Burgado 1, Realejo Alto. Tel. 342012. 461 rooms.

Reforma, (****), Urbanización Tierra de Oro, Realejo Alto. Tel. 341000. 311 rooms.

Mencey, (*****), Calle José Naveiras 38, Santa Cruz. Tel. 276700. 30 rooms.

Plaza, (***), Plaza de la Candelaria 9, Santa Cruz. Tel. 247587. 64 rooms.

Anaga, (**), Calle Imeldo Seris 19, Santa Cruz. Tel. 245090. 126 rooms.

Taburiente, (**), Calle Doctor Guigou 25, Santa Cruz. Tel. 276000. 90 rooms.

LA PALMA

This island does not have the same concentration of tourists as Tenerife, nevertheless there is a wide range of accommodation available ranging from the Parador Nacional in Santa Cruz de la Palma to hostels and apartments in most places on the island.

Full details of room availability can be obtained from Tourist Information Centres in both La Palma and Tenerife.

Nambroque, (**), Calle Montelują́n, El Paso. Tel. 485279. 10 rooms.

Eden, (*), Calle Angel 1, Los Llanos de Aridane. Tel. 460104. 15 rooms.

Parador Nacional de Santa Cruz, (***), Av. Maritima 34, Santa Cruz. Tel. 412340-41. 32 rooms.

San Miquel, (***), Av. El Puente 31, Santa Cruz. Tel. 411243. 70 rooms.

Canarias, (**), Calle A. Cabrera Pinto 27, Santa Cruz. Tel. 413182. 14 rooms.

Bahia, (*), Plaza de la Luz 26, Santa Cruz. Tel. 411846. 30 rooms.

GOMERA

The three centres of accommodation in Gomera are San Sebastian, Santiago and notably Valle Gran Rey. Hotels as such do not exist with the exception of the beautiful but expensive Parador in San Sebastian and the Hotel Tecina, a new upmarket resort hotel in Santiago. Apartments and rooms are available in these towns but availability can be restricted as many people from Tenerife spend holiday periods in Gomera. Easter, Christmas and the months of July and August are to be avoided unless you book in advance. New hotels are planned.

Parador Nacional de la Gomera, (****), San Sebastian. Tel. 871100. 20 rooms.

Garajonay, (**), Calle Ruiz de Padrón 15. San Sebastian. Tel. 870550. 21 rooms.

Canarias, (*), Calle Ruiz de Padrón 3. San Sebastian. Tel. 870355. 19 rooms.

Colombina, (*), Calle Ruiz de Padrón 81. San Sebastian. Tel. 871257. 25 rooms.

Amaya, (*), El Paso. Vallehermoso. Tel. 800073. 7 rooms.

HIERRO

Hierro is not a tourist centre and therefore accommodation is extremely restricted. Advance booking would be a wise precaution. Possible choices are:

Parador Nacional El Hierro (***), Valverde. Tel. 550101. 47 rooms.

Boomerang (**), Calle Doctor Gost 1. Tel. 550200. 17 rooms.

Casañas (*), Calle San Francisco 5. Tel. 550254. 11 rooms.

Morales (*), Calle Licenciado Bueno 7. Tel. 550162. 14 rooms.

Sanflei (*), Calle Santiago 18. Tel. 550857. 13 rooms.

CAMPING

There are few official campsites on the islands but nevertheless many people do camp in the mountains. It is imperative to avoid camping within the National Parks because this is illegal. On the more out-of-the-way beaches people often sleep over-night with or without a tent.

In Tenerife there are three official sites, namely:

Las Calletas, Urbanizacion el Palmar - Tel. 785027

Las Rosas (Arona), Carretera Guaza - Tel. 785118

San Miguel, Urbanization las Chafiras - Tel. 700400

There are no **Youth Hostels** on the islands.

FOOD DIGEST

WHAT TO EAT

Canary Island cooking can best be described as good but basic. In the past only essential food products were imported due not only to the isolation of the islands, but also to economic factors. The islands do not have the terrain to maintain large amounts of livestock, although many varieties of fruit are grown. The local residents are happy with their standard diet and are seldom tempted to try the more international cuisine available in Indian, Chinese and indeed English restaurants in the large tourist centres. However, Italian cooking is quite popular.

If you are cooking for yourself fish, meat, vegetables, fruit, bread and wine are cheap in comparison to other European countries. Tinned foods and drinks can be more expensive. Choose a shop or supermarket away from tourist areas, where the prices can be highly inflated. Local markets in the major towns are always the best bet.

SNACKS

Many bars in towns will serve sandwiches and rolls (*bocadillos*) with various fillings such as steak, cheese, bacon, and *chorizo* which is a type of garlic sausage.

A *tapa* is a small snack which is served in Spain to accompany a drink. In the Canaries the choice of *tapas* is not as varied as in mainland Spain but nevertheless most bars will have some on offer. *Tapas* are normally displayed in a glass cabinet along the bar and it is therefore easy for the non-Spanish speaker to indicate his or her requirements. Typical *tapas* are octopus in vinegar and salad; Russian salad which is a mixture of potato salad and vegetables (mayonnaise goes off quickly in the heat and therefore should be avoided); *boquerones* or fresh anchovies; prawns in garlic salad; and *tortilla*, a Spanish omelette but without the strange British addition of peas!

BREAKFAST

This usually consists of coffee and a sandwich or cake in a local bar or cafe. Tea is unreliable, ranging from a cup of hot milk with a tea bag in it, to microwaved tea. The coffee is good but possibly too strong for some tastes. It comes in several shapes and strengths:

A *cortado* is a small white coffee, very strong.

A *cafe solo* is a small, strong black coffee.

A *cafe con leche* is a large white coffee.

Freshly squeezed orange juice is also plentiful and relatively cheap. Bars will normally give you a glass of mineral water free if you ask for *agua*. The tap water is unreliable.

LOCAL DISHES

Goats' cheese is often served along with *Morcia*, a typical Spanish black pudding which is distinctive in the Canaries by being sweetened with added sultanas. *Salchicha* or sausage is also a favourite and will normally arrive at your table flamed with lighted brandy. Garlic mushrooms is another dish often provided, and many bars and restaurants have hocks of ham hanging from the ceiling; these are called *Jamon Serrano* and slices are served as a complement to goats' cheese.

A selection of local favourites is as follows:

Rancho Canario—Vegetable and meat stew.

Gofio—A powdered barley or maize traditionally the staple food given to children at an early age. *Gofio* come in various forms, for example mixed into milk or coffee, mixed with chocolate and honey for the sweet tooth, or added to soups and stews.

Arroz con Pescado—Fish and rice soup.

Garbanzo Compuesto—Chick pea and potato stew. Beans and pulses are very popular on the islands.

Meat dishes—Rabbit (*conejo*) is popular in the mountains and goat could be on the menu if you have the taste for it. More usual however, is chicken (*pollo*), steak (*bistec*), and pork chops (*chuleta de cerdo*).

Fish—A wide variety of fish surround the islands. Most commonly eaten are squid (*calamares*) and octopus (*pulpo*). The good thing about fish restaurants is that one is invited to choose the fish from the kitchen and can therefore match shape and size to appetite without having to know the local names for the fish. Shellfish are particularly plentiful.

Fish is normally served with *papas arrugadas* (potatoes cooked in their skins) and *mojo* sauce, again typical of the islands. The sauce comes in two varieties, red, which is very hot, and spicy and green, which is slightly less so.

Portions are usually huge. An order for chicken results in a complete half-chicken; chops and steaks are of cartoon-like proportions. Meat dishes are normally served with salad and chips.

PRICES

In general, prices in Canary restaurants average less than 2,000 pesetas or £10 per person for a meal comprising a starter, main dish and a sweet with wine, coffee and a liqueur. A service charge is often not levied: tipping should be around 10 percent.

WHERE TO EAT

Typical Canary restaurants are usually decorated in basic style, rather like garages, but this does not affect the quality of the food. Remember that in Spain people eat their main meal in the middle of the day, and many restaurants do not serve after 16.00 hours and some may not reopen in the evening.

Various villages in Tenerife are famous for their restaurants.

For fish: **Taganana** in the north of the island is a spectacular drive through the Anaga Mountains and has three good, cheap fish restaurants. The same can be said for **Playa de Los Abrigos** which is located near the southern airport, although here the price of fame has made the menus more expensive. **Playa de San Juan** is another centre for fish, as is **San Andrés** in the north near Santa Cruz.

The village of **La Esperanza**, on the road from La Laguna up to the Cañadas, boasts more than 10 restaurants which all serve the basic meat dishes already described above. There are also well known restaurants on the motorway between La Laguna and Tacoronte, very popular with people from Santa Cruz who eat out at weekends. On Sunday afternoons the restaurants are crowded with large local extended family groups, ranging from babies to the elderly, not conducive to a quiet Sunday lunch. Icod, Tacoronte, Candelaria, Garachico and Adeje all have a selection of typical restaurants.

The following restaurants are particularly recommended:

In Esperanza: Casa Ramallo
In Candelaria: Meson La Rueda
In Garachico: Mirador de Garachico
In Tacoronte: El Campa
In Santa Cruz (Playa del Principe): Kiosco

Gomera: The island is particularly famous for its fish restaurants. Local tuna fish comes virtually straight from the sea on to the customer's plate. The best restaurants are in Valle Gran Rey and in San Sebastian. In the latter, the El Pejin fish restaurant in Calle del Medio has an excellent reputation.

Hierro: Restaurants in Hierro are extremely limited and all will serve typical Canary cooking, as there are practically no tourists to cater for. The wine here is the best on all the islands.

La Palma: In Santa Cruz de la Palma the following are worth trying:

Restaurante la Abuela in Calle la Conception and the Restaurant los Àlmendros in Calle San Vicente.

DRINKING NOTES

One of the advantages of a holiday abroad for Northern Europeans is the availability of alcohol at low prices. Tenerife and the other islands have even cheaper prices than mainland Spain because of their tax-free status. The good local lager, Dorada, comes on tap and in bottles. It is cheaper and often better than imported beer, but you should ask for it by name. In some bars the hygiene is not of a high standard and visitors would be safer to ask for a bottle of beer rather than risk a beer from an unclean supply pipe.

The Canaries have an incredible selection of spirits from all over the world and on average the measures are triple or quadruple an equivalent British measure. Ask specifically for a brand name, particularly with gin or vodka, because there are plenty of cheap Spanish alternatives which can leave the most hardened head with a hangover.

Wine is produced on the islands but, with the exception of Hierro wine which is bottled for the other islands, it is usually presented in carafes and can distinctly vary in quality. Locally produced wine is also often more expensive than imported mainland bottled wine.

Bars stay open late and in consequence people tend to drink more slowly than in more hurried northern climes. Normally bar tips are quite small—of the order of 10 to 25 pesetas. Barmen are not usually allowed to drink behind the bar and therefore will seldom accept drinks from customers.

CULTURE PLUS

MUSEUMS

Both Tenerife and La Palma have interesting museums containing many artefacts from Guanche culture. The usual opening times are 10.00 until 13.00 and 16.00 until 18.00.

In Santa Cruz de Tenerife:

Municipal Museum, Plaza del Principe. Contains many objects of local art.

Archaeological Museum, Palacio Insular, Calle Bravo Murillo. Concentration of Guanche culture from the province.

In Santa Cruz de la Palma:

Museo Insular, Convent of San Francisco. Contains local art and objects of historical interest.

CULTURAL EVENTS

Theatre, opera, ballet and concerts are concentrated in the provincial capital of Santa Cruz in Tenerife. The Teatro Guimera in the centre of town has a full programme of opera and concerts from visiting artists as well as being the base for the Tenerife Symphony Orchestra. Pop concerts are usually held in the bull-ring. All events are advertised in the local papers. La Laguna, being a university town, often has concerts and plays in the Teatro Leal and also has an annual Jazz Festival with guest artists from abroad.

During the summer months concert seasons are often organised in the open air, particularly in the Plaza Principe and the Plaza Architecto.

CINEMA

Canarios are keen cinema-goers, as are mainland Spaniards. The films are normally dubbed into Spanish, and subtitles are seldom used. The Cine Victor in the Plaza de la Paz in Santa Cruz, Tenerife, is a good example of 1920s cinema architecture and the billboards advertising the current film are actually hand-painted, depicting scenes from the films.

ARCHITECTURE

A particular feature of the architecture of the Canaries are the beautifully carved wooden balconies. Probably the best examples of this can be seen in La Orotava. All the older towns on the islands have houses with this feature, particularly La Laguna and Garachico on Tenerife and Santa Cruz and Los Llanos de Aridane on La Palma. San Sebastian (Gomera) and Valverde (Hierro) also have fine examples.

Another feature is courtyards or patios in the centre of the older houses. The rooms surround an open central area which is often filled with plants and flowers. You can often catch a glimpse of these courtyards in the older quarters of town.

NIGHTLIFE

Tenerife is the only one of the four islands in the province which provides a full range of nightclubs and discos. The remaining three islands do not offer the same entertainment facilities.

Santa Cruz, being a port, does have late night bars and a few discos. During the week however, these places can be relatively deserted by the majority of the locals, who have to be fit for an early start each morning. Weekends are different. A series of bars along the Avenida Anaga are open until the early hours of the morning, also are the bars on Calle Ramon y Cajal. Behind the bullring in the Rambla General Franco late bars such as Espacio 41, La Calle and Cactus cater for the more bohemian element of the Santa Cruz populace, whereas the Residencia Anaga is more geared towards the "yuppie" element. The best disco in Santa Cruz is probably Daida where a certain standard of dress is required before entering. The other discos tend to attract the under-20s.

La Laguna is a thriving university town during term and consequently has a series of disco bars centred around the university. Under orders from the local town hall these bars have to close by 3.00 a.m. Equilibrio (Avenida Trinidad) and Districto (Calle Catedenor) are worth visiting.

In Puerto de la Cruz the nightlife continues all through the night, particularly at El Coto Disco under the Hotel Botanico (opposite the Botanical Gardens) and the Victoria Disco in the Avenida Colón.

Playa de las Américas and Los Cristianos have numerous bars and discos open all night but these are normally frequented by tourists. Avoid the Veronicas complex in Playa de las Américas, the scene of frequent trouble with rowdy tourists.

Nightlife on the other smaller islands is

limited to late-night bars, although Santa Cruz on La Palma does actually have a disco.

GAMBLING

The Casino Taoro in Puerto de la Cruz is probably one of the best casinos in Europe. There is also a casino in Plaza Candelaria in Santa Cruz.

Horse racing is not popular but this is substituted by various lottery competitions where the prizes could be in the region of £3 million. Santa Cruz also has a bingo hall in Calle Candelaria but this is only to be recommended for those who can understand numbers in rapid Spanish.

SHOPPING

WHAT TO BUY

Most goods are imported, which obviously has an effect on the prices. To compensate for this the Canaries have tax-free status, although this could change prior to 1992. Alcohol, cigarettes, and perfume are much cheaper than in many European countries and also cheaper than in duty-free shops at airports or on the plane.

Main towns have shops specialising in electrical goods such as radios, personal stereos and televisions as well as cameras and watches. Although watches can be cheap, prices of the other goods are often comparable to Europe-wide prices. Check prices in your country of origin before you leave because it is difficult to return goods once you are back home. Take care with miniature TVs which may not function on some broadcast frequencies.

Clothes are not cheap at all, with the exception of some leatherwear and (surprisingly) fur goods. Few locals ever wear fur coats.

Typical Canary products are limited to ceramics and embroidery. Tablecloths and cushion covers with detailed patterns are a speciality from these islands. Buy from a shop, not from a street seller, or you may find your "genuine" tablecloth comes from Taiwan.

SHOPPING AREAS

Try to buy goods in the main towns rather than the tourist centres. Do not buy anything unless the price is marked, and even if it is you may still be able to negotiate a lower price. In Santa Cruz the shop Sovespan in Residencia Anaga is a Russian Supermarket where leather and fur goods as well as vodka are particularly cheap

SHOPPING HOURS

Normal hours are 10.00 until 13.00 or 14.00. Most shops close until 16.00 or 17.00 and are then open until 20.00. Saturday is normally half day closing and on Sunday you may have difficulty even buying a bottle of milk, so remember to buy food before 14.00 on Saturday. Shops in tourist centres will open on Sundays.

EXPORT

Unless you are a Spanish resident and wish to take goods to mainland Spain, there are no restrictions on exporting goods from the Canary Islands. There will of course be the usual restrictions on imports from the country of your origin. Remember that you are entitled to import fewer duty-free items into your own country from the Canaries than from Mainland Spain and other EEC countries, because in the latter cases you have already paid VAT whereas in the Canaries you have not. No-one is allowed to export more than 500,000 pesetas from the Canaries without declaring it.

COMPLAINTS

Spanish law does cover the return of faulty goods in line with other EEC countries. Most shops will exchange faulty goods, but it is unlikely they will give you your money back although there is a legal obligation for them to do so. It is possible to make a "denuncia-tion" to the local police but the wheels of justice are slow.

All bars and restaurants are obliged to keep a complaints book. If more than two complaints are registered then the local town hall can withdraw their licence. Simply asking for this book is likely to obtain an apology, but it has been known for irate chefs to chase complainants up the street.

SPORTS

PARTICIPANT

Water Sports are well provided for in Tenerife, but restricted in La Palma, Gomera and Hierro. Swimming can be dangerous in some areas because of strong undercurrents. Pay very close attention to red flag warnings.

The resort of El Médano in Tenerife is renowned among windsurfers, and top international competitions are held here. Many tourist centres provide windsurfing lessons as well as water-skiing and scuba diving. Boats are available for hire for fishing trips at most major resorts.

Golf is increasingly popular in Tenerife. In La Laguna the Tenerife Golf Club is next to Los Rodeos airport and on the Costa del Silencio in the south there are two other courses, Golf del Sur and Amarillo Golf Club. Further courses are under construction. There are very few public tennis courts, but many hotels allow non-residents to hire their facilities. The Palacco Desportes in Santa Cruz does have public courts.

Horse riding is available in the north of Tenerife, particularly in La Laguna

SPECTATOR

Bull fighting has never been particularly popular in the Canaries and the bull ring in Santa Cruz is now used for concerts. Tenerife Football Club is worth visiting if you are interested in soccer, Tenerife currently being in the second division. The ground is situated in Torni Carno in Santa Cruz.

One of Tenerife's two first division basketball teams plays next door, in the Palacco Desportes. The other plays in the La Laguna stadium. Basketball is a passion in Spain and top quality mainland teams are usually on the fixture list. The newspapers give full details of these games.

You may be lucky to see a bout of Canary Wrestling, peculiar to these islands. Specific fixture details vary but watch out for signs saying *La Lucha Canaria*; some bouts are televised, some advertised in the local press. Demonstration fights are common at festival time.

Special Information

CHILDREN

Tenerife provides most opportunities for children. La Palma and Gomera can provide good swimming conditions but offer little else to occupy the very young. In Hierro, even the possibilities for swimming are limited.

Puerto de la Cruz has a Loro Parque or parrot park with dolphinarium which can prove an interesting visit. Puerto also has a spectacular botanical garden.

Bananera El Guanche in La Orotava is also an interesting visit (free buses run from Puerto de la Cruz), with a guided tour around a banana plantation. La Orotava also has the only zoo on the Canaries, although this is quite small.

In the south there is the Octopus Water Park in Playa de las Américas, with a series of water slides which vary in complexity to suit the age group. Very popular with tourists, you may have to queue a long time for thirty seconds of fun.

GAYS

There are several gay bars and discos on Tenerife, particularly in Puerto de la Cruz, where Vampires is known as a gay disco. The nearby bars also have gay clientele.

DISABLED

The newer hotels often provide facilities for the disabled, but this is by no means universal. Toilets for the disabled are few and far between. There are a few telephone kiosks designed for the disabled in the large towns.

STUDENTS

Museums will sometimes give discounts to students, but otherwise a student union card will be of little benefit with respect to travel or hotel costs.

PILGRIMAGES

The Basilica of Candelaria contains the statue of Our Lady of Candelaria. Many pilgrimages are made to the Basilica, usually on foot, from all over Tenerife.

In the mountains above the capital, Santa Cruz, on La Palma, is the church of Nuestra Señora de las Palmas which serves the same purpose on this island as Candelaria does for Tenerife.

WALKING

Both the Tenerife and La Palma Tourist Information Centres provide a very good service of maps and suggested walks giving distances and estimated time.

On Tenerife: Walks of particular interest include San Andrés to Antequerra, which should take the best part of a day. In the mountainous area in the centre the best short walking is around Los Raices and La Esperanza. One of the best-loved island walks is from Masca on the island's westerly point down to the beach, a walk of about two hours down and five to get back.

Art/Photo Credits

Beatty, David	226/227
Dunkin, Neil	127
Eames, Andrew	27, 28, 31, 32, 34, 35, 37, 43, 45, 49, 52, 54, 56, 59, 60, 74, 85, 88, 89, 90, 91, 92, 93, 98, 101, 136, 138, 167, 173, 236, 244, 254, 256, 257, 280
Eddy, Mike	242, 268, 270
Expo Tenerife	29, 46, 53, 55, 57, 58, 67, 68, 69, 70, 72/73, 77, 80/81, 82, 83, 84, 100, 135, 143, 145, 206, 255, 263, 271, 272/273, 277
Gatti, Tulio	3, 18/19, 24/25, 36, 38, 86/87, 102/103, 104/105, 106/107, 114, 116, 118, 119, 132, 140/141, 153, 172, 175, 182, 184, 187, 188, 191, 194/195, 210/211, 218/219, 222, 223, 245
Gravette, Andy	96
Godfrey, Dave	26
Kanzler, Thomas	20/21, 42, 44, 161, 166, 169, 170, 171, 174, 178/179, 192, 232/233, 238
Kew Gardens	75, 76, 246/247, 248, 249, 250, 251, 253
Murray, Don	40, 48
National Portrait Gallery	79
Naylor, Kim	228
Reuther, Joerg	9, 16/17, 30, 50, 51, 64/65, 71, 99, 117, 121, 122, 126, 139, 144, 146, 152, 156, 158, 159, 160, 162/163, 176/177, 181, 185, 186, 190, 193, 196, 197, 198/199, 200, 201, 203, 204, 205, 208, 234/235, 237, 239, 240/241, 243, 262, 265, 266, 267, 269, 274/275, 276, 278, 279
Sailing boat postcard	61
Shaw, Ian	22, 142, 150, 214/215, 220
Spanish Connection	212/213
Spectrum	97, 131, 134, 151, 155, 221
Tisdall, Nigel	33, 157, 207, 209
Tony Stone Worldwide	Cover, 94/95, 148/149, 258/259
Wassman, Bill	14/15, 62/63, 66, 108/109, 120, 123, 124/125, 128/129, 130, 137, 154, 216, 217, 260/261, 264
Wright, George	164/165, 180, 189
Wolfgang, Fritz	230/231

Index

H - I

J - L

M

N - O

P

R - S

T

V -W